Perfecting the Union

Perfecting the Union

National and State Authority
in the US Constitution

MAX M. EDLING

OXFORD
UNIVERSITY PRESS

OXFORD

UNIVERSITY PRESS

Oxford University Press is a department of the University of Oxford. It furthers
the University's objective of excellence in research, scholarship, and education
by publishing worldwide. Oxford is a registered trade mark of Oxford University
Press in the UK and certain other countries.

Published in the United States of America by Oxford University Press
198 Madison Avenue, New York, NY 10016, United States of America.

Library of Congress Cataloging-in-Publication Data
Names: Edling, Max M., author.
Title: Perfecting the union : national and state authority in the US
Constitution / Max M. Edling.
Description: New York, NY : Oxford University Press, [2021] |
Includes bibliographical references and index.
Identifiers: LCCN 2020024084 (print) | LCCN 2020024085 (ebook) |
ISBN 9780197534717 (hardback) | ISBN 9780197534731 (epub)
Subjects: LCSH: Constitutional law—United States. |
Constitutional law—United States—States.
Classification: LCC KF4550 .E37 2019 (print) | LCC KF4550 (ebook) |
DDC 342.73/042—dc23
LC record available at https://lccn.loc.gov/2020024084
LC ebook record available at https://lccn.loc.gov/2020024085

DOI: 10.1093/oso/9780197534717.001.0001

1 3 5 7 9 8 6 4 2

Printed by Sheridan Books, Inc., United States of America

To Peter Onuf, mentor extraordinaire

CONTENTS

Acknowledgments ix

Introduction: Revisiting the Critical Period 1

1. Peace Pact and Nation: The Constitution as a Compact between States 16

2. Union: Empowering a New National Government 35

3. Internal Police: The Residual Power of the States 75

4. Legislation: Implementing the Constitution 105

Conclusion: Toward a New Understanding of the Founding 134

Notes 151
Index 183

ACKNOWLEDGMENTS

About a decade ago I decided I wished to return to research on the American founding, the subject of my first book, to write about the political and social order that sprang from the American Revolution. My decision meant I had to come to terms with new work on the Constitution, which, as far as my intended project was concerned, was in equal parts stimulating and worrisome. The new scholarship argued that the causes and consequences of the Constitution could be found not in the national but in the international history of the United States, and that the Constitution mattered much less than previously thought to domestic developments. I was myself part of the problem, for I had written a book that interpreted the Constitution as an attempt to create a *fiscal-military state* that could defend US interests against international competitors. But my interest was now in domestic changes, in how American Independence "laid the foundation for a democratic social order that combined unsurpassed equality and opportunity with institutionalized inequality and oppression," as I put it in one of my essays. Innovative work on the founding suggested that the solution to this puzzle lay in the actions and inaction of the American states rather than the federal government. But how could one write in a convincing manner about liberty and rights, exclusion and subjugation in the era of the American founding without referencing the Declaration of Independence, the US Constitution, and the federal Bill of Rights? It seemed to me that before I could start on my story of American liberty and American oppression, I had to explain why the Constitution mattered to the story in some ways, but not in others. This book is my attempt at explanation.

In the spring of 2014, Nicolas Barreyre invited me to spend a month at the Centre d'études nord-américaines at the École des hautes études en sciences sociales in Paris. The presentations that formed part of my visiting appointment were the stimulus that first prompted me to visualize my ideas about the Constitution as a book. I presented three papers at CENA, which laid the groundwork for chapters 1 and 3. I would like to extend my warmest thanks to Nicolas for the invitation and to the CENA director, Cécile Vidal, and secretary, Camille Amat, as well as the other *membres* of CENA for their gracious hospitality, stimulating seminars, and delightful lunchtime conversations.

Most of the book was written in the academic years 2015–2017 in Uppsala, Sweden. I gratefully acknowledge a financial grant from the Swedish Research Council, which allowed me to spend 2015–2016 as a researcher at the Department of History, Uppsala University. I also thank the department for hosting me. In September 2016 I carried my boxes of books and papers across Thunbergsvägen to the Swedish Collegium for Advanced Study, where I had the great fortune to be a fellow in the academic year 2016–2017. Housed in the glorious Linneanum building in the Botanical Gardens, SCAS is an unrivaled sanctuary dedicated to undisturbed research, reflection, and writing. I would like to thank the staff and the other fellows at the collegium for their support and excellent company, and above all the director, Björn Wittrock, for making my fellowship such a productive time. I would also like to thank Adam Sutcliffe, who as my Head of Department kindly accepted my extended leave from King's College London and supported the research that made this book possible. Angel O'Donnell covered my teaching at King's perhaps too well. My absence was barely noted.

I presented an advanced version of chapter 1 to the American History Seminar at Cambridge University in October 2017 and benefitted greatly from the comments and criticisms of the participants, especially from Gary Gerstle and Nicholas Guyatt. The paper was subsequently published as a viewpoint article in *Past and Present*, no. 240 (August 2018) and before publication was further improved by the thoughtful comments of four anonymous reviewers and the editor, Alexandra Walsham. I am grateful to the editors of *Past and Present* for permission to republish a slightly revised version of the article here.

In February 2016, with my customary resolve weakened by a mild depression brought about by the darkness and sense of isolation that are part and parcel of northern winters, Gerald Leonard lured me into writing a short pamphlet on the creation of the Constitution for his New Essays on American Constitutional History. Gerry convinced me it would amount to "no more than a summer's work, if that" and said he was "hoping for speed." I foolishly chose to believe him. Gerry's hopes slowly crumbled to dust as the summer turned to autumn, the autumn to winter, and the winter to spring. But he showed commendable patience and when the pamphlet was finally delivered, Gerry turned into a meticulous, astute, and constructive editor. George Van Cleve read an advanced draft and pointed out errors and questionable claims, although he cannot be held responsible for all those that remain. When the pamphlet went into production, Amy Hughes did a wonderful job as copyeditor. Material from the pamphlet make up chapter 2 and parts of the introduction. I am grateful to the American Historical Association for permission to reprint.

An early draft of chapter 3 saw first light at a workshop on American political economy in the long nineteenth century that I organized together with Daniel Peart in April 2015. Financial support from King's College London and Queen Mary University London made the workshop possible. I would like to thank the participants for perceptive comments and in particular Nicolas Barreyre, who once again showed himself to be a careful reader and constructive critic. At different points in my research John Brooke, Gary Gerstle, Joel Isaac, Richard John, and Niall O'Flaherty have discussed the arcane topic of eighteenth-century *police* with me and have pointed me to useful references. Lloyd Ross was a King's College Undergraduate Research Fellow in the summer of 2015 and helped me find and analyze newspaper and pamphlet material on internal police. I am grateful to them all.

In April 2016, together with Peter Kastor, I organized a workshop on the Washington administration and the creation of the federal government. King's College London and Washington University in St. Louis provided financial support, and the Fred W. Smith National Library for the Study of George Washington at Mount Vernon generously provided us with accommodation and a state-of-the-art workshop venue. I would like to thank the library's Founding Director, Douglas Bradburn, and the Director of Library Programs, Stephen McLeod, for hosting us. At Mount Vernon I presented an early version of chapter 4, which was much improved by the comments of the participants, a stellar group of experts on early American government. At a later stage Richard John read and commented on a more advanced draft. Julian Hoppit very generously shared with me his data on the legislation of the British Parliament in the 1790s. Ira Katznelson helped with legislative classification. Christopher Pearl kindly answered questions about Pennsylvania in the American Revolution and Lindsay Chervinsky about the aborted Home department.

In addition to the seminars and workshops mentioned here, many other audiences have sat through my attempts to explain the significance and insignificance of the Constitution. I would like to thank the audience of seminars and talks at Eidsvoll 1814, Oxford University, and the Swedish Collegium for Advanced Study, and the participants of panels and roundtables at conferences of the British Group of Early American History, the European Early American Studies Association, the Omohundro Institute for Early American History and Culture, and the Réseau pour le développement européen de l'histoire de la jeune Amérique, for their interest, criticism, questions, and comments.

The book took a long and circuitous route to publication. Along the road, Mary Sarah Bilder, Daniel Hulsebosch, Peter Onuf, Susanna Rabow-Edling, Christopher Tomlins, and an anonymous reviewer for Oxford University Press took time out of their busy schedules to read the manuscript. I owe them a great debt of gratitude for their help in improving my argument, but also for much-needed encouragement to believe that the project was worth pursuing. As always, Susanna has helped me to sharpen my ideas and to stay on point.

Although I wrote this book to equip myself for my future quest in search of the true meaning of the American founding, it is also a mea culpa. When Peter Onuf read the manuscript of my first book, *A Revolution in Favor of Government*, for Oxford University Press, he stressed that my argument should emphasize much more than it did the role of the states in the American federal system of government. But I was then a (reasonably) young man, eager to publish the book and to get on with my career. I did no more than a minimum of what Peter asked and not nearly enough. My light-touch editing certainly did not fool one of the most perceptive reviewers of the published book, who pointed to my criminal negligence of American federalism. I hope the pages that follow go some way toward making amends.

Readers familiar with his scholarship will recognize how much I owe to the work of Peter Onuf. More than anyone else he has shaped my understanding of the American founding. Indeed, what I contribute is no more than a variation on the themes that dominate his writing. It therefore seems fitting to dedicate this book to Peter, as a heartfelt thanks for his mentoring and inspiration over the last two decades, but also as a belated apology for not taking his insights more seriously all those years ago. I should have.

Introduction

Revisiting the Critical Period

Early in the summer of 1783, George Washington concluded that the military and political situation at last allowed him to tender his resignation as commander of the Continental army. After eight long years the American War of Independence was over, and George III had reluctantly acknowledged that his erstwhile colonies were now independent states. As the central leader in the struggle against Britain, Washington felt obliged to add to his letter of resignation a few "sentiments respecting some important subjects which appear[ed] to [him] to be intimately connected with the tranquility of the United States." Washington's sentiments offer a snapshot of the political circumstances of the newly independent United States, a nation that from then on had to make its own way in the world. His letter can therefore serve as a useful starting point from which to begin an investigation into the nature of the American union and the challenges that led to the Philadelphia Convention and the creation of the Constitution in 1787.

Washington addressed his letter of resignation neither to Congress nor to the American people but to the governors of the thirteen states, asking them to relay his sentiments to their respective legislatures. This is a poignant reminder of where both formal and de facto power resided in the United States in 1783. Washington served a union of thirteen republics, not a nation-state or an American people. The future of this union and its role in maintaining the liberty and independence of its member-states were the core concerns of his circular. As commander in chief of the American army, Washington had witnessed at close range the defects of the union and its inability to organize and pursue the War of Independence in an efficient manner. "I could demonstrate to every mind open to conviction," he wrote,

> that in less time & with much less expence than has been incurred,
> the War might have been brought to the same happy, conclusion if the

Perfecting the Union. Max M. Edling, Oxford University Press (2021). © Oxford University Press.
DOI: 10.1093/oso/9780197534717.003.0001

resources of the Continent could have been properly drawn forth—that the distresses and disappointments, which have very often occurred, have in too many instances resulted more from a want of energy in the Continental Government, than a deficiency of means in the particular States—That the inefficacy of measures, arising from the want of an adequate authority in the supreme Power, from a partial compliance with the requisitions of Congress in some of the States and from a failure of punctuality in others, while it tended to damp the Zeal of those which where [*sic*] more willing to exert themselves, served also to accumulate the expences of the War and to frustrate the best concerted plans.

Washington was describing the administration of union affairs under the Articles of Confederation and the lack of effective power in what contemporaries referred to as the "general" government. No one doubted the need for such a government. It was "indispensible [*sic*] to the happiness of the individual States that there should be lodged somewhere, a supreme power to regulate and govern the general concerns of the confederated Republic," Washington wrote. But unless the states would allow Congress "to exercise those prerogatives" invested in it by the confederation articles, "every thing must very rapidly tend to Anarchy and confusion."

Washington's words echoed a growing concern among a group of politicians who had been closely involved in directing the war against Britain that the American union was on the road to dissolution. "Anarchy and confusion" was eighteenth-century shorthand for the civil wars and domestic disturbances many observers foresaw should the union disintegrate into a North American state-system in which thirteen unconnected republics would vie for supremacy and reproduce the interstate tensions and conflicts that were typical of contemporary Europe. Ultimately, disunion spelled the end to both liberty and independence. Anarchy would compel the people to support any tyrant who promised to restore order, even if the cost were giving up popular liberties. Independence could be maintained only if foreign predatory nations could be kept at bay. But without a strong and effective union the American states would become "the sport of European Politicks." The great powers of the Old World would "play one State against another" to prevent the "growing importance" of America and "to serve their own interested purposes."

Despite his anxiety about the union's future, Washington's letter fell short of formulating a program for the reform of the Articles of Confederation. He was content to merely highlight two specific concerns. The first was the need to honor the debts to public creditors, army officers, and wounded veterans that the union had incurred fighting the War of Independence. The second was the need to provide for the defense of the United States by setting up an efficient military peace establishment. In addition to an "indissoluble Union of the States under one federal Head," justice to creditors, officers, and soldiers, and a viable peace establishment, Washington added one more thing that he believed "essential to the well being" and even "to the existence, of the United States as an independent Power": a readiness of the American people to set aside state interests in favor of the common good of the union. Yet he offered no recipe for cultivating that readiness, but left it "to the good sense and serious consideration of those immediately concerned." Those most "immediately concerned" were of course the very same state governors and state legislators who were the recipients of Washington's letter. On their actions the future of the union now depended.[1]

Washington's missive reflected concerns about the needs and shortcomings of the American union that reform politicians would repeatedly identify and air between the conclusion of the War of Independence and the adoption of the Constitution. Although political union was a prerequisite for the preservation of liberty and independence, the union was under constant strain from the fallout of the War of Independence. Common obligations had been incurred during the war, and independence created a range of problems that the American colonies had not faced as dependents of the British Empire. The pressure from common obligations and external forces caused political tension because the United States was a confederation of thirteen heterogeneous republics, each of which reacted differently to the same stimulus. A constant balancing act between the need for union, on the one hand, and the interests of the states, on the other, therefore became the distinctive feature of national politics in the early United States.

I

American historians have always regarded the years between the signing of the Peace of Paris in September 1783, which ended the War of Independence, and the framing of the new federal Constitution four years later, as a particularly important period in the nation's history. The peace treaty signaled Britain's acceptance of the bid for independence that the colonies had made on July 4, 1776. Yet to many historians it was the Constitution, rather than the Peace of Paris, that secured independence and thereby served as the ending point of the American Revolution. The new nation had faced many difficulties after the conclusion of the war with Britain, and the Constitution was the means to resolve them. Popular authors and commentators who celebrate the achievements of the so-called Founding Fathers also typically embrace this view. Most historians, however, are much more critical of the Constitution. To them, the framing and adoption of the Constitution meant the destruction of egalitarian and democratic promises introduced by the American Revolution.

Both views have impressive pedigrees that can be traced all the way back to the founding generation. Yet the discussion among modern historians owes more to works published in the late nineteenth and early twentieth centuries, when history was becoming an academic discipline. In 1888, the lawyer-turned-philosopher and historian John Fiske published an essay in which he argued that "the period of five years following the peace of 1783 was the most critical moment in all the history of the American people. The dangers from which we were saved in 1788 were even greater than the dangers from which we were saved in 1865." Although his book is rarely read today, Fiske made a lasting contribution to American historiography by popularizing the term *critical period*, first used by John Quincy Adams in his 1787 Harvard valedictory address, in reference to the 1780s. Fiske's account of the dangers of the critical period also subsequently made its way into monographs and textbooks that shaped perceptions of the period.[2]

To Fiske, the core problem facing the new nation was its dysfunctional central government, which was unable to meet challenges to American sovereignty and national interests. But while it was a major problem that Congress was weak and the union fragile, this state of affairs was hardly surprising. In the aftermath of independence, most Americans still identified with their own states rather than with the United States. Without a common sense of nationality, there was no popular basis for a movement to firm up the union and build a stronger national government. In fact, the thirteen states had come together only to defend their independence against Britain. Once that conflict was resolved, the natural tendency was for their union to disintegrate into its foundational elements, the states. At the same time, the states shared a number of concerns that served like a centripetal force to counterbalance the centrifugal tendency to disintegration.

Perhaps the most fundamental reason to stay united was that the United States was recognized as one nation, rather than thirteen republics, by the monarchies and empires of Europe. That the center of this nation was weak was evident already in the peace treaty that created it. Several passages of the Paris treaty spoke not of what the United States would do as a signatory but of what Congress would "earnestly recommend . . . the Legislatures of the respective states" do. Although foreign powers often doubted the United States' ability to live up to treaty obligations, in the context of the law of nations, the American union was nevertheless regarded as one nation. Another incitement to continued union lay in the western reaches of the nation. Several of the states had ceded territorial claims west of the Appalachian Mountains to Congress, creating a vast public domain north of the Ohio River that was administered by Congress, not the states. When the Constitutional Convention met this was a new development, but there was widespread expectation that the region would absorb thousands of settlers from the thirteen states and from Europe in years to come. Finally, the struggle for independence had left a legacy of shared obligations in the form of a large foreign and domestic debt contracted by Congress in the name of the United States. Defaulting on these debt obligations would cause moral as well as economic and political problems. Quite apart from these tangible causes for continued union, there was also reason to think that the states would be more successful in defending and promoting their interests both in North America and on the Atlantic Ocean as a federal union than they would be as thirteen separate republics.[3]

But if there were good reasons for the states to continue in the union, their Articles of Confederation had not established a central government with sufficient strength to manage their common concerns. In a list often repeated since, Fiske identified a number of areas where Congress could not fulfill international obligations or stand up for American interests: Congress could not enforce international treaties, principally the peace treaty; it could not force the British to abandon military posts on United States soil held contrary to the treaty; it could not adopt countermeasures against Britain's discrimination against American shipping or Spain's closure of the Mississippi River to American traders; it could not impose a common navigation act on the states; it could not prevent conflicts between the states over interstate commerce (among other incidents, Fiske claimed that New York's customs duties deliberately discriminated against New Jersey and Connecticut traders) and territorial boundaries (Connecticut and Pennsylvania clashed over the Wyoming Valley; New York and New Hampshire over the Green Mountains); it could not service its foreign debt or secure new loans on good terms; it could not retaliate against the Barbary States' depredations on American trade in the Mediterranean; it could not secure the loyalty of citizens in Kentucky and New England who contemplated secession, and so on.

In Fiske's account, the Philadelphia Convention came together to address these challenges, and in the absence of a popular movement for reform of the union and the national government, he naturally came to stress the role of influential statesmen rather than the people out of doors in bringing about reform. Fiske called the Constitution the "Iliad, or Parthenon, or Fifth Symphony, of statesmanship," revealing not only his admiration for the work of the founders, but his belief that they were selfless politicians hoping to promote the common good. Although Fiske's narrative ended with the inauguration of George Washington as first president in April 1789, the implication of his work was that the new federal government under Washington's lead defused the dangers of the critical period. The Constitution thereby ensured that the national independence that was declared in name in 1776 became a reality in 1789.[4]

Fiske wrote his essay a century after the founding and two decades after the Civil War, at a time when sectional conflict and international weakness had an immediacy now long lost. Neither continued union nor international great power status was taken for granted by Fiske, and the consequences of disunion were very real to him. In a passage grounded in equal measures in his evolutionary theory of history and his triumphant Anglo-Saxonism, Fiske wrote that the fortunate outcome of the critical period had determined that "the continent of North America should be dominated by a single powerful and pacific federal nation instead of being parcelled out among forty or fifty small communities, wasting their strength and lowering their moral tone by perpetual warfare, like the states of ancient Greece, or by perpetual preparation for warfare, like the nations of modern Europe."[5]

A quarter-century after the publication of Fiske's essay, there appeared a work in many ways its inversion, which has ever since exercised enormous influence on historians' understanding of the nation's founding. Whereas Fiske saw the 1780s as a period of interstate and international rivalries, Charles Beard's *An Economic Interpretation of the Constitution of the United States* concentrated on domestic struggles between social groups representing antagonistic interests. Beard and his followers in the so-called Progressive school of interpretation deemphasized the problem of independence and argued that the fears over disunion and international depredations so often raised by the founding generation were no more than a ruse. The crucial question at the heart of the founding was not whether the United States would remain independent, but what sort of society it would become. In the Progressive interpretation, the founding was a struggle over the distribution of scarce resources, and the Constitution was the means by which one class gained control over the central government to further its own material interests.

Whereas Fiske's approach downplayed the opposition to the Constitution— he dismissed anti-federalism as "purely a policy of negation and obstruction," for example—Charles Beard, with Mary Beard, argued that the Constitution was adopted not by the American people but by an interested segment of the population: "Broadly speaking, the division of the voters over the document ran along economic lines. The merchants, manufacturers, private creditors, and holders of public securities loomed large among the advocates of the new system, while the opposition came chiefly from the small farmers behind the seaboard, especially from the men who, in earlier years, had demanded paper money and other apparatus for easing the strain of their debts."[6]

It followed from the Beards' analysis of the struggle over ratification that they approached the idea of a critical period with considerable skepticism. "When it is remembered," Charles Beard asserted in his *Economic Interpretation of the Constitution*, "that most of our history has been written by Federalists, it will become apparent that great care should be taken in accepting, without reserve, the gloomy pictures of the social conditions prevailing under the Articles of

Confederation." In fact, the critical period was little more than "a figment of political imagination." Although the Beards accepted that some socioeconomic groups, essentially those who supported the Constitution, suffered in the 1780s, they ventured the guess that the country as a whole "was in many respects steadily recovering order and prosperity even under the despised Articles of Confederation."[7]

Despite his reputation as an iconoclast, Beard's analysis of the founding was in fact always measured. A much more uncompromising attitude was adopted by Merrill Jensen, a historian thirty years Beard's junior who has also been extremely influential among his peers. Not only did Jensen claim that the 1780s was a period of "extraordinary economic growth," he also made explicit the struggle over democracy that was only implicit in Beard's work. To Jensen, the revolutionary era was dominated by a struggle between "radicals" and "conservatives," which followed on "the democratization of the American society by the destruction of the coercive authority of Great Britain and the establishment of actual local self-government within the separate states under the Articles of Confederation." Jensen's radicals were democrats and supporters of state sovereignty, while his conservatives were aristocrats and nationalists. Whereas the Declaration of Independence and the Articles of Confederation were the institutional manifestations of radical ideals, the Constitution was the work of the conservatives. The Federalists, said Jensen, "engineered a conservative counterrevolution and erected a nationalistic government whose purpose in part was to thwart the will of 'the people' in whose name they acted."[8]

For most of the twentieth century, the tradition established by Beard and Jensen has dominated scholarship on the creation of the Constitution. The founding has been interpreted as a struggle between social classes over issues arising primarily within, rather than outside, the United States. This holds true also for the work that for the last five decades has served as the standard interpretation of the period between the Peace of Paris and the adoption of the Constitution, Gordon Wood's *Creation of the American Republic.* But in recent years there has been a renewed interest in the twinned questions of federalism and international relations that featured so prominently in Fiske's account of the critical period. Such *unionist* or *internationalist* interpretations, in contrast to the economic interpretations of the Progressives, reflect a general turn in the profession that has compelled historians to analyze the many ways in which separate national histories are connected to, or entangled with, one another. Peter Onuf and David Armitage have written about the international and global history of the Declaration of Independence. David Golove and Daniel Hulsebosch have interpreted the Constitution as "a fundamentally international document"—not a counterrevolutionary negation of the promise of the Declaration but a continuation of its attempt to secure international recognition of the fledgling United

States. Eliga Gould has presented a similar argument, showing how American statesmen struggled to make their new nation assume its rank "among the powers of the earth." Robbie Totten has argued that the Constitution was the solution to a two-sided diplomatic crisis of how to work out the relationship between the thirteen new American republics and their collective relationship to foreign powers. Leonard Sadosky and Gregory Ablavsky have pointed to the importance of settling the new nation's relationship not only with European states and empires but also with Native American nations in order to secure the promises of independence.[9]

These newer works point to international and intraunion, rather than domestic, relations in their analysis of both the causes and the consequences of the Constitution. Where the Progressives believe the principal political agents to be classes, the new literature concentrates on polities: European monarchies, American states, the federal union, and American Indian nations. Where the Progressives see the principal historical dynamic springing from class struggle, these authors find it in geopolitical competition and sectional tension. Where the Progressives find the principal political agenda of the constitutional reform movement to be the redistribution of property and status from "ordinary people" to the elite, recent scholarship describe it as an attempt to defend US territorial integrity and the national interest from competitors in the western borderlands and on the Atlantic Ocean. And where the Progressives identify the principal outcome of the founding to be the creation of a bourgeois state that faced inward to make North America safe for capitalism, Unionist interpretations identify it as the creation of a stronger federal union that faced outward to stand up to European powers and to conquer the North American continent.

Unionist interpretations therefore call for a return to, and a reassessment of, the so-called dual revolution-thesis that Progressive historians have used to make sense of the American nation-building process. The term *dual revolution* was coined by a contemporary of Beard, Carl Becker, to capture how the American founding was at the same time "a struggle for home rule," or independence, and "a struggle over who should rule at home," or, in Becker's words, a struggle over "the democratization of American politics and society." Although the Progressive tradition has never denied the significance of independence, it has always emphasized the struggle over democratization as the more important development. Representing a return to Fiske's approach, interpretations focusing on international and intraunion relations reverse this priority by arguing that neither political independence nor the creation of a stable federal union were foregone conclusions of the American Revolution.[10]

The following pages draw on the insights of scholars who have studied foreign affairs and federalism in the founding era. It presents the framing and ratification of the Constitution as the outcome of a perceived need to secure the survival of the American union of republics as an independent nation. Multiple challenges arose from the American colonies' transition to independent nationhood, and after independence the conviction rapidly grew that these challenges could not be effectively addressed within the framework of the Articles of Confederation. By 1787, the American states faced the choice of either reinvigorating their union or dissolving it. Both main routes contained alternatives. Many people who accepted the need for reform still believed that the best way to make the American union fit for purpose was to amend the Articles of Confederation. Others came to think that a completely new compact of union had to be substituted for the old. Similarly, the dissolution of the union did not necessarily mean that the states would be on their own. A more common projection was for the existing union of thirteen states to be replaced by two or three smaller regional confederations of economically and culturally more homogeneous sections. The outcome of the political crisis of the confederation was therefore not preordained. Nor does the Constitution represent the realization of a single master plan. Rather, it was shaped by an extended debate and repeated compromises in which the need for union to preserve the independence and well-being of the states confronted and sometimes clashed with the impulse to defend state and sectional identities and interests.

The reform of the union effected by the Constitution restructured and strengthened the general or national government. But the Constitution did not obliterate the states, nor did it make the states redundant. As Mary Sarah Bilder has shown, the framers at first found it anything but easy to precisely delimit the respective duties and remits of the different levels of government in the union. The problem was not new. It had been central to the critique of the British Parliament before the American Revolution and to the debates surrounding the framing of the Articles of Confederation after the break with Britain. In the Constitutional Convention, James Madison said that it was "impracticable" or even "impossible" to draw a "precise line" between the jurisdictions of the states and the national government. Yet what Madison found impracticable and impossible became necessary to win over the majority of the Convention and the majority of American citizens, who had no wish to see the states absorbed by Congress. In the ratification debates, Federalists defended the Constitution against its critics by arguing that the new national government was a government of enumerated powers that would not infringe on essential state authority and rights.[11]

In his opinion on the constitutionality of the Bank of the United States, Alexander Hamilton pointed out that the principle of enumeration did not in fact result in a clear-cut "division of the legislative power." The Constitution created a tripartite division of authority under which "there will be cases [of legislation] clearly within the power of the National Government; others clearly without its power; and a third class, which will leave room for controversy & difference of opinion." The third class that Hamilton identified were at the center of the party struggles between Federalists and Jeffersonian Republicans in the 1790s. But the viciousness of these party conflicts should not prevent us from recognizing that most legislative activity of Congress and the state assemblies belonged in, respectively, the first and the second class. Just like the Bank, such laws could be fiercely contested on party principles, but in contrast to the chartering of the Bank of the United States, they did not raise questions over the nature of the federal union or the boundary between national and state authority. Even more important, the existence of the contentious third class should not prevent us from recognizing that the states retained extensive political authority under the Constitution. In the early republic and well beyond, the states rather than the national government regulated the economy, education, communications, infrastructure investments, religion, property, and civic rights. Understanding the respective roles of the national and the state governments in the federal union is central to understanding the Constitution and the American state-building project.[12]

II

This book presents the framing and adoption of the Constitution as a reform of the American union. Its focus is the division of government duties and powers between Congress and the states. The thesis can be summed up like this: the Constitution profoundly transformed the *structure* of the American union, thereby making the national government more effective, but it did not transform the fundamental *purpose* of the union, which remained a political organization designed to manage the relations between the American states, on the one hand, and between the American states and foreign powers, on the other. In other words, the Constitution created a national government but did not significantly extend its remit. Despite the challenge identified by Madison, the framers succeed in their attempt "to draw a line of demarkation [sic] which would give to the General Government every power requisite for general purposes, and leave to the States every power which might be most beneficially administered by them." The result was a dual structure of government, in which the federal government and the states were both essential to the people's welfare. Getting the story about the Constitution straight matters because it makes possible a broader assessment of the American founding as both a transformative event, aiming at territorial and economic expansion, and as a conservative event, aiming at the preservation of key elements of the colonial sociopolitical order.[13]

The book starts in a review of new interpretations of the American founding that invites us to reconsider what we mean by the term *constitution* when we speak of the federal constitution of 1787. Today, we tend to think of a constitution as "the basic legal order of the polity, which holds a special rank vis-à-vis laws and other sources of the law and which radiates into all spheres of the legal system," as one constitutional theorist puts it. But there exists an older meaning of constitution as a federal treaty, or international agreement, whereby "several states join into a lasting political entity without giving up their own political independence in the process." The US Constitution contains both of these elements. It is at the same time a form of government creating and defining the federal government, and an agreement between the American states recreating the American union. Chapter 1 puts the spotlight on the Constitution in its incarnation as a compact of union between sovereign states, a compact that allowed them to maintain interstate peace and to act in unison as a single nation vis-à-vis other nations in the international state-system. There are two key features to the American compact of union: the voluntary circumscription of the member-states' sovereignty, and the creation of a national government through the delegation of enumerated powers from the states to the union. Interpreting the Constitution as an agreement between states, creating what early modern political writers called a "federal republic," makes clear that the instrument was a limited, if also a very important, reform of the American union. It did not aim at a wholesale transformation of American social and economic life, but sought to equip the union with the means to address challenges that arose from intraunion tensions, on the one hand, and from international competition in the Atlantic marketplace and the Western borderlands, on the other.[14]

Chapter 2 continues the investigation into the meaning of the Constitution by taking seriously the preamble's declaration that the framers sought to create "a more perfect union." This statement suggests that their labor was intended as an improvement over the less than perfect union established by the Articles of Confederation. But what did the framers mean by *union*, and what was their American union meant to achieve? Too often answers to these questions are shaped by what the United States would become in the twentieth century— that is, a polity where the state governments, although possessing considerable autonomy, can be forced by the federal government to conform to national standards in the organization and management of their social, economic, and civic life. Yet what the United States would become is not what the framers envisioned. To understand the framers' concept of union it is necessary to consult how early modern political thinkers approached unions or confederations, and to investigate the first American compact of union—the Articles of Confederation. Against this background, chapter 2 argues that there was significant continuity between the Articles of Confederation and the Constitution.

Although the latter laid the basis for a national government that was founded on popular sovereignty and had the capacity to act independently of the states, the fundamental purpose of the American union and the remit of the national government remained the management of intraunion and international affairs. Beyond the national government's remit, the American union reserved to the states the power to regulate the social, economic, and civic life of their citizens and inhabitants with only limited supervision and control from the national government.

The division of labor whereby the national government was tasked with intraunion and international affairs, and the state governments remained responsible for domestic affairs, does not mean that the actions of the federal government played no role in internal state development after 1787. Most obviously, Article VI of the Constitution makes all international treaties "the supreme Law of the Land." Trade agreements had a direct impact on the economic life of the states. Other federal government activity, such as the organization of federal territories and the opening up federal land for settlement, also had consequences for the development of the states. The creation of a common market mattered too. Nor is it the case that US foreign policy was insulated from what took place in the states. To the contrary, the actions of the federal government were shaped by the needs and wishes of the states, which the states made known in Congress through their representatives. Rather than their competitor, the federal government was the collective instrument of government of the states. Finally, it would of course be a mistake to think of domestic and international politics as separate rather than interdependent. But the fact that no watertight bulkhead separated domestic from international politics in the American ship of state does not mean that the distinction between the two is meaningless. To the contrary, the distinction between the domestic and the international has been an organizing principle of political organization and political reflection at least since the early modern period.

Chapter 3 delves deeper into the question of the division of governmental authority between the states and the national government. In the form of an investigation of the concept of *internal police*, it asks in what, precisely, the duties of eighteenth-century states consisted. Now largely forgotten, but much in use in the decades surrounding the American Revolution, *internal police* was a term employed to describe a range of activities, other than the administration of justice, that eighteenth-century states did to regulate their societies and their economies. But if its range of application was broad, its exact meaning went undefined. Part of chapter 3 therefore seeks to recover the different meanings of internal police in eighteenth-century European and American social and political discourse in the years preceding the framing and adoption of the Constitution. The chapter then turns to an analysis of the distribution of authority between the states and the national government in the Constitution with a special emphasis on internal police powers. This analysis reinforces the point made in chapter 2, that under the Constitution domestic regulation in the early United States was overwhelmingly the concern of the states.

No matter how much they disagree on the causes, aims, and consequences of the Constitution, virtually all scholars agree on two things. First, they agree that the Constitutional Convention was called to address matters that the framers of the Constitution believed to be highly pressing. Second, they agree that the first Congress was dominated by representatives and senators sympathetic to the program of the Constitution's framers. It is therefore reasonable to assume that the first Congresses under George Washington's presidency did their best to implement the political program that had propelled the framers to Philadelphia and that had informed their actions in the Constitutional Convention. The administration lost majority support in the House of Representatives in the third and fourth Congress but kept control of the Senate. If treated with care, the record of the early Congresses can shed light on the implementation of the Constitution. Acting on this assumption, chapter 4 investigates the legislative record of Congress between 1789 and 1797. It uses several different classification schemata to establish whether the actions of the national legislature focused mostly on domestic social and economic matters, or mostly on intraunion and international affairs. To highlight the specificities of the federal government, the legislative record of Congress is analyzed alongside that of the legislature of one of the member-states of the American union, the Commonwealth of Pennsylvania, and that of a unitary nation-state, the former mother country Great Britain, in the same period.

III

The perspective shift provided by a Unionist interpretation of the founding invites us to reconsider claims about the Constitution that are deeply entrenched in the literature. Based on an ironic reading of the framing and adoption of the federal constitution, historians have interpreted the Constitution as a failure. Called together to turn the tide of democratization that had swept over the state legislatures in the wake of the struggle for independence, and which had led local majorities to trample on the rights of minorities and to disregard the greater good of the nation, the Constitutional Convention tried to relocate power from the people to a distant central government removed from popular pressure. According to this view, the framers envisioned the creation of a central government that could reach deeply into society to protect individual rights, principally property rights, against democratic majorities in the states. But if the

Constitutional Convention succeeded in the immediate goal to frame and adopt the Constitution, it soon became evident that "their Constitution failed, and failed miserably, in what they wanted it to do." The federal government did not replace the states as the central locus of power before the middle of the twentieth century. Until then its influence on the nation's internal development proved to be negligible. Whereas the states grew in importance and power in the early nineteenth century, "governance in Washington barely mattered in the lives of ordinary Americans."[15]

According to the Unionist interpretation, however, the federal government was never created to regulate domestic affairs. It therefore raises the question if scholars have mischaracterized both the Constitution and the American union and thereby exaggerated the degree to which the founding generation sought to radically recast early American social and political life. The proper measure of the Constitution's success is not the federal government's regulation of domestic affairs but its regulation of the western borderlands and the Atlantic market-place. In the early years of the federal government, there were endless difficulties and government blunders in both the continental interior and on the Atlantic Ocean. But the Constitution set in motion a long process of territorial and commercial expansion that would turn the United States first into a continental, and eventually into a global, power.

The Unionist interpretation inserts the Constitution into a narrative of American empire. But this does not mean that the questions formulated by alternative interpretations are now redundant. To the contrary, and perhaps counterintuitively, a reinterpretation of the Constitution's origins that emphasizes the importance of "home rule" allows for a fresh look at the old question of "who should rule at home" once American independence was secured, and thus for a reinvigoration of the tradition of constitutional analysis initiated by Beard and others well over a century ago. However, the Unionist interpretation has two consequences for the Progressive analysis. First, it shifts the focus from the nation to the states as the principal arena of economic change. New work on the American Revolution shows that the break with Britain was accompanied by demands for government intervention in economic and social life. The extent of that intervention in the early republic and antebellum eras is well documented by economic historians. But all too often this intervention has been ignored because of the assumption that real change can only happen at the national level. The evidence suggests otherwise. For example, the federal government spent $60 million on transportation projects and incorporated two banks between 1790 and 1860. In the same period, the state governments invested more than $450 million in transportation ventures and incorporated thousands of banks. What is more, such state action was often controversial and gave rise to political struggles that furthered the democratization of American government. Scholars have to pay greater attention to state politics if they are to show how independence and the founding reshaped American society.[16]

Second, the conventional view of the American founding as a transformative event in the history of liberal democracy still dominates investigations into the causes and consequences of the Constitution. More than anything else, the assumption that leading framers aimed to create national citizenship rights has led to their project being deemed a failure. But if the true aim of the Constitutional Convention was not civic rights but the reform of the federal union, scholars interested in the origins of liberal democracy need to turn their attention to the sources of law that actually regulated civic rights in early America. Although the Constitution strengthened the rights of foreign nationals and out-of-state citizens, for the vast majority of Americans, rights and entitlements continued to be determined by state constitutions, state statutes, and state common law. The degree to which the American founding was an emancipatory event therefore cannot be meaningfully investigated at national level. Just as the case is with economic change, inquiries into civic rights have to concentrate on developments in the states. Although such an inquiry is beyond the scope of this study, the book ends with some reflections on how the Unionist interpretation makes possible a complex and decentered understanding of the founding as an event that partly changed but mostly conserved an older tradition of civic rights in America.

1

Peace Pact and Nation

The Constitution as a Compact between States

At the time of the Constitution's two-hundredth anniversary, there was widespread agreement that founding scholarship was languishing. A special issue on "The Constitution and American Life" in the *Journal of American History* failed to include a single article on the founding because "experts on the drafting and ratification of the Constitution" had told the editor, David Thelen, "that there was little fresh thinking in their field." In a long review article published a few years earlier, James Hutson had concluded that founding historiography was "at a standstill." According to Hutson, before around 1960 historians had been busy debating the value of Charles Beard's 1913 classic *An Economic Interpretation of the Constitution of the United States*. In the decades that followed, the profession largely turned its back on political history and the few brave souls who soldiered on went with the general scholarly flow in a turn toward cultural and intellectual history that downplayed institutions like the Constitution in favor of mapping broad ideological transformations.[1]

Their turn uncovered a rich and largely unexplored intellectual world that provided material for new scholarly milestones in books by the likes of Bernard Bailyn and Gordon Wood. Together with John Pocock and his disciples, they challenged a long-held view among scholars that the American founding was fundamentally a Lockean, or liberal, moment. This shifted the terrain away from Progressive interpreters like Beard and his followers, for whom the liberal outcome of the founding had never been in doubt—if for the most part regretted. Instead, the new intellectual history presented the founding as a classical republican vanguard action fought to contain the inevitable advance of liberalism in a struggle for the soul of America. With their attention fastened on culture and ideas, historians no longer had time for institutions. The Constitution, along with its clauses sanctifying contract and banning paper money, which Beard and others had once presented as the heralds of economic liberalism, were deemed

Perfecting the Union. Max M. Edling, Oxford University Press (2021). © Oxford University Press.
DOI: 10.1093/oso/9780197534717.003.0002

irrelevant as scholars concentrated on changes in a collective American "mind" or a nebulous American "political culture." It is symptomatic that the most intense debates about when exactly liberalism replaced republicanism as the dominant ideology in America revolved not around the framing and ratification of the Constitution, but around the formulation of a Jeffersonian ideology in the 1790s.[2]

Historiographical milestones became millstones when scholars failed to demonstrate that the founding discourse was structured by sharply demarcated republican and liberal worldviews that followed on each other in succession. Instead, they found a polyglot "confusion of idioms" and "clatter" of tongues. Polyglotism indicates that to the framers of the Constitution, ideas and concepts were means to persuade and to make the world intelligible. But the estrangement of the Ideological historians from agency, institutions, and materiality prevented them from making the intellectual leap required to pursue this lead. By 1987, the republican synthesis was dying from consumption. There is nothing to suggest that its resurrection is nigh.[3]

And so we find ourselves in the intellectual desert of the bicentennial. Yet the ground was perhaps not quite as barren as Hutson and Thelen had indicated. A lone dissenting voice argued that "prematurely pessimistic assessments" had failed to notice "how the field itself is being redefined." To Peter Onuf, the founding was a period marked neither by class struggle between the people and the elite, as the Progressives believed, or by the transition from republicanism to liberalism, as suggested by the ideological interpretation, but by the crisis of the American union in the wake of the War of Independence. More than anything else, the Constitution represented "the efforts of constitutional reformers to construct—and conceptualize—a workable federal system." A decade later, the ongoing redefinition of the field that Onuf had spotted had matured into a complex but cohesive explanation of the form and function of the Constitution. Although the works of scholars approaching the founding from the perspective of federalism and international relations is now both known and appreciated, there is still a need to present their core arguments in cogent form.[4]

I

Onuf's prescience at the founding's bicentennial came from his own role in forcing historiographical change. His scholarly trajectory began in 1983 with a study of how "jurisdictional controversies" over state land claims and secessionist movements in the trans-Appalachian west during the American Revolution fed into the creation of the Constitution. It was soon followed by a book on the Northwest Ordinance. At the time, the West was a highly unusual vantage point from which to write the history of the founding, but it meant that Onuf's analysis came to foreground interstate conflict and federalism and to identify the creation of a viable union as the single most important political problem of the founding era. He next brought this outlook to bear on the making of the Constitution in a series of essays written for publications marking the bicentennial, which were then reworked into a book coauthored with Cathy Matson, *A Union of Interests: Political and Economic Thought in Revolutionary America*, which appeared in 1990. It added to the analysis of western expansion and state conflict an account of how the immersion of the American states in the Atlantic marketplace also gave rise to intraunion tensions. It was the first fully fledged Unionist interpretation of the origins of the Constitution.[5]

Onuf owed an intellectual debt to his advisor Jack P. Greene, who in 1986 published *Peripheries and Center: Constitutional Development in the Extended Polities of the British Empire and the United States, 1607–1788*, a book based on decades of research into the British Empire and colonial America, which in turn drew extensively on Onuf and Jack Rakove for the postindependence period. In *Peripheries and Center*, Greene acknowledged his own debt to Andrew McLaughlin and Charles McIlwain, constitutional scholars of the British Empire and the United States active in the 1920s, and thus sank historiographical roots for a Unionist interpretation. Greene made the case for the persistence of a fundamental political problem in the English and British imperial project: how to govern a geographically "extended polity." From the establishment of the first colonies in North America to the outbreak of the American Revolution, Britons on both sides of the Atlantic struggled to maintain a central power strong enough to keep the far-flung Empire together without endangering the liberty and safety of its constituent parts. The American Revolution removed Britain from the equation but otherwise left organizational issues unaddressed when the problem of empire turned into the problem of union. Attempts to resolve the tension between the whole and the constituent parts "provide an underlying unity to early American constitutional history from the colonial through the early national periods," Greene says. To Onuf, "the definition of the federal union" remained "the central problem in American political discourse" to the Civil War.[6]

Economic and administrative limits meant that the English Crown colonized North America by proxy using charter companies and proprietary lords. Two important consequences followed from this mode of colonization. First, there was not one but many colonization ventures, which resulted in a number of distinctive colonies largely autonomous from the imperial center. Second, because the sponsors, too, had limited economic and administrative resources at their command they could only attract settlers by extending the rights and privileges of native-born Englishmen to the American colonies. Chief among these was the right to extensive self-rule in legislative assemblies representing local landowners. These "contracts" between sponsors and settlers formed the basis for every colony's "peculiar constitution." In the century and a half that followed on the establishment of Jamestown and Plymouth Plantation, the understanding that the colonies had a separate identity as bodies politic with distinctive privileges became entrenched in North America. "Consisting of a well-defined body of territory, each of these colonies had its own peculiar constitution, institutions, laws, history, and identity, to which its inhabitants were, for the most part, both well socialized and strongly attached."[7]

The colonists' belief that their satellite states were separate bodies politic raises the question why the struggle against England produced not thirteen independent nations but one. This mystery dissolves when the act of declaring independence is scrutinized more closely. In an insightful essay from the time of the Constitution's bicentennial, John Pocock asked what it meant that the rebelling colonies chose to call themselves "united states." According to Pocock, *state* was not the default term for a political organization at the time, at least not in the Anglophone world, but was derived from the law of nations to signal that the colonies assumed for themselves the status of sovereign polities vis-à-vis other sovereign states. Their declaration of independence announced that they were henceforth "Free and Independent States" possessing "full Power to levy War, conclude Peace, contract Alliances, establish Commerce," and the right "to do all other Acts and Things which Independent States may of right do." As Pocock points out, this presents us with "the problem of what happens when thirteen 'states' are made to claim that they are 'free and independent' and that they are 'united.'"[8]

The answer is that the colonies used the federative powers they had assumed as independent states to enter into union. In *Spirit of the Laws*, Montesquieu had explained how federations—what he and other writers on natural law called "federal republics"—were the fruit of "an agreement by which many political bodies consent to become citizens of the larger state that they want to form. It is a kind of society of societies that make a new one, which can be enlarged by new associates that unite with it." These societies were formed, Pocock writes, when states exercised their "power to conclude peace and war by means of treaties or *foedera*." The American union, announced to the world in the Declaration of Independence, should therefore be seen as a treaty organization. In July 1776 the American *foedus* was implied rather than explicit, the result of a decade of consultation between, and concerted action by, the colonies, but it would soon be spelled out in the Articles of Confederation. The "firm league of friendship" established by the ratification of the articles constituted the United States not as "a body politic but an association of bodies politic." The *Novus Ordo Seclorum* motto to the contrary, such a political organization

was nothing new but was well-established in the law of nations and "readily recognizable" to European "eighteenth-century taxonomists of political forms as a
'league of firm friendship,' a '*république federative*,' or a 'system of states.'" That a
treaty could create a union that made it possible for several states to act as one
nation explains why a portfolio of American organic laws, aimed at impressing
European observers, described the Articles of Confederation as a "Treaty," that
formed a "Constitution, or mode of Government, for the collective North-
American Commonwealth."[9]

The goal of the American union that was created by the Declaration and
formalized by the Articles was, in Onuf's analysis, twofold: to "constitute a more
perfect world order for the colony-states," on the one hand, and to serve as "a
legitimate (recognizable) government" of the union "in the larger world," on
the other. But the first union failed miserably on both counts. After independence, critical issues confronted the United States in the western marchlands
of the continental interior as well as in the Atlantic marketplace. In the West,
the Continental Congress had only nominal control over American Indians
and European American settler colonists who resided there. Britain violated
the new nation's territorial integrity by maintaining military posts on American
soil and diplomatic relations with Indian nations living within the borders of
the United States. On the Atlantic Ocean and beyond, the expulsion of the
American colonies from the common market of the British Empire had led to
a sharp downturn in exports and shipping, which in turn had caused an economic depression. A third challenge lay in the cracks that had begun to appear
in the federal union, where conflicts of interest between the member-states over
the Revolutionary debt, commercial regulations, and territorial claims were
producing tension. Times were bad, the future of the Union in doubt. In this
climate the Constitutional Convention met in May 1787 to "render the federal
constitution adequate to the exigencies of government and the preservation of
the Union."[10]

The principal purpose of the Constitutional Convention was therefore not
to restrict democracy, promote property interests, or turn America into a liberal society—although such outcomes may well have been unintended, if not
necessarily unwelcome, consequences—but to repair the union. In political
scientist Michael Zuckert's words, the leading reformers were critical of the
Confederation for "its failures to achieve the ends for which it was instituted, not
its failure to seek ends beyond these." Looking back at the Convention from a distance of five decades, James Madison, the putative "father of the Constitution,"
presented the Constitution as a plan of union between sovereign republics.
Throughout ancient and modern history, he wrote with a nod to Montesquieu,
"feeble communities, independent of each other, have resorted to a Union ... for
the common safety ag[ain]st powerful neighbors, and for the preservation of

justice and peace among themselves." The American Constitution was but another addition "to those examples."[11]

The idea that a union could preserve peace and justice among member-states harked back to a long tradition of peace plans. When the Americans formed their union "Montesquieu, Vattel, and before them, a whole series of early world federalists had imagined a world of confederated states, freed from war," Onuf points out.[12] Although Onuf was the first to analyze this aspect of the union, the most elaborate discussion is found in the works of two political scientists: David Hendrickson's *Peace Pact: The Lost World of the American Founding* from 2003, preceded by an influential article on the "Philadelphia System" by Daniel Deudney. Union as a means of nation-building, another central part of Onuf's analysis, has recently been the subject of detailed inquiries by Eliga Gould and Daniel Hulsebosch focusing on the problem of international recognition, and by Leonard Sadosky and others focusing on the organization of the national domain in the trans-Appalachian West.[13]

II

The term *constitution*, like most key terms that organize political life and reflection, is a complex word with multiple meanings. Today it typically refers to the institutions, practices, and principles that define the government of an organization or state, on the one hand, and to the written document that creates those institutions, practices, and principles, on the other. Already Samuel Johnson's *Dictionary of the English Language,* from the middle of the eighteenth century, defined *constitution* both as an "established form of government" and as "the act of constituting, enacting." It is the existence of these alternative meanings that makes it possible to say that Britain has a constitution in the first, but not in the second, sense of the term. But irrespective of their existence as a written document, modern constitutions are said to share certain core characteristics. A constitution is the fundamental law of a state or polity, which, as the supreme law of the land, trumps other sources of law. A constitution also determines the structure of the government and the functions of governmental institutions. Doing so, it both enables and empowers, and limits and restricts, government. Finally, a constitution regulates the relationship between individual citizens and the government. Through bills of rights, constitutions safeguard civic rights and limit government action.[14]

On both sides of the Atlantic, the late eighteenth-century Age of Revolution was a golden age of constitution-making and constitution-writing. The new American states were at the forefront of this development. From 1776 and onward, all but two of the states wrote new constitutions. These not only expressed and embraced a republican system of government that has persisted to this day, but also established the importance of *written* constitutions. Constitution-writing encouraged commentators to claim that wherever a constitution "cannot be produced in a visible form, there is none," as Thomas Paine put it in a jibe at Edmund Burke's praise for the English constitution. Typically, the American state constitutions were divided in two parts. The first part was a bill of rights that contained not only an enumeration of civic rights but, just as important, the central political principles on which the new government rested. It mixed sweeping assertions with detailed prescriptions. The Virginia Declaration of Rights of 1776, for example, stated both that all men were by nature equally free and independent, and that the government should not issue general warrants. The second part, which followed on the bill or declaration of rights, was the constitution proper, that is, the form of government. Again, Virginia is a case in point. After the Declaration of Rights followed "The Constitution or Form of Government" of the Commonwealth. The Pennsylvania political writer and medical doctor Benjamin Rush illustrated the relationship between the two parts of the American state constitutions when he wrote that a bill of rights should "contain the great principles of *natural* and *civil* liberty" and that the constitution proper should form "the executive part of the Bill of Rights."[15]

Largely lost today is an older meaning of *constitution* as a compact of union or federal treaty, the means by which "several states join into a lasting political entity without giving up their own political independence in the process." This understanding harks back to early modern ideas about European international relations. In the seventeenth to nineteenth century, writers on international politics and law presented Europe's sovereign states as bound together by the rules of sociability and cooperation, and the rules governing conflicts of interest and war, which informed the great peace settlements of European international history. They spoke of the European state-system as a "federal system" governed by a "constitution." In a similar way, American writers often claimed that the relationship between the American colonies and the mother country, the composite parts of the British Empire, was governed by an imperial "constitution," although the nature of that constitution was much contested. Alongside such larger, uncodified European and transatlantic federal systems, political and legal thinkers also wrote about *federal republics*, or *perpetual unions*, that were created when sovereign states entered into union by means of a treaty. In the eighteenth century, the United Provinces of the Netherlands and the Swiss Cantons were the best-known examples of such "federal republics." It is noteworthy that they were typically referred to as the Swiss and the Dutch *republic* in the singular, despite being federal unions of several republics. The treaty of union that created such federal republics was often called a *constitution*.[16]

As Mary Sarah Bilder and David Hendrickson have shown, American statesmen of the founding period were no strangers to the use of the word *constitution* to refer to a treaty creating a "federal republic." In framing and adopting the Articles of Confederation, they created an American republic alongside the Dutch and the Swiss republics. Although modern commentators tend to present the Constitution of 1787 as a qualitatively different instrument from the Articles of Confederation of 1781, presenting the former as a constitution and the latter as a treaty of union, this was hardly the view of the 1780s. Bilder convincingly argues that the framers had not yet conceptualized several of the features that we now consider central and integral to the Constitution, and that the exact nature of the document was anything but clear to them. Although the framers were convinced that the Constitution was an improvement on the Articles of Confederation, there is nothing to suggest that they thought of the Constitution as a different kind of instrument from the articles. We should note that when Congress called the Constitutional Convention it referred to the articles as "the federal *constitution*," not as the treaty of union or the treaty of confederation. When the convention met, so did Madison. His notes from the Constitutional Convention opened with the words "Monday May 14 was the day fixed for the meeting of the deputies in Convention for revising the federal Constitution." Only decades later did Madison scratch out the word "Constitution" and replace it with the words "system of government," thus retrospectively marking the summer of 1787 as a watershed in American political organization.[17]

The *federal republic* described by eighteenth-century political writers created supra-state institutions of authority and transferred powers from the states joining in union to these institutions. Yet the ultimate aim of the federal republic was the preservation and protection of the separate identity and the particular interests of the treaty parties. One way in which it did this was by offering states entering into union a way to escape war, the default means of conflict resolution in the anarchic international state system and a principal existential threat to states. By replacing anarchy with union, Hendrickson argues that the US Constitution of 1787 fulfilled a role comparable to the great peace settlements of early modern European history: Westphalia in 1648, Utrecht in 1713, and Vienna in 1815.[18]

This understanding of the founding implies that the bonds of affection that held the American states together after independence were not strong enough to prevent them from acting out their self-interest to the detriment of sister states. Absent union, anarchy and interstate competition would characterize their relationship and thereby extend to North America the European balance of power system with its arms races, bloated governments, and frequent wars. This prospect posed an existential threat to the newly independent American republics in two ways. Most obviously, a single state or group of states, with or without a

European ally, could achieve hegemony and subject the other states to its will. Less obviously, the republican system of government could be expected to corrode if external pressure became too pronounced. War always centralizes power and if wars were frequent, or the danger of war constant, there was a significant risk that centralized power would develop into despotic rule and the circumscription of civic rights. "America was without kings or military establishments; it would acquire both in circumstances of disunion," Hendrickson remarks. "It had no class of white men who, profiting from the 'military system' so deeply entrenched in Europe, made the European laborer 'go supperless to bed, and to moisten his bed with the sweat of his brows.' Disunion would bring that as well." Because the "internal character of states" was perceived to be "a function of powerful systemic pressures generated by the structure of the 'international system,'" the preservation of republican rule in the American states depended on the creation and maintenance of a benevolent international environment in North America. Union was the means to do so. By defusing the danger of interstate war, the federal treaty of union protected both the independence of the American states and their republican system of government.[19]

To maintain union the centrifugal force of state interests had to be somehow neutralized without watering down state self-determination to the point where the states were no longer politically independent. Entering into a federal republic entailed a voluntary circumscription of the treaty parties' sovereignty. In Emer de Vattel's words, the states "put some restraint on the exercise of [their sovereignty], in virtue of voluntary engagements." But in the American case this did not mean that the thirteen states were consolidated into one nation-state. The framers of the Constitution steered a careful course between the twin dangers of national consolidation and civil war. They wrote into the Constitution protection both for the states' separate identity as bodies politic and for their essential interests, while at the same time they attempted to remove sources of interstate conflict and the power of the states to make war.[20]

The Constitution protected the separate identity, or sovereignty, of the states by guaranteeing their territorial integrity and self-determination. Large states could not be subdivided and small states could not be merged with other states without their consent (Article IV, section 3). States were protected from invasion and rebellion and guaranteed a "Republican Form of Government" (Article IV, section 4). They were made essential elements of the federal government structure by the provision for equal state representation in the Senate (Article I, section 3 and further protected by Article V), but also by the creation of a House of Representatives elected by "the People of the several States" (Article I, section 2) and an executive chosen by state electors appointed "in such Manner as the Legislature [of each state] may direct" (Article II, section 1). But the most important protection of state identity as distinctive bodies politic was the framers' design of a national government of limited and enumerated powers, which was geared toward the management of diplomacy, international trade, and war, but left domestic matters mostly alone. Federal government powers were explicitly listed in Article I, section 8. Powers that were not enumerated there belonged to the states, a principle that was most clearly expressed in the constitutional postscript of the tenth amendment, which stated that "the powers not delegated to the United States by the Constitution, nor prohibited by it to the States, are reserved to the States respectively, or to the people."[21]

As newly independent states with a long colonial history of the facto autonomy, all American states were concerned with their territorial integrity and self-determination. Onuf and others have stressed how they were also keen to protect their particular economic interests. Social and economic diversity between the member-states in the American union meant that the states had potentially antagonistic material interests. Preserving the peace pact therefore required that the treaty parties accepted both that other states had legitimate interests and that such interested states could nevertheless coexist in a "union of interests." Matson and Onuf argue that this understanding of the American union was absent when the Constitutional Convention assembled in Philadelphia and was worked out only in the course of its proceedings.[22]

The two interests most clearly articulated in the convention were the slave interest of the southern states and the shipping interest of the northern and middle states. An intersectional agricultural interest was also voiced, with demands for action by a stronger national government to open foreign markets for American exports and western lands for European American settlers, and to keep open sea lanes and transportation routes, and maintain peace in the trans-Appalachian West. To a degree these demands worked at cross purposes. If settlement was stepped up, a backlash from the American Indian nations controlling the region, and from Britain and Spain that still had ambitions there, could be expected.

The Constitution provided both explicit and implicit protection for state economic interests. The slave states were strikingly successful in getting explicit protections written into the document, guaranteeing numerical advantage in the House of Representatives (Article I, section 2) and presidential elections (Article II, section 1) as a result of the "three-fifths clause," which counted 60 percent of the slave population for purposes of representation; return of escapee slaves in the fugitive clause (Article IV, section 2); and a continuation of the slave trade to at least 1808 (Article I, section 9; Article V). The Constitution also banned export duties (Article I, section 9), which would have affected southern staples like rice and tobacco, and introduced a comity clause (Article IV, section 1) that forced non–slave states to recognize the legality of slavery. So pronounced was the Southern victory that recent works by George Van Cleve and David Waldstreicher have placed protection of slavery at the center of the

American compact of union, vindicating an understanding once embraced by radical abolitionists and slave owners alike that the Constitution was a pro-slavery document.[23]

The gains of the shipping interest were much more limited. Northern delegates defeated the slave states' insistence on a qualified majority for Congress to pass navigation acts, but a two-thirds majority in the Senate was required to ratify commercial treaties (Article II, section 2). The Northwest Ordinance was adopted by Congress in July 1787 thanks to delegates from the Constitutional Convention, who were also members of Congress, taking time out of the convention to attend Congress. It was very likely part of sectional bargain over slavery. The Ordinance held out the promise to the northern agricultural interest that the West would be opened up for white settlement and that in time the region north of the Ohio River would be turned into three to five self-governing republics. The exclusion of slavery ensured the future of the Northwest Territory as a free soil region, but also implied slavery's legality in future territories to be created south of the Ohio River. North and South, the argument was also made that economic interests would be promoted by the creation of a stronger national government with power to conclude beneficial trade agreements in the Atlantic marketplace and to pacify American Indian nations in the western borderlands.[24]

Explicit guarantees for state economic interests were of course important. But just as important was the development in the convention of a general understanding of how to balance state interests with the need to preserve the union. This involved accepting that the interests of other states were real and that the pursuit of self-interest was legitimate. Up to a point, the framers argued that claims about sectional antagonism—based on slave, shipping, and agricultural interests centered in the South, North, and West—were exaggerated and that the sections could coexist in a harmonious "union of interests." But whenever state interests clashed, compromise alone, achieved by bargaining, could prevent disunion. *Union* and *independence* became inseparable concepts in American political culture, the *Staatsräson* of the American union in Hendrickson's terms, due to the conviction that only the peace pact could guarantee a republican system of government in the states and protection of vital state interests. This acceptance laid the foundation for a distinctive American style of politics, as the statesmen of the antebellum era became adept at developing the art of the sectional compromise.[25]

If constitutional guarantees for the separate identity and the interests of the treaty parties was one way of maintaining the peace pact, another was the removal of sources of interstate conflict. There were limits to such endeavors. Southern planters would not abolish slavery, and Northern merchants would not abandon the shipping industry. But beyond these confines, something could still be achieved. The landed states ceded their western territory to the nation in the mid and late 1780s. The right of Congress to make "Rules and Regulations" to govern this common national domain was established by the Constitution (Article IV, section 3) and the rules themselves were spelled out in the Northwest Ordinance. In a single stroke, the discontent of the landless states for not having a stake in western expansion, and the repeated conflicts between states with overlapping western land claims, disappeared.

Other sources of conflict were removed by the monopolization of commercial policy by the federal government, which prevented the enactment of competing tariffs by the states and competition in the Indian trade. The Constitution also prohibited the states from issuing paper money and interfering with contracts. In the postwar period such policies had defrauded out-of-state creditors and caused interstate friction. After the Constitution's adoption, the fiscal resources of the new federal government made possible both payments on the national debt and the nationalization of large parts of the state debts, another source of conflict between the states. Should interstate conflict still arise, the Constitution reduced the chance of escalation by depriving the states from the right to enter into alliances, to maintain troops, or to wage war without the consent of Congress (Article I, sections 8 and 10). Conflict resolution instead took the form of adjudication by the Supreme Court, which had judicial power over "controversies between two or more States" (Article III, section 2). Yet if the Constitutional Convention expected that the boundary disputes which had dominated interstate conflicts before the adoption of the Constitution would continue, they were mistaken. Such cases only rarely came before the federal court in the decades that followed. Rather than the Supreme Court, Congress came to provide the principal forum for interstate conflict resolution through bargaining and compromise.[26]

III

If the peace pact was one main purpose of the federal compact, the other was to allow thirteen sovereign republics to act in unison as one nation against external powers. In the words of a contemporary jurist, the federal government became "the organ through which the individual states communicate with foreign nations." The law of nations established that all nations were equal. "A dwarf is as much a man as a giant," Vattel wrote, "a small republic is no less a sovereign state than the most powerful kingdom." But the equality of states extended beyond their size to also apply to their form. Whether they were democratic or monarchical, unitary states or federal republics, they were all *nations* in relation to each other.[27]

The ability to act as one nation provided protection against foreign aggression, which, just like the peace pact, guaranteed the continued independence of the American republics. Typically militarily weaker than monarchies, confederation was a conventional solution to the security concerns of republics. Although the principal security threat to the American states was civil war, a limited threat existed also in the western borderlands from American Indian nations and their European allies, and from naval attacks and amphibious assaults on Atlantic port cities by European naval powers, as evidenced in both the War of Independence and the War of 1812. But as long as the United States was at peace with European North American powers, a borderlands war would likely be instigated by Americans, either through brash government action or freelance aggression by European American settlers. Stronger national government was held out as a means to make the former more likely of success should that path be taken, but also as a way to prevent unwanted occurrences of the latter.[28]

Concerted international action also promised to protect and promote material interests by expanding white settlements in the western borderlands and by promoting Atlantic and global trade. The cost of war and the relative weakness of the United States meant that negotiation rather than armed aggression was the most realistic means to reach such goals. To make that possible, however, the power over foreign affairs and Indian diplomacy had to be transferred from the states to the national government by the process of voluntary circumscription of state sovereignty that Vattel had identified as an intrinsic part of the construction of a federal republic. In 1787, the Atlantic marketplace was structured by trading nations' attempts to exclude or restrict political and economic competitors from access to their home markets and colonial dependencies. These restrictions could be circumvented by trading illicitly, but commercial agreements were a more effective means to promote economic interests.[29]

To conclude a commercial agreement a nation had to be seen as "treaty-worthy," in Eliga Gould's phrase, and under the Articles of Confederation, the United States was not. In their extended essay "A Civilized Nation: The Early American Constitution, the Law of Nations, and the Pursuit of International Recognition," David Golove and Daniel Hulsebosh argue that the Constitution of 1787 was both caused and profoundly shaped by the need for the United States to pass muster as a member of the European "civilized family of nations." "The fundamental purpose of the Federal Constitution," they write, "was to create a nation-state that the European powers would recognize, in the practical and legal sense, as a 'civilized state' worthy of equal respect in the international community." Gould, too, has shown that independence raised the problem of exactly how the United States would take its place among the "Powers of the Earth."[30]

The "family of civilized nations" consisted of countries that continually demonstrated their readiness to abide by the law of nations, a system of norms established by European diplomats and promulgated by European jurists to govern interactions between European nations and nationals. The decision by American political leaders and their constituents that the United States, too, would live by the law of nations, signifies that American independence was less the start of American exceptionalism than "an attempt to remake the former colonies in Europe's image." That decision was first pronounced with the Declaration of Independence and was followed by the state constitutions and the Articles of Confederation. It took the form of written constitutional documents in part because of the need for Americans to convey it to, and display it in, European courts and courts of public opinion. Printed and bound in a "revolutionary portfolio," the documents were carried abroad by American envoys to demonstrate to the world that the law of nations now spanned the Atlantic.[31]

The Constitution continued the attempt to make the United States pass as "treaty-worthy" by rectifying the failures of the Articles of Confederation. Historians agree that the violations of the peace treaty of 1783 by several of the American states were "the most dramatic manifestation" of the union's inability to conduct foreign affairs in accordance with European norms. Such diplomatic incompetence repeatedly torpedoed postwar attempts to realize American international aspirations, "as painfully evidenced by the repeated failures and humiliations experienced by American diplomats." In particular, it proved impossible to make Britain agree to a treaty that would extricate the United States from its neocolonial dependence on the former mother country to place American commerce and international status on par with that of European nations.[32]

The management of foreign affairs was the duty of Congress also under the Articles of Confederation and the issue facing the Constitutional Convention was not so much to increase as to make the powers of the national government effective. Doing so involved preventing "illegal acts of hostility on the part of Americans themselves," most importantly acts perpetuated by the state governments against foreign nationals. Accordingly, the Constitution gave the new federal government a monopoly on foreign affairs and restricted the powers of the states. Congress was granted war-making powers and the right to regulate commerce (Article I, section 8), the latter of which was a new authority. A federal judiciary was created and given sole jurisdiction over disputes in maritime and admiralty law, where the vast majority of cases arising under the law of nations would originate, as well as all cases involving foreign nationals (Article III). By establishing a single executive who was both commander in chief and empowered to make treaties (Article II, section 2), the convention equipped the United States with a president that carried some resemblance to the British monarch.[33]

Progressive historians working in the tradition of Beard are correct to argue that the framers intended to shield the national government from state and popular influence over foreign affairs. Under the Constitution, treaties take effect on ratification by the Senate, the less popular of the legislative branches, and when ratified automatically become the supreme law of the land "any Thing in the Constitution or Laws of any State to the contrary notwithstanding" (Article VI), thereby overriding state sovereignty in foreign affairs. By granting the federal courts jurisdiction over all cases arising under international treaties, the framers ensured "that the federal judiciary would be available to uphold federal authority against recalcitrant states." In a parallel move (Article I, section 10), the states were stripped of their foreign affairs power by explicit proscriptions against entering into any "Treaty, Alliance, or Confederation" or making any "Agreement or Compact" with another state or foreign nation without congressional consent. The states were also prohibited from regulating commerce by imposing import and tonnage duties and they had neither the right to make war or to maintain troops or warships in peacetime. The restrictions on the states from issuing paper money or impairing the obligation of contracts reassured foreign nations that the rights of their subjects under international treaties and the law of nations would henceforth be honored.[34]

The Constitution and the rulings of the federal courts went a long way to convince British merchants and diplomats that the United States would in future act in accordance with the law of nations and the law merchant. Although it would take several years before that conviction bore fruit, the United States signed commercial treaties with Britain in 1794 and with Spain in 1795. At long last, the new nation was seen as "treaty-worthy."[35]

In the Age of Revolution, the law of nations governed the western borderlands only imperfectly. Consequently, Golove and Hulsebosch limit their analysis of "the international Constitution" to relations between the federal union and the powers of Europe. In contrast, scholars like Gould and Leonard Sadosky have employed a broader concept of international history that incorporates borderlands relations and treats them as deeply intertwined with Atlantic diplomacy. The borderlands diplomatic regime recognized American Indian nations as sovereign actors with legitimate interests and territorial rights, on the one hand, but denied them the status of "civilized nations" on par with European powers, on the other. At the same time American Indian strength and European American weakness meant that a precarious peace could only be maintained by continuous negotiation influenced as much by indigenous beliefs and practices as by the law of the imperial powers. When the military and administrative capacity of the national government grew after the adoption of the Constitution, the United States gradually reshaped the legal geography by extending the law of nations into the borderlands. Because the European diplomatic regime recognized only "civilized nations," the sovereign status of American Indian polities was thereby undermined. To American Indian peoples, the success of the United States in becoming the only recognized sovereign nation in the trans-Appalachian West "proved to be a profoundly disruptive event, as the intrusion and growing authority of European notions of peace and treaty-worthiness created new hierarchies of value, new forms of dependency, and, often, new languages of exclusion." The end point of that development was the Supreme Court's definition of American Indian tribes as "domestic dependent nations" in its 1831 *Cherokee Nation v. Georgia* ruling, which effectively ended the tradition of recognizing American Indian nations as independent and accelerated the process of Indian removal.[36]

Like Gould and Sadosky, Gregory Ablavsky insists in his analysis of the "Savage Constitution" that American Indian relations were central to the framers. Along with Atlantic trade, American economic success depended on the successful development of the West. As Ablavsky points out, the Indians "possessed the most valuable commodity in early America"—land. Rebelling against Britain, the American people and their leaders had banked on their ability to lay their hands on that commodity after independence. Visions of the future wealth of the region were legion long before the fertile lands of the Ohio and Mississippi River valleys became the home to a large population of European American settler-migrants. But unlocking the economic potential of the West required not only the transfer of western territory from the states to Congress, a process well under way by 1787, but also the creation of a legal framework for federal rule of the national domain.[37]

That legal framework had to provide both for the management of a vast geographic space predestined for fundamental transformation, and for the management of two distinctive population groups: the indigenous inhabitants that controlled the land and the white settlers that the government hoped would replace them. The Constitution gave Congress the "power to dispose of and make all needful Rules and Regulations respecting the Territory or other Property belonging to the United States" (Article IV, section 3), but these rules and regulations were only fleshed out in the Northwest Ordinance, which to that extent forms an inseparable part of the Constitution in the American founding. The Constitution also extended Congress's right to regulate commerce to include "the Indian Tribes" (Article I, section 8) and the same principle that made treaties with "civilized nations" the supreme law of the land applied also to Indian treaties (Article VI).[38]

The Northwest Ordinance made possible the transformation of the territory north of the Ohio River from what contemporary white Americans were apt to call a "wilderness" into a space governed by the common law, republican principles of government, Christian morals, and patriarchal authority. It was a space reserved for white immigrant settlers and the Ordinance had little to say about American Indians other than that they should be treated with "good faith" and that "their lands and property" would never be "taken from them without their consent." The government's intention was to people the Northwest Territory with white family groups managing freehold farms under the watchful eye of a male household head. Production would be partly for the market and settlement would be relatively dense, allowing for both local self-government and market integration. Educated and kept in line by missionaries and government agents, the people of the Northwest Territory would be prevented from backsliding into barbarity. The ultimate aim was for white migrants to the West to reproduce their republican homelands in the East.

This transposition of Atlantic republics into the continental interior required intervention by the national government in several steps. First was the transfer of land titles from American Indian nations to the United States through a process of negotiation and purchase ratified by treaty; second, the removal of the American Indian inhabitants beyond a treaty line demarcating the land cleared for European American settlement; third, the process of surveying and selling this land to white settlers in farm-sized parcels; and fourth, the creation of a colonial government to oversee the process of immigration and the gradual development of settler sovereignty that would eventually turn the Northwest Territory into sovereign republics that would join the American union as equal treaty parties.[39]

Bethel Saler has shown how in contrast to the detailed form of government guiding the federal government's rule over white settler colonies, it ruled Indian nations by creating a much less formalized "treaty polity," which regulated Indian territorial possession and rights. As the term suggests, the principal governing instrument in this polity was the Indian treaty. These documents ratified Indian land transfers to the United States and established a border line separating American Indians from European American settlers. Treaties also attempted to sever commercial and political links with Britain and Spain to replace them with ties to the United States. Treaties, finally, formulated the route by which the Indians would be "civilized" and made to conform to European American norms of socioeconomic organization. The long-term goal of United States policy was not the physical but the cultural annihilation of Indian society, to "civilize" the indigenous population by imposing on them ideals of sedentary farming, private property rights, and patriarchy. Meanwhile, in a transitional period, the Indian nations were treated as "quasi-foreign political bodies" over which the federal government "claimed a paternalistic colonial rule" or "a guardianship until they metamorphosed from perceived culturally alien and backward peoples into 'civilized' Americans ready for membership in the republic."[40]

IV

In the twentieth century, scholarship on the founding focused overwhelmingly on domestic challenges and domestic interest-group conflict when analyzing the origins and outcomes of the Constitutional Convention. To both Progressive historians in the tradition of Beard and Ideological historians like Bailyn, Pocock, and Wood, and their many disciples, the key question was the degree to which the American founding represents a transition to a liberal social order characterized by a market economy, representative democracy, and individual rights. The Unionist interpretation, in contrast, puts the spotlight on international and intraunion affairs and on interstate competition both within the American "federal republic" and between the American nation and foreign powers.

The perspective shift promoted by the Unionist interpretation presents specialists on the founding with a dilemma. Academics may well be content to investigate the international causes and consequences of the founding and to downplay the Constitution's role in domestic developments. Yet in American political life and popular culture, the Constitution and the Declaration of Independence are held to be symbols of the nation's ideals and values. Such beliefs are unlikely to go away. For academic scholarship to be relevant to a wider public, it cannot turn its back on questions about the type of society that the founders hoped to create. The Unionist interpretation has therefore to demonstrate its significance to entrenched claims about the Constitution's role in shaping domestic institutions. Contrary to first impressions, a Unionist view of the founding has important implications also for how to best understand domestic developments in the founding era despite its focus on federalism and international relations. It thereby offers means with which to dispute established truths and national myths about the Constitution.

The Unionist interpretation claims that the Constitution was significant to domestic developments only in some areas of national life, such as territorial and commercial expansion. It thereby points to the need to turn to other political arenas and agents than Congress, the federal government, and the Supreme Court to discover who and what shaped American society after the independence. Territorial expansion and commercial diplomacy were regulated by the Constitution, the North West Ordinance, and international treaties, and were driven by the actions of the federal government. Both phenomena can be fruitfully analyzed by the kind of *economic* interpretations associated with Progressive scholarship, that is, an analysis that places class struggle over material resources center stage. But many other areas of social and economic development were governed by developments in the states, which constituted the main arena for the struggle over who should rule at home, and to what effect, in the early republic and antebellum period.

Perhaps most importantly, the Unionist interpretation draws attention to the Constitution's role in preserving rather than changing the existing order. Bilder has argued that in the Constitutional Convention Madison proposed a dramatic redistribution of power within the American union. Although he later excised these remarks from his famous notes, other delegates reported how Madison denied that the American states were sovereign, pronouncing them "corporations" possessing only the power to pass "bylaws." Had Madison's vision prevailed, the Constitution could have created a national government with far-ranging powers to regulate American social and economic life. Instead the outcome of the convention suggests that the majority of the delegates believed that the state government should retain the powers they had assumed in the Declaration of Independence. The constitutions and laws that these governments passed, and the actions they pursued, in the founding period raise troublesome questions about how to correctly label the political system of the new American republics, and not least what we mean when we describe it as a landmark on the road to liberal democracy.[41]

The conclusion of this book seeks to explain at greater length how the Unionist interpretation should alter our perspective on both the domestic and the international history of the founding. But the chapters that follow expands on the Unionist interpretation by analyzing the Constitution as an immensely important, yet carefully limited, reform of the American union.

2

Union

Empowering a New National Government

Only rarely do attempts to capture the meaning of the Constitution begin in the actual text of the compact. This is a missed opportunity, because the key to the document's interpretation is present in plain sight already in the pre-amble. The Constitution was presented to the people of the American states for their adoption or rejection. In an age of poor communication, with no national newspapers or other media, the framers had every reason to let the charter itself speak as clearly as possible about their aspirations. Thus, the Committee of Style, appointed at the Philadelphia Convention, introduced the Constitution with the declaration that its aim was "to form a more perfect Union." The preamble would therefore suggest that the most fruitful way to unravel the meaning of the Constitution should take the form of an investigation of the concept of *union*. At the same time, the wording "more perfect" signals that the Constitution has to be analyzed alongside the imperfections of the compact of union that preceded it, the Articles of Confederation.

In the history of the American union, the transition from the Articles of Confederation to the Constitution is a story of both change and continuity. Adoption of the Constitution signified important changes to both the legitimating principles and the structure of the union. The authority of the Constitution rested on popular sovereignty whereas the Articles of Confederation had been an agreement between the states. In contrast to the articles, the Constitution was adopted by the people of the states, through their representatives in special state ratifying conventions, rather than the state governments. The Constitution also created a national government that could act independently of the states, whereas the Continental Congress had depended on the state governments to execute its decisions. Furthermore, the Constitution invested in Congress new powers to regulate commerce and to tax, and it circumscribed certain powers of the states, most significantly by forbidding them from issuing paper

Perfecting the Union. Max M. Edling, Oxford University Press (2021). © Oxford University Press.
DOI: 10.1093/oso/9780197534717.003.0003

money and from "impairing the obligation of contracts." Returning to the dual meaning of the term *constitution* discussed earlier, the Constitution of 1787 was both an instrument of union and a form of government, whereas the Articles of Confederation was only an instrument of union. But in other respects there was continuity. The principle that the union and the national government were designed primarily to govern the common affairs of the states—that is, interstate matters, the western territories, and foreign affairs, including commerce—rather than the domestic affairs of the states, remained. Nor did the Constitution challenge the principle that the union was primarily a political organization meant to further the interests of the states. Despite significant changes, the Constitution should therefore be seen first and foremost as a reform of the organization of the federal union, not of its rationale or aims.

I

Federal union and *federal republic* were well-known terms in eighteenth-century political discourse, used to describe the means whereby weak states could safeguard their sovereignty. Its rationale was security. States associated in a federal union to preserve peace between themselves and to provide protection from external aggression. Republics in particular were inclined to confederate because they were smaller and weaker than monarchies and faced different security concerns. In a chapter titled "How republics provide for their security," Montesquieu's *Spirit of the Laws* described a "federal republic," in words frequently cited by Americans, as "a kind of constitution that has all the internal advantages of a republican government and the external force of monarchy." It was "a society of societies," composed of republics that enjoyed "the goodness of the internal government of each one," yet which "with regard to the exterior" had "by the force of the association all the advantages of large monarchies." In another influential treatise, *The Law of Nations*, Emer de Vattel explained that a "federal republic" was a political organization that bound together states that had voluntarily restrained the exercise of their sovereignty to better preserve their standing as independent states. Other writers used other terms. Jean-Jacques Burlamaqui spoke of "a union of several particular states" and Samuel von Pufendorf of "systems of states." They all agreed that union allowed independent states to band together to provide for their security needs by investing a common council with powers over war and diplomacy and the authority to act on their behalf in the international state-system.[1]

Inherent in the concept of federal union was the principle of a division of governmental duties and authority between a confederation government and the governments of the member-states. This division followed the distinction conventionally made by early modern political theorists between international and domestic governmental affairs. There was no universally accepted nomenclature, however. John Locke used the terms *executive* and *federative* powers, with the latter referring to "the management of the *security and interest of the publick without,* with all those that it may receive benefit and damages from," including "the Power of War and Peace, Leagues and Alliances, and all the Transactions with all Persons and Communities without the Commonwealth." Montesquieu instead spoke of two forms of executive power, one pertaining to "the things depending on civil rights" and the other to "the things depending on the rights of nations." By means of the latter form of executive power, he wrote, the magistrate "makes peace or war, sends or receives embassies, establishes security, and prevents invasions." When they entered into union, states delegated the exercise of their federative powers, or, in Montesquieu's words, their executive power pertaining to "the things depending on the rights of nations," to a common confederation government.[2]

When American constitutional commentators of the founding generation looked back at the origins of the United States, they agreed that security and international relations had been the main rationales also behind the formation of the American union. In the early years of the 1790s, James Wilson, a Federalist, paraphrased Montesquieu in saying that the federal republic combined the "vigour and decision of a wide spreading monarchy" with "the freedom and beneficence of a compacted commonwealth." A decade later St. George Tucker, a Jeffersonian, described the "American confederacy" as an association "formed by terror," an explanation far removed from any notion of a unifying sense of American national identity. Like every other confederation in history, said Tucker, paraphrasing Pufendorf, the American union was "chiefly founded upon this circumstance, that each particular people choose to remain their own masters, and yet are not strong enough to make a head against a common enemy." The primacy of security was put more bluntly by a congressional committee report from early 1781, which dealt with the need for stronger union. The origins of the American "Confederate Republic," it said, lay in the need "to crush the pr[esent] & future foes of her Independence."[3]

The principle that union was a necessary means for independence—that is, that the states had to restrict their sovereignty to guarantee it—became the first axiom of American political theory. In the struggle against Britain in the early 1770s, several people who would go on to become leading statesmen developed what historians have termed a *commonwealth* conception of the British Empire. They stressed the corporate status and rights of the colonies against the right of Parliament to legislate for Britain's American dependencies and they argued that the Empire was a conglomeration of sovereign polities held together by their voluntary subjection to the rule of the British monarch. They thereby came to depict the British Empire as a kind of federal union. When the time came to create a union of independent states, their understanding of the British Empire would influence their work.[4]

An early example of American views of the status of the colonies within the British Empire was made by Virginian Richard Bland. In a pamphlet published in 1766, Bland claimed that ever since the first settlements in North America, English colonists had been "respected as a distinct State, independent, as to their *internal* Government, of the original Kingdom, but united to her, as to their *external* Polity, in the closest and most intimate LEAGUE AND AMITY, under the same Allegiance, and enjoying the Benefits of a reciprocal Intercourse." In 1775, a youthful Alexander Hamilton wrote in his *Farmer Refuted* that a "state" could be understood as "a number of individual societies, or bodies politic, united under one common head." In the British Empire it was "the person and prerogative of the King . . . that conjoins all these individual societies, into one great body politic," so as "to preserve their mutual connexion and dependence, and make them all co-operate to one common end the general good." Thomas Jefferson told a similar story to Bland. On emigrating to America, he claimed, Englishmen had chosen to "continue their union" with the mother country "by submitting themselves to the same common sovereign, who was thereby made the central link connecting the several parts of the empire thus newly multiplied." In an essay written in 1766 but published in 1774, James Wilson concluded that "all the different members of the British Empire are distinct states, independent of each other, but connected together under the same sovereign in right of the same crown." Under the penname "Novanglus," John Adams argued that the colonies were sovereign polities equipped with their own legislative assemblies that "have, and ought to exercise, every power of the house of Commons."[5]

The commonwealth concept of imperial organization accepted that Parliament had the right to regulate trade within and without the British Empire. But this arrangement, Adams said, "may be compared to a treaty of commerce, by which those distinct states are cemented together, in perpetual league and amity." In other words, it did not negate the identity and interests of the American colonies as distinctive bodies politic. At least in the abstract Adams seems to have accepted the potential problem that the individual "states" might pursue their own "particular interests" to the detriment of the common good of the whole. A "superintending power" might therefore be necessary to ensure that all states acted in concert, at least in the event of war or commercial conflicts. Nevertheless, Adams claimed that serious conflicts of interests were unlikely and called for the continuation of the status quo "by letting parliament regulate trade and our own assemblies all other matters."[6]

The notion that Britain's American colonies were in effect self-governing polities bound together in union with the mother country for purposes of trade and defense also colored the flurry of formal plans for imperial reform that appeared as the imperial crisis unfolded in the 1770s. According to one count there were as many as thirty-seven between the years 1774 and 1777 alone. On the Loyalist side, the Philadelphia merchant and politician Joseph Galloway authored the most important plan. In the opposing camp Benjamin Franklin wrote one and Silas Deane two, the first on his own and the other with his fellow Connecticut delegates to Congress. These plans shed much light on how Americans perceived the purposes of union, whether it was the union of the British imperial "commonwealth" or a union of American independent states. They also show how indeterminate the concept of union was in this early phase of the struggle for independence.[7]

Galloway, Franklin, and Deane all adopted the familiar distinction between internal and external powers. They proposed that what Locke called "federative" powers be delegated by the American states to a union, but carefully preserved other powers in the colonial assemblies. As a Loyalist, Galloway suggested that a "Grand Council" of American colonies would have the right to administer intercolonial affairs and relations with Britain but that Parliament would continue to manage defense and trade. In his scheme, each colony was to "retain its present Constitution and powers of regulating and governing its own internal Police in all Cases whatsoever." Rarely used today, the term *internal police* was common in late eighteenth-century political and social discourse. Derived from the ancient Greek word πολιτεία (politeia) over the French *police* and often rendered "policy" or "policie" in English, internal police referred to a wide and eclectic range of government regulations of health, morals, education, communications, and the economy, covering virtually everything an eighteenth-century government did domestically apart from taxation and the administration of justice. The term could therefore serve as a convenient shorthand for the powers over which American statesmen envisaged the colonies and states would retain full control also after they had delegated their "federative" powers to the union.

Franklin, Dean, and the Connecticut delegation promoted the creation of "a firm League of Friendship" between the colonies, to provide "for their common Defence, against their Enemies, for the Security of their Liberties and Propertys, the Safety of their Persons and Families, and their mutual and general Welfare." An American "General Congress" would have power to declare war and peace; to send and receive ambassadors; to enter into alliances with foreign powers; to arbitrate intercolonial conflicts; to create new colonies; and to administer Indian affairs. Congress would also make ordinances necessary to "the General Welfare," a term that would later cause such concern among states' rights' advocates. But Franklin explained that "general welfare" referred only to the management of international commerce, the currency, and the military. Like Galloway, Franklin proposed that the American states would be self-governing in domestic matters.

Every member of the union would "enjoy and retain as much as it may think fit of its own present Laws, Customs, Rights, Privileges, and peculiar Jurisdictions within its own Limits; and may amend its own Constitution as shall seem best to its own Assembly or Convention." Deane's plan and that of the Connecticut delegation added that every confederate would "have the sole direction and government of its own internal police."[8]

The concept of a union of self-governing states delegating authority over international and interstate matters to a common council reflects the understanding that the colonies were sovereign polities. Yet many of the details of their confederation were not worked out at this early stage. The plans are surprisingly vague about the need for the states to be represented as distinctive bodies politic in Congress, for example. Most authors proposed representation proportionate to population and delegates voting as individuals. Only the Connecticut plan insisted that representatives should vote both as individuals and as state delegations. The implication of these recommendations is that Franklin and others imagined a Congress that represented an American people rather than thirteen sovereign states. But it is not clear if this was a carefully considered position or not. If it was, it found few supporters in Congress.

Neither Dean nor Franklin were members of the congressional committee that drew up the first American compact of union. Leading this task was John Dickinson, a veteran of the pamphlet wars against the British Parliament but a reluctant convert to independence. The Articles of Confederation were long in the making. On June 7, 1776, Richard Henry Lee, acting on instructions from the Virginia assembly, moved that the American colonies "are, and of right ought to be, free and independent States" and that their political connection with Britain should be dissolved. Lee's motion called for a declaration of independence and also asked Congress to form foreign military alliances against the mother country and to prepare "a plan of confederation." Congress quickly appointed a committee to draw up a declaration of independence and another to "prepare and digest the form of confederation to be entered into between these colonies." After a few weeks, Dickinson's committee presented a first draft to Congress, which was debated, amended, and recommitted. A second report followed in the summer of 1777, but pressing matters postponed the adoption of an amended version to November 15. Ten states then ratified within five months but Delaware, Maryland, and New Jersey delayed action. Although the Articles served as the de facto compact of union, they were not formally adopted until ratified by Maryland in February 1781.[9]

Thomas Burke of North Carolina was the first delegate in Congress to articulate a fully fledged view of the American union as a confederation between sovereign states that had delegated only *expressly enumerated* powers to a common national council. As Congress debated the draft Articles of Confederation, his view that the union was created by the states through a voluntary restriction of their sovereignty gradually took hold. The success of this concept of the union in overcoming ideas implicit in earlier plans can be seen in the stipulation in the fifth article in the Articles of Confederation that each state, regardless of size, had one vote in Congress, and in the thirteenth article, which demanded unanimous agreement by all states to any alteration of the articles. It has often been pointed out that Article XIII gave each state a veto on amendment proposals. But far from an oversight, this right was necessary if the articles were to be a compact among sovereign states, which by definition could only be altered by the unanimous consent of all contracting parties. That the articles were in fact regarded as such a compact is evident from Article II, which stated: "Each state retains its sovereignty, freedom and independence, and every Power, Jurisdiction and right, which is not by this confederation expressly delegated to the United States, in Congress assembled."[10]

The full title of the agreement between the American states, habitually referred to as the Articles of Confederation, was "Articles of Confederation and Perpetual Union." Although rarely commented upon, the second part of the title is as important as the first. Dickinson's committee was well versed in the law of nations and no doubt picked a name that would correctly convey the nature of the American compact. In his highly influential treatise *Of the Law of Nature and Nations*, Samuel von Pufendorf had explained that what he called "systems of states" could be formed either by the common subjection of states under the same monarch or "when two or more States, are linked together in one Body by virtue of some League or Alliance." The "commonwealth" concept of the British Empire was an example of the former system. Pufendorf called the latter type "perpetual" leagues to distinguish them from temporary agreements between sovereign nations that did not aim to establish "any lasting Union, as to the chief Management of Affairs." The "chief Occasion" for the formation of perpetual leagues was the by now familiar recognition "that each particular People loved to be their own Masters, and yet each was not strong enough to make Head against a Common Enemy." When entering into a perpetual alliance for these purposes, states agreed not to "exercise some parts of the Sovereignty . . . without the General Consent of each other." The most important powers that the states in perpetual alliances ceded to their confederacy were "the Affair[s] of Peace and War" that could henceforth be exercised only with "the general consent of the whole Confederacy."[11]

As adopted, the Articles of Confederation conformed even better to Pufendorf's ideas of perpetual leagues and alliances than did the Dickinson committee drafts. Article III stated that "the said states hereby severally enter into a firm league of friendship with each other, for their common defence, the security of their Liberties, and their mutual and general welfare, binding themselves to assist each other, against all force offered to, or attacks made upon them, or any of them, on account of religion, sovereignty, trade, or any pretence whatever." The states ceded their "federative powers" to a congress of states, which was given exclusive power over war and peace, treaties and alliances with foreign powers, the exchange of ambassadors, the creation and regulation of prize courts and courts trying felonies committed on the high seas, and the issuing of letters of marque and reprisal. Dickinson's first draft prevented the states from levying trade duties that interfered with the union's commercial treaties. But opposition from states' rights advocates meant that the final version of the articles compromised Congress's ability to pursue an effective commercial policy by stipulating that "no treaty of commerce shall be made, whereby the legislative power of the respective states shall be restrained from imposing such imposts and duties on foreigners, as their own people are subjected to, or from prohibiting the exportation or importation of any species of goods or commodities whatsoever" (Article IX).[12]

By amending the original Dickinson plan, Congress also rolled back many of the powers over interstate arbitration and the western lands that Dickinson's committee would have delegated to the general government and which would eventually be restored to the federal government in 1787 by the Northwest Ordinance and the Constitution. But the adopted Articles of Confederation carefully guarded the sovereignty of the states by restricting congressional intervention in interstate conflicts to situations in which a state had petitioned for arbitration. In the West, the adopted articles stopped short of investing Congress with an exclusive right to regulate American Indian affairs. Instead, Congress was granted the right of "regulating the trade and managing all affairs with the Indians, not members of any of the states; provided that the legislative right of any state, within its own limits, be not infringed or violated," a formulation that left diplomacy with American Indian nations open to competition between the national government and the states.[13]

The articles also conformed to the concept of a perpetual league by reserving for the confederating states the power over internal matters, with only a few exceptions. Congress was given authority to create a common market by regulating coinage and the standards of weights and measures and by managing the postal service. Interstate exchange was also facilitated by the interstate comity stipulations in Article IV. This article guaranteed freedom of movement by granting to "the free inhabitants of each of these states, paupers, vagabonds and fugitives from Justice excepted . . . all privileges and immunities of free citizens in the several states" as well as "free ingress and regress to and from any other state," together with "the privileges of trade and commerce, subject to the same duties, impositions and restrictions as the inhabitants thereof respectively, provided that such restriction shall not extend so far as to prevent the removal of property imported into any state, to any other State of which the Owner is an inhabitant." But all other domestic matters were left to the states to order as they saw fit.

The origins of the first American federal union, institutionalized in the Articles of Confederation, suggests that it is best understood as an organizational solution to security concerns that allowed thirteen small and weak republics to join together to defend their independence and interests. In accordance with the precepts of early modern political theorists, the American union invested powers over war and international matters in a congress of states, but the state governments retained their right to govern their own internal affairs. Despite the fact that Congress was charged with very extensive duties, the Articles of Confederation created little in the way of national governmental institutions. Nor did the articles create a sovereign American people. They provided no method to collect the popular will outside the thirteen states. Hence, although the United States became a *nation* within the international system of states, and in the eyes of the law of nations that governed it, the American union did not become a *nation-state*. As a result, there could be no national will separate from the interests of the member-states. At the same time, there was always aware-ness that the union was necessary for the states to survive and flourish as inde-pendent polities. To a degree not always appreciated, this understanding of the federal union survived the transition from the Articles of Confederation to the Constitution.[14]

The continuity between the Articles of Confederation and the Constitution is reflected in the iconography of the new nation. In the summer of 1776, in the midst of directing the war against Britain, Congress appointed Thomas Jefferson, John Adams, and Benjamin Franklin to propose an official coat-of-arms, or seal, for the United States. Far from a trivial matter, the seal was urgently needed in American interactions with foreign nations and the composition of the com-mittee alone signals that the task was important. The committee approached a Swiss-born artist with some skill in heraldic design, Pierre-Eugène du Simitière, who developed a devise centered on the union of the "Six principal nations of Europe from whom the Americans have originated" and the union of the thir-teen states. However, Congress rejected du Simitière's design and only the motto *E Pluribus Unum* came to survive. No record explains the rationale behind Congress's rejection. But it is telling that subsequent committees abandoned the idea of representing a united people or nation on the seal of the United States. Instead they developed a devise that spoke to the structure of the American fed-eral union and its place in the world.

The seal that Congress finally adopted in 1782 showed a red, white, and blue shield on the breast of an American eagle. It was a device full of symbolism pertaining to federal union. Thirteen red and white stripes on the lower part of the shield, the *pale*, denoted the American states. The stripes supported the blue upper part of the shield, the *chief*, which signified Congress. As the committee report penned by Charles Thompson explained, "the pales in the arms are kept closely united by the chief and the Chief depends upon that union & the strength resulting from it for its support, to denote the Confederacy of the United States of America & the preservation of their union through Congress." Du Simitière's motto, placed on a scroll held in the eagle's beak, it was now declared, "alludes to this union" rather than to the union of six transplanted European peoples. In the talons of the eagle were thirteen arrows and an olive branch, representing "the power of peace & war which is exclusively vested in Congress." Over the eagle's head were a constellation of thirteen stars against a blue background, symbolizing "a new State taking its place and rank among other sovereign powers."[15]

The adopted seal depicted the American states as distinctive bodies politics and the federal union as a political organization facing outward toward the international state system. Approved a year after Maryland's belated ratification had brought the Articles of Confederation into effect, it was never replaced after the adoption of the Constitution. Historians have often argued that the substitution of the Constitution for the Articles signified a qualitative transformation of the United States from a loose confederation to a polity that gave the central government precedence over the states. But contemporaries apparently found that the symbolism conveyed by the seal applied to the American union also under the Constitution. In one of its first acts of legislation, the first federal Congress simply stated that "the seal heretofore used by the United States in congress assembled, shall be, and hereby is declared to be, the seal of the United States." To this day it remains the Great Seal of the United States.[16]

II

The Articles of Confederation were written to better organize the armed struggle against Britain and to signal to European powers that the American states were serious in their pursuit of independence. Though the articles provided for de facto union upon their adoption by Congress in 1777, the politics of state interest nevertheless delayed formal ratification until 1781, when the war was all but over. During the conflict, the Articles fell considerably short of their intended aim. Once the war ended, and Britain recognized American independence, securing state compliance with decisions of Congress proved even harder than during the struggle against Britain. By the middle of the 1780s, the United States faced a number of challenges that called into question the viability of the existing union. These challenges are most easily appreciated by focusing on the two geographic zones where the new American states interacted with the outside world: the Atlantic marketplace and the western borderlands. Economic historians believe that the standard of living in the free white population of North America was the highest in the world on the eve of the Revolution, and the colonists were accustomed to continuous economic growth. But their wealth was in large part based on easy access to new agricultural land and foreign markets. Once liberated from the British Empire, the new nation could provide neither.

Important sectors of the American economy were heavily trade-dependent, and the colonists had flourished in the extensive common market of the British Empire. Yet they expected to do even better once freed from the shackles of Britain's mercantilist policies. However, such hopes were put to shame when expulsion from the Empire instead caused a severe economic shock. Exports fell by as much as a quarter compared to pre-Revolution volumes despite a rapidly growing population. As a result, the economy slowed. According to one economic historian, the War of Independence may have set back gross domestic product per capita by as much as fifty years.[17]

Scholars disagree on the meaning and usefulness of the term *mercantilism*. But there is no question that the Atlantic marketplace was shaped by the wish of European maritime empires to restrict foreign ships and goods from full access to their markets. Their reasons were partly economic and partly military. Shipping services generated income, but early modern navies also depended on being able to recruit skilled seamen from merchant ships in wartime, and a large merchant fleet underpinned naval power. Military concerns also dictated the need for maritime empires to be self-sufficient in essential naval stores, such as hemp, tar, and timber for ship masts and ship construction.[18]

After the Peace of Paris, American trade faced an altered political landscape. Britain offered generous terms for American exports to the British Isles because it was perceived to be in its best economic interest. However, Britain was much more restrictive about American trade with the West Indies, traditionally an important American export market. In 1783 Britain banned American ships from trading with its Caribbean possessions and also prohibited the importation of many American products that Britain hoped to secure from Canada and the Maritime Provinces of British North America. Meanwhile, the non-British markets that were expected to welcome American custom failed to materialize. In 1784, France prohibited the importation of flour and wheat from the United States to the French West Indies and the export of sugar from the islands to North America. France also tried to corner the trade in fish from the Newfoundland fishing banks to the French West Indies, an action of particular concern to New England. Spain was not more forthcoming. Rather than opening markets, it closed the Mississippi River to American boats and goods, thereby imperiling the economic prospects of settlements in the continental interior. Although commercial agreements were signed with minor powers such as Prussia and Sweden, the major trading nations showed scant interest in commercial negotiations with the United States. With no new trading routes or trading partners, the American states remained stuck within the economic orbit of the British Empire but on terms considerably worse than in the colonial period. In 1783 the British politician Lord Sheffield brought this view home in his *Observations on the Commerce of the American States,* in which he argued that as long as disagreements between the states persisted, "it will not be an easy matter to bring the American states to act as a nation." Hence, he concluded, "they are not to be feared as such by us."[19]

The United States could improve its position only by punitive countermeasures. By 1783, members of Congress had realized that Britain and former allies France and Spain were intent on preventing the United States from acquiring a position of power in North America. Late in the year a committee proposed that ships from nations without a commercial treaty with the United States be banned from American ports. Foreign merchants operating in American ports would be allowed to import goods directly from their home countries only if their government had signed a trade agreement with Congress. But such restrictions required amendment of the Articles of Confederation, which in turn required the unanimous support of all thirteen member-states. Such support was not forthcoming in either 1783 or 1785, when a more radical proposal was made. As Lord Sheffield had implied, in the eyes of Europe's empires, the American union seemed anything but a formidable enemy in a trade war.

In the Mediterranean trade, American ships suffered from raids by the North African Barbary States. Nominally part of the Ottoman Empire but in reality autonomous, these principalities had long claimed sovereignty over, and the right to intercept ships on, Mediterranean waters. European trading nations therefore paid tribute to Algiers, Tunis, and Tripoli to secure safe passage in the Mediterranean Sea. Cast out of the protection of the British Crown and lacking the funds to arrange treaty payments, US-flagged ships were fair game, and their cargo and crew were often taken and held for ransom in North Africa. The spectacle of white Christians enslaved by African Muslims troubled Americans and was well publicized in early American plays and novels, such as Susanna Rowson's *Slaves in Algiers* (1794) and Royall Tyler's *The Algerine Captive* (1797). To Americans it seemed that European maritime empires were only too pleased to see American commercial activity in the Mediterranean stall. In a frequently quoted report, Benjamin Franklin claimed to have overheard a London merchant remark, "*If there were no Algiers it would be worth Englands* [sic] *while to build one.*"[20]

The economic prospects of the United States also hinged on developments in the trans-Appalachian West. The peace treaty had awarded the vast territory between the Appalachian Mountains, the Mississippi River, and the Great Lakes to the United States. With rich soils and plentiful natural resources, the Ohio and Mississippi River Valleys were universally held to be a region of great potential. Jedidiah Morse, for example, wrote in his *Geography Made Easy* that the Ohio River Valley was "the most healthy, the most pleasant, the most commodious and most fertile spot on earth, known to the Anglo Americans." In an age when the economy was still overwhelmingly agrarian, the fertility and abundance of land there meant that the North American interior was destined to become the heartland of a populous and powerful nation.[21]

Yet unleashing the West's potential was not easy. In a gradual process completed by 1784, the states ceded their colonial claims to land north of the Ohio River to Congress, creating a 260,000-square mile public domain. By surveying and selling this land to settlers Congress hoped to reduce the substantial public debt run up during the War of Independence. But surveying took longer than expected and the yield from sales was disappointing. Furthermore, payment was made mostly in domestic debt certificates rather than the gold and silver Congress needed to meet the demands of foreign creditors. No matter how much money the western lands might one day be worth, western land sales was not the solution to the union's immediate financial woes.

The problem was primarily geopolitical. The rapid population growth in the early nineteenth century demonstrates that the region was highly attractive to migrants. But in the early 1780s, the Ohio country was a perilous land. Although Congress's land and government ordinances that laid out the future of the West presented it as an empty space, no one was unaware that the region was inhabited and ruled by strong American Indian nations. Between 1784 and 1786, Congress negotiated treaties with the Iroquois or Six Nations, the nations of the Northwest Confederacy (the Wyandot, Delaware, Chippewa, and Ottawa, and others), and the Shawnee to acquire territory for European American settlers north and west of the Ohio River. But these nations soon had second thoughts and became determined to prevent white settlers from crossing the river.

The indigenous nations' position was bolstered by the continued presence of British traders and army posts south of the Great Lakes. The American Indian economy revolved around the exchange of pelts for textiles, tools, small arms, and gunpowder. As long as the native nations could be supplied by the British, they would be able to mount effective resistance to white settler expansion. Adding insult to injury, the posts that the British maintained in the region were located well inside US territory and should have been evacuated in accordance with the treaty of Paris. In order to open up the Ohio Country for settlement, American traders and army garrisons had to replace the British. But the US Army was in no state to mount an attack against the British forts, and in any event the political will to do so was lacking. The diplomatic road was also closed. Several states had breached the 1783 peace treaty by refusing to allow British creditors to sue for debts in American courts. Britain had no cause to surrender its forts before the United States granted British merchants their treaty rights. But under the Articles of Confederation, Congress did not have the means to prevent state legislatures or state courts from violating international agreements.

Spain, too, prevented western expansion. Its long-term aim was to stop the Americans from establishing positions on the Gulf Coast, from which they could threaten Spain's transportation routes to Mexico, its principal American possession. Due to North America's topography, its rivers generally flow from north to south or, less commonly, vice versa, rather than from west to east. The limitations of eighteenth-century communications technology made riverine navigation the only viable means of transportation. Because the majority of rivers empty into the Mississippi, most transports from the interior had to pass through New Orleans. Had Americans been subsistence farmers this would hardly have mattered. But in fact almost all farmers in the early United States produced at least in part for the market, and southern planters did so primarily. To complicate matters, many farmers and most planters produced not for the domestic but for foreign markets. The colonization of the Ohio and Mississippi river valleys by the United States therefore depended on providing settlers with access to national and international markets by allowing them to ship produce down river to New Orleans. Spain's closure of the Mississippi River to American traffic in 1784 was a fundamental blow to American prospects in the region. Westerners made clear to political leaders on the Atlantic seaboard that come what may, the river had to stay open. If Congress could not deliver this, settlers were better off as subjects under the Spanish Crown.

In addition to the inability to assert American interests in the Atlantic marketplace and the continental interior, Congress also faced a critical financial situation. The War of Independence had been fought primarily on borrowed money and in 1783 both the states and the union were heavily indebted to soldiers, contractors, and foreign allies. Under the Articles of Confederation, Congress was expected to requisition money from the states, which were under obligation to meet congressional demands. The system never worked, and its failure became a principal reason for the confederation's downfall. Congress made six requisitions between 1781 and 1786 that together generated an income of slightly more than $5 million. A substantial figure, it was still no more than a third of the sum requested. To make matters worse, the returns on every requisition declined. By the summer of 1786, the financial situation was critical. Congress struggled to avoid default on its Dutch loans and stopped payments on its French and Spanish loans. It could pay neither its small army nor its handful of civil servants.[22]

Several states tried to meet the demands of the union. In the middle years of the 1780s, taxes were three to four times higher than prewar levels, and many states, at least on paper, enforced harsh collection measures. Without ready money and faced with the threat of losing their property through fore-closure, the people protested. Their protests soon paid off when state after state abolished or postponed taxes and provided relief legislation that stayed court proceedings and issued paper currency. Relief measures preserved or restored the social peace but had negative consequences for Congress. When creditors lost faith in the union they demanded that their home states step in to guarantee their investments, and many state governments answered the call. Out-of-state and foreign creditors had no such option, which lead to tensions between states and between the union and other nations. Congress could pay its creditors in Amsterdam only by taking up a new loan to cover interest payments on the old. It was not a sustainable policy, and the credit of the United States plummeted.

The risk of sovereign default had important implications for the ability of the United States to hold its own against other powers. Just as nations do today, eighteenth-century states financed wars and emergencies with borrowed money. As Alexander Hamilton pointed out, "in the modern system of war, nations the most wealthy are obliged to have recourse to large loans," and public credit was therefore of "immense importance" to "the strength and security of nations." But to borrow, a state had to have sufficient income to service its debts. Unless the system of state requisitions was reformed, Congress's credit was unlikely to re-cover. There was real danger that the young United States would be left to the mercy of stronger nations.[23]

When Congress failed to address the challenges facing American merchants, fishermen, sailors, settlers, land speculators, and creditors, the states stepped into the breach. In doing so, they undermined the case for union. Sometimes their actions also went against the interests of sister states, which further weakened the ligaments of union. Georgia made war on and entered into treaties with the Creek Nation; Virginia went to war against the Wabash Nation in the Ohio Country; and Virginia and Maryland concluded a commercial agreement. Some states adopted commercial legislation that discriminated against not only foreign nationals but also out-of-state citizens. Emissions of paper money and adoption of legal-tender laws (which forced creditors to accept paper money as payment for debt) were other sources of interstate and international irritation because they unilaterally altered contracts with foreigners and citizens of other states. State assumption of United States debt obligations made the value of gov-ernment securities depend not on Congress's credit but on the creditor's domi-cile, because not all states could afford to assume US debt and those that could serviced only the debt held by their own citizens.

On the occasions when Congress did act, the consequences were not always positive. The negotiations led by John Jay and Diego de Gardoqui between the United States and Spain over trade and the Mississippi caused the states to fall out along sectional lines. Northern states valued Atlantic commerce more than the Mississippi River trade and were ready to give up the latter for advantages in the former. Southern states, in contrast, were the main source of western migration at the time, and they demanded that the Mississippi River stay open to secure continued migration. In the end, sectional conflict brought the negotiations to a standstill. The Jay-Gardoqui negotiations represent the last attempt of the Confederation Congress to address any of the major challenges facing the new nation. This failure put an end to Congress's role as an effective decision-making body already by August 1786, almost a year before the Constitutional Convention met.[24]

Although historians have disagreed in their assessment of the 1780s, it is evident that the War of Independence was followed by a severe economic depression. It is also evident that in the postwar period the American union consistently proved itself incapable of performing its basic function to defend and promote the independence and interests of the American states. As a consequence, the language of crisis and despondency was everywhere in the newspapers and pamphlets of the period. The reform-minded Alexander Hamilton summed up the sentiment of despair well when he wrote that the United States had "reached almost the last stage of national humiliation. There is scarcely any thing that can wound the pride, or degrade the character of an independent nation, which we do not experience."[25]

III

Demands for changes in the Articles of Confederation began even before Maryland, as the last state to do so, ratified the agreement in 1781. They would continue right up to 1787, and the Constitutional Convention was but the last in a series of reform attempts. Invariably, these attempts focused on four issues. The first concerned the organization of the federal union and called for a coercive mechanism to secure state compliance with congressional demands. The second concerned the need to create and organize the national domain in the trans-Appalachian West. The two remaining issues concerned the needs to invest Congress with the power to regulate commerce and the power to collect taxes independently of the states. Increased fiscal powers of Congress and the coercion of recalcitrant state governments were closely related questions, because the most serious and persistent state delinquency was the failure of state governments to comply with Congress's requisitions for money. With the exception of the management of the national domain in the West, there was little progress, however. Amendments addressing the other three issues faltered because sectionalism prevented either sufficient support in Congress or the unanimous state approval of amendments demanded by the Articles of Confederation.

In the summer of 1783, two months before the signing of the peace treaty between the United States and Britain, a British order in council closed the British West Indies to American ships. In response, Congress began to consider amending the Articles of Confederation to give Congress the power to regulate commerce. It seemed that strong countermeasures alone could give the United States "reciprocal advantages in trade." Inaction, in contrast, would lead to American commerce slowly expiring in the face of commercial discrimination by rival powers. But effective countermeasures required the coordination of thirteen disparate state policies into one common navigation act. An amendment giving Congress the power to prohibit foreign ships and merchants from trading in American ports was therefore adopted and sent to the states in the spring of 1784. It was never ratified, however. The demand for the centralization of the power to regulate commerce was repeated in 1785 and 1786 in a more sweeping proposal to invest "the United States in Congress Assembled" with the power "of Regulating the trade of the States as well with foreign Nations as with each other and of laying such prohibitions, and such Imposts and duties upon imports, and exports, as may be Necessary for the purpose." On neither occasion did the proposal secure sufficient support in Congress.[26]

In contrast to commercial discrimination, which became an issue only after peace was secured, the problems of the union's empty treasury and of state failure to meet congressional demands had already begun in the midst of the War of Independence. Contemporary critics had no difficulty discerning that the shortage of money arose from a structural flaw in the design of the American confederation. Although the Articles of Confederation invested enough powers in Congress "to answer the ends of our union," there was "no method of enforcing [Congress's] resolutions," the lexicographer and political commentator Noah Webster wrote in the mid-1780s. In other words, the problem was not that the formal powers of Congress were insufficient, but that the union was organized in a manner that prevented Congress from exercising them. According to Article VIII, "All charges of war, and all other expences that shall be incurred for the common defence or general welfare, and allowed by the united states in congress assembled, shall be defrayed out of a common treasury." The same article also stated that the "taxes for paying that proportion shall be laid and levied by the authority and direction of the legislatures of the several states within the time agreed upon by the united states in congress assembled." There was therefore no question that the states were constitutionally bound to honor the requisitions and resolutions of Congress. Yet they did not. Critics of the

Articles of Confederation believed that the crux of the matter was the absence of a mechanism by which Congress could force states to comply with congressional demands. The articles provided Congress with no sanction or means of coercion to employ against recalcitrant state governments. Instead, the union rested on voluntary compliance. But the "idea of governing thirteen states and uniting their interests by mere *resolves* and *recommendations*, without any penalty annexed to a non-compliance," Webster remarked, in no uncertain terms, "is a ridiculous farce, a burlesque on government, and a reproach to America."[27]

The inadequacies of the union were readily apparent to critics both within and without Congress. In one of the most comprehensive treatises on the problem of union from the early 1780s, the Philadelphia merchant and political economist Pelatiah Webster laid down as his "first and great principle": "That the constitution must vest powers in every department sufficient to secure and make effectual the ends of it."

> The supreme authority must have the power of making war and peace— of appointing armies and navies—of appointing officers both civil and military—of making contracts—of emitting, coining, and borrowing money—of regulating trade and making treaties with foreign powers— of establishing post-offices—and in short of doing every thing which the well-being of the commonwealth may require, and which is not compatible to any particular state, all of which require money, and can't possibly be made effectual without it, they must therefore of necessity be invested with a power of taxation.

To ensure compliance with Congress's resolutions, Webster suggested, Congress should have the right to summon and convict any individual who in either a private or a public capacity disobeyed its authority. Should a state government resist by force any act or order of Congress, it would "be lawful for Congress to send into such state a sufficient force to suppress it."[28]

As Pelatiah Webster's pamphlet suggested, the coercive mechanism needed to make states comply with congressional resolutions might have to take severe form. To address this issue Congress appointed a three-man committee, which included James Madison. The committee report dated March 1781 pulled no punches when suggesting

> that in case any one or more of the Confederated States shall refuse or neglect to abide by the determinations of the United States in Congress assembled or to observe all the Articles of the Confederation as required in the 13th Article, the said United States in Congress assembled are fully authorised to employ the force of the United States

as well by sea as by land to compel such State or States to fulfill their
federal engagements, and particularly to make distraint on any of the
effects Vessels and Merchandizes of such State or States or of any of
the Citizens thereof wherever found, and to prohibit and prevent their
trade and intercourse as well with any other of the United States and the
Citizens thereof, as with any foreign State, and as well by land as by sea,
untill full compensation or compliance be obtained with respect to all
Requisitions made by the United States in Congress assembled in pur-
suance of the Articles of Confederation.

It was an extreme proposal that laid bare the inherent flaw of the requisitions
system. Expropriating the property of individual citizens to compensate for the
delinquencies of their governments was an exceptionally heavy-handed way of
administering the nation's finances. It is hardly surprising that the proposal went
nowhere. Nor is it surprising that later proposals to invest Congress with coercive power over the states took much milder forms.[29]

The need to replenish the confederation's treasury was the principal reason
for amending the Articles of Confederation with the insertion of a coercive
mechanism. An alternative means to the same end was to bypass the states and
the requisitions system altogether. If Congress were given the right to levy and
collect taxes directly from the citizens, the finances of the union could operate
without the assistance of the states. This would be the method later favored by
the Constitutional Convention in 1787. The ground for the convention's decision had been well prepared by a series of amendment proposals presented in
Congress in the years leading up to the Philadelphia Convention.

In 1781, a committee charged with the preparation of "a plan for arranging the
finances, paying the debts and economizing the revenue of the United States"
advised that Congress be given the right to levy a 5 percent import duty and a
5 percent duty on lawful prizes captured by American privateers. The committee
tied taxation directly to the nation's debt obligations by stating that "the monies
arising from the said duties be appropriated to the discharge of the principal &
interest of the debts already contracted or which may be contracted on the faith
of the United States for supporting the present war." Eventually all states except
Rhode Island ratified the amendment. Rhode Island remained adamant, and in
December 1782, Virginia killed the proposal by rescinding its earlier ratification. The following spring another committee, which included both Alexander
Hamilton and Madison, repeated the impost proposal as part of a more extensive tax package that also asked the states to contribute $1.5 million annually
to Congress. Again the money would be reserved for payment of the union's
debt. To make the proposal more palatable to the state governments, this grant
of power would run for only twenty-five years. The $1.5 million contribution

proved unpopular, but this time both Rhode Island and Virginia accepted the proposal. The amendment now fell instead on New York's refusal to deliver up its lucrative customs income.[30]

After repeated failures to amend the articles, the reform initiative finally passed from Congress to the states. In 1785 Virginia negotiated an agreement with Maryland over the navigation of Chesapeake Bay, and in the following year Virginia invited all states to meet in convention in Annapolis to consider the national regulation of commerce. Only five states sent delegates. No New England state was represented, and apart from Virginia there was no state from the South. Because of poor attendance the convention adjourned almost immediately. But the delegates did at least write a report that spoke of "important defects in the system of the Foederal Government" and of "national circumstances" serious enough "to render the situation of the United States delicate and critical." The Annapolis convention also recommended the calling of a second convention "to devise such further provisions as shall appear to them necessary to render the constitution of the Foederal Government adequate to the exigencies of the Union."[31]

The meeting in Annapolis has traditionally been seen as the prelude to the Philadelphia Convention. But recent research has demonstrated that as late as September 1786, there was little appetite for sweeping reforms of the union in the larger states. In Congress, some delegates argued that the appointment of a constitutional convention undermined Congress's status as the representative assembly of the states and would be the death of the existing confederation. But 1786 saw the woes of the confederation deepen. Lack of revenue meant that default on the foreign debt was imminent and that Congress could protect neither American merchants from Barbary pirates nor frontier families from Indian attacks. Already in February, a congressional committee on the revenue had reported that a "crisis" faced the confederation, which would determine the future of the American union. In May, Americans learned that Britain had yet again refused to vacate military posts in the Northwest, thereby encouraging Native Americans to step up their raids across the Ohio River. Meanwhile, the impasse in the treaty negotiations with Spain further stoked the discontent of western settlers and encouraged talk of secession. As Congress proved unable to address any of the challenges facing the states individually and collectively, the rhetoric of crisis dominated. Yet Congress grew only weaker. Attendance plummeted in 1786 and Congress struggled even to find a quorum.[32]

The sense of escalating crisis made leading reform opponents discontinue or tone down their opposition to a constitutional convention. In November 1786, Virginia authorized the election of delegates to the Philadelphia meeting. New Jersey, Pennsylvania, North Carolina, Delaware, and Georgia followed in the next few months. On February 21, 1787, Congress agreed to call a convention. Nevertheless, skeptics limited its mandate to "revising the Articles of Confederation," thereby hoping to safeguard the continuation of the existing confederation. States accepted the need for reform for different reasons and had different and sometimes conflicting hopes about the outcome. To Virginia the need for revenue and forceful action on the frontier were paramount. In Massachusetts, the protests against taxation and debt litigation that erupted in Shays's Rebellion united a previously divided political class behind the need for a stronger national government. Reformers in Massachusetts also hoped that a revamped Congress would be able to pursue effective commercial policies. In contrast, their allies in Virginia worried that this would increase the cost of shipping to the detriment of planters. Virginia politicians' wish to strengthen Congress's fiscal powers was not popular in New York where the government was funded by the productive state impost. A shared sense of crisis and support for reform therefore did not mean that the delegates who gathered in Philadelphia in May 1787 shared the same analysis of the dysfunctions of the union or agreed on how to fix them. Rather, their individual trajectories to the Constitutional Convention were shaped by experiences in their respective states and sections. These varied experiences would guide the convention's deliberations and ultimately shape its outcome.[33]

IV

No delegate prepared more diligently for the Constitutional Convention than James Madison, who therefore remains the natural starting point for any discussion of its work. In the months leading up to the convention Madison wrote two memoranda about the political evils that plagued the United States. These texts are rightly famous, but the most striking fact about them is rarely mentioned: Madison prepared for the convention not by investigating democracies or republics, or even constitutions, but by examining confederations. His "Notes on Ancient and Modern Confederacies" were not concerned with domestic politics or the excesses of democracy as much as with the international and internal relations of past and present unions. He commented extensively on the failure of such confederations to effectively withstand foreign powers and maintain peace and concord among member-states. When he turned to an enumeration of the "Vices of the Political System of the United States" in his second memorandum, this focus remained. Only four out of twelve vices referred to the internal affairs of the states. The list instead began with the failure of the states to comply with congressional requisitions. It continued with state encroachments on federal authority; violations of treaties and the law of nations; encroachments by the states on one another's rights; disagreement over commercial regulations and fiscal measures; and the failure to protect the member-states from domestic unrest. The long discussion about social interests and factions, which made up Madison's eleventh vice and constitutes the part of the memorandum that has attracted by far the most interest from scholars, was most likely an addition that Madison wrote either late in, or after, the Constitutional Convention.[34]

Madison outlined his recipe for remedies in a series of letters to fellow Virginia politicians. He concluded that the organizational structure of the federal union, which made Congress dependent on the voluntary compliance of the states, was the fundamental problem facing the American confederation. In this he was far from alone. But Madison had thought further and harder than others about how to fix the problem. Commentators such as Noah Webster and Pelatiah Webster saw the need for a coercive mechanism in the union but had only begun to grasp the need for a separate federal administrative structure. Madison, in contrast, had come to see that the federal government had to be designed so that it could "operate without the intervention of the states." The key to an efficient national government was to keep the states out of the administration of government at the national level and allow Congress to legislate directly on individuals. The national government also needed administrative agencies and a court structure to implement its decisions. Such a drastic change in the operation of government required that the equal representation of states in Congress be replaced by the proportional representation of the citizens. If the federal government would act independently of the states and directly on individuals, the people rather than the states should elect the new government. Finally, to counteract state legislation threatening the common good of the union, the federal government had to have the power to veto state laws. All of these points made their way into the so-called Virginia Plan, which opened and set the agenda for the Constitutional Convention.

Whereas Madison devoted much effort to detailing the reorganization of the union, he was reticent about the specific powers that his new national government would wield. In a letter to Jefferson, written after the convention had adjourned, he claimed that the Constitution aimed not to correct the internal legislation of the states but to secure "the objects of the Union." Unfortunately, he did not reveal what these objects were but spoke merely of the convention's intent "to draw a line of demarkation [sic] which would give to the General Government every power requisite for general purposes, and leave to the States every power which might be most beneficially administered by them." A preconvention letter to George Washington shed only a little more light on this matter. Here Madison noted that the national government would possess all the "federal powers" of the old together with "positive and compleat authority in all cases which require uniformity, such as the regulation of trade, including the right to tax both exports & imports, the fixing the term and forms of naturalization &c. &c." In the convention, some of Madison's interventions implied that he wished to see a national government with the power to interfere in the domestic affairs of the states. But his wish was not widely shared among other delegates. Consequently, Madison's later assertion in *The Federalist* that "if the new Constitution be examined with accuracy and candour, it will be found that the change which it proposes, consists much less in the addition of *new powers* to the Union, than in the invigoration of its *original powers*," remains perhaps the best characterization of the achievements of the Constitutional Convention, if not of his own aspirations.[35]

In all, fifty-five delegates from twelve states attended the Constitutional Convention. Rhode Island alone declined to send any representatives. The delegates were political leaders in their home states, and many of them had served in Congress or held a commission in the Continental army. A majority were lawyers, and almost half were college educated. If they were not quite the assembly of demigods they have sometimes been made out be, and even if some luminaries were absent—John Adams, Patrick Henry, Thomas Jefferson, and Richard Henry Lee among them—they were undoubtedly a group of men highly qualified to address the problems of the American union. Their discussions were kept frank and open thanks to the decision to meet behind closed doors, making sure that no details of the convention's debates and its sometimes controversial propositions reached the public.[36]

Ever since their posthumous publication in the nineteenth century, the principal source to the Constitutional Convention has been the notes taken by James Madison. Despite their obvious limitations—it is evident that Madison often summarized long speeches in a sentence or short paragraph, for example—scholars have largely accepted Madison's claim that his notes were a full, accurate and impartial record of the convention's proceedings. However, the recent careful scrutiny by Mary Sarah Bilder shows that Madison's notes are in fact a deeply problematical text, which Madison doctored extensively throughout his long life. The most problematic feature of the notes is Madison's replacement of whole sheets of text that recorded several of his major speeches in the Convention. Written sometime between late 1789 and the end of 1792, the new versions eradicated statements that later became controversial and ensured that Madison's convention speeches matched the political views he adopted after he became an opponent to the first Washington administration. But Madison's many revisions of the notes also added and altered speeches of other delegates. As a source to the proceedings of the Constitutional Convention the notes are subjective and biased and have therefore to be treated with some care.[37]

The convention did not reach a quorum until May 25, 1787, a week after the designated start, and the delay allowed the Virginia delegation to prepare a set of opening resolutions that came to set the agenda for the convention. The acceptance of these resolutions on May 30 signaled the delegates' readiness to supersede their mandate to merely revise the Articles of Confederation and instead establish a national government with a separate legislature, judiciary, and executive. The Virginia resolutions opened by stating that the "articles of Confederation ought to be so corrected & enlarged as to accomplish the objects proposed by their institution; namely, 'common defence, security of liberty and general welfare.'" In his accompanying speech, Virginia delegate Edmund Randolph expanded on this recommendation. He spoke of the "defects of the confederation," pointing to the familiar financial and commercial difficulties that had plagued the American union over the last decade. The most pressing matters confronting the Confederation were the "inefficiency" of requisitions, "commercial discord" between the states, the urgency of the foreign debt, the violation of international treaties, and the recent tax revolt in Massachusetts associated with Daniel Shays. To address them it was necessary to set up a national government, Randolph asserted, that was able to "secure 1. against foreign invasion: 2. against dissentions between the members of the Union, or sedition in particular states: 3. to p[ro]cure to the several States various blessings, of which an isolated situation was i[n]capable: 4. to be able to defend itself against incroachment: & 5. to be paramount to the state constitutions." Although the third item has an expansive ring to it, Randolph had quite specific blessings in mind, such as "a productive impost," "counteraction of the commercial regulations of other nations," and the ability to increase American commerce "ad libitum."[38]

The Virginia Plan generated strong resistance from the small-state delegates in the convention, but the propriety of the basic remit of the national government outlined by Randolph was not questioned. Connecticut delegate Roger Sherman, who was an outspoken critic of the Virginia resolutions, acknowledged that "the Confederation had not given sufficient power to Congs. and that additional powers were necessary; particularly that of raising money," which, he said, "would involve many other powers." A few days later he defined "the objects of the Union" in a manner quite similar to Randolph as "1. defence agst. foreign danger. 2. agst. internal disputes & a resort to force. 3. Treaties with foreign nations 4 regulating foreign commerce, & drawing revenue from it." It was these and "perhaps a few lesser objects alone" that "rendered a Confederation of the States necessary." The New Jersey Plan, which was developed as the small states' counterproposal to the Virginia resolutions, also focused on commerce and revenue as the critical issues that had to be addressed by the convention. Like the Virginia Plan it stipulated that the national legislature would possess "the powers vested in the U. States in Congress, by the present existing articles of Confederation." In addition to these inherited powers, it would also be given the right to levy import duties and a stamp tax and the right to regulate commerce with foreign powers and between the members of the union.[39]

The Philadelphia convention saw only one early attempt to explicitly enumerate the proper powers of the national government. Introduced by Charles
Pinckney of South Carolina, the Pinckney Plan was largely ignored by the other
delegates but later came to be used by the Committee of Detail in its draft constitution. By way of this draft, much of Pinckney's enumeration of powers would
eventually make its way into the finished Constitution. The South Carolinian's
proposal further demonstrates how the convention worked with a rather conventional conception of the proper distribution of powers between the states and the
national government along the internal–external distinction. The Pinckney Plan
repeated the battery of powers already wielded by Congress under the Articles of
Confederation but added the right to levy taxes, including duties on exports and
imports, and the right to regulate interstate and international trade.[40]

During the first half of the convention, delegates battled over the principle of
representation and postponed debate on the exact powers of the national government. The Virginia plan had stipulated that the new "National Legislature"
be elected by the people rather than the states and that the allocation of seats
"ought to be proportioned to the Quotas of contribution [i.e., taxes], or to the
number of free inhabitants." This was in marked contrast to the rule under the
Articles of Confederation giving all the states an equal vote. Opposition to the
Virginia plan arose from the delegations of New York, New Jersey, Delaware,
and Maryland, which at critical points were joined by Connecticut. During the
convention these delegations were called "small-state" members, a name that has
stuck, despite the fact that some of them represented states that did not differ
much in size from some of the so-called large states.[41]

The alternative small-state plan, or New Jersey Plan, presented by William
Paterson of New Jersey on June 15, left the principle of representation in
Congress untouched. Had the plan been accepted, Congress would have continued to be an assembly appointed by and representing the states, and each
state would have continued to have one vote in the national council. When the
convention rejected the New Jersey plan on June 19, the small-state members
fell back on their second line of defense: demand for state appointment to, and
state equality in, one of the two branches of the legislature. They secured this
goal in the so-called Connecticut Compromise, which was reached on July 16.
The compromise was an important watershed that came approximately halfway
into the convention's work.[42]

The animated debate over representation that was resolved by the Connecticut
Compromise is usually presented as a question of size: large states favored proportional representation, small states did not. But underlying the debate in
June and July were questions about the nature of the states and of the American
union, as Convention delegates "struggled to describe what a *state* should be,"
in Bilder's words. In inflammatory speeches, Alexander Hamilton and Rufus

King both argued that the states should be viewed as "corporations" or "subordinate jurisdictions." Hamilton even said that that their sovereignty should be "abolished." It appears likely that Madison shared this view. In speeches that he later removed from his notes, other note takers heard him claim that the states were "not sovereign" but "Corporations with power of Bye Laws." In one of the speeches that was not removed, Madison recorded his suggestion that the union ought to be reformed to turn the states into "mere counties of one entire republic, subject to one common law."[43]

Redefining the states as corporations was highly provocative because Anglo-American law typically understood a corporation to be created through an act of incorporation by the sovereign authority. A corporation was a legal person whose actions were "cognizable by the superior power of the state, and regulated by its laws," as a contemporary jurist put it. Turning states into corporations therefore meant stripping them of their sovereignty and investing it in Congress. Scholars are right to call this vision of the American union *nationalist*. Had it prevailed it might possibly have given rise to a national government with a mandate to intervene broadly in the domestic affairs of the states. However, even delegates who spoke of the states as subordinate corporations recognized that they filled important functions. Although nationalists did not specify those functions, they recognized a need to guarantee "to each State the right of regulating its private & internal affairs in the manner of a subordinate corporation." Regardless of their intentions, the nationalist assault on the sovereignty of the states was repulsed by the convention. A majority of the delegates refused to accept that the states were, or ought to be, subordinate corporations. Equal and direct state representation in the Senate, secured by the Connecticut Compromise, is the strongest indication of this. But even in the House of Representatives, which would be directly elected by the people, the states maintained their presence. Seats in the House of Representatives were allocated on the basis of state population, and congressional electoral districts did not cross state borders. The Connecticut Compromise left Madison and his allies severely disappointed. But it allowed the convention to move forward.[44]

Less well-known than the Connecticut Compromise is the equally important solution to Congress's near total inability to enforce its policies. The Virginia plan offered no fewer than three institutional solutions to this problem. The first was the creation of a separate national government that could act directly on the people without assistance of the states. By simply leaving the states out of the implementation of the union's decisions, there would be no need to compel them to act. For this reason the Virginia Plan called for a national government that could both make and enforce the law. This government had to possess executive and judicial branches, because a government "without a proper Executive & Judiciary," Madison said in a telling metaphor, "would be a mere trunk of a body without arms or legs to act or move." The proposal to establish a national government capable of acting independently of the states ran headlong into the problem of representation. How could the national government be constructed so that the states would trust it with power to operate beyond their control? After the large and the small states had worked out an agreement in the Connecticut Compromise, the North and the South would clash over the same issue later in the convention. Nevertheless, the creation of a national government that could act directly on the people was the mechanism that would eventually be adopted by the convention to overcome the problem of state delinquency.[45]

The Virginia delegation's other two proposals fared less well, even though they did not raise the problem of representation. The sixth resolution proposed to invest the national legislature with the right "to negative all laws passed by the several States, contravening . . . the articles of Union." In Madison's mind this veto power would shield the union from selfish and shortsighted state legislation. Without it, "every positive power that can be given on paper" to the national government "will be evaded & defeated" by the states. "The States will continue to invade the national jurisdiction, to violate treaties and the law of nations & to harass each other with rival and spiteful measures dictated by mistaken views of interest." The negative proposed by the Virginia Plan was actually a diluted version of Madison's original call for "a negative in *all cases whatsoever*," which his fellow Virginians presumably found too great an interference with states' rights. Madison's later attempts to introduce this broader power were also unsuccessful. Although the convention at first accepted the resolution, this milder veto was eventually also rejected. Delegates believed that the negative would be both unpopular and impractical. "Are all laws whatever to be brought up" to the national legislature, Virginia delegate George Mason asked on one occasion. "Is no road nor bridge to be established without the Sanction of the General Legislature? Is this to sit constantly in order to receive & revise the State laws?"[46]

The convention delegates could reject the idea of the veto because they had begun to flesh out their concept of parallel structures of state and national governments. If the national government could act without the involvement of the state governments, the problem of their inaction, such as the noncompliance with congressional requisitions, would disappear. Positive state actions contrary to the interest of the union would remain a problem, however. Had the convention aimed to set up a national government to actively regulate the internal affairs of the states, this would have been a real concern as the states and Congress would have found themselves acting and possibly competing in the same sphere of government activity. But Madison was one of the few delegates who had such an expansive government in mind. The majority of the delegates did not, and they preferred to trust to the judiciary to invalidate unconstitutional state laws. "A law that ought to be negatived will be set aside in the Judiciary departmt.,"

Pennsylvania delegate Gouverneur Morris said, "and if that security should fail; may be repealed by a Nationl. law." Sherman added that the veto involved "a wrong principle, to wit, that a law of a State contrary to the articles of the Union, would if not negatived, be valid & operative."[47]

In the finished Constitution the problem of unconstitutional state legislation was solved by the "supremacy clause" (Article VI), according to which the Constitution itself and all laws and treaties made under it became "the supreme Law of the Land," which "the Judges in every State" were bound to uphold. The right to appeal from state courts to the Supreme Court was implicit in Article III of the Constitution and made explicit in the 1789 Judiciary Act. The convention also wrote into the Constitution prohibitions against certain state laws that had appeared especially troubling to the delegates, including those allowing for the printing of paper money and other measures that tended to undermine contractual obligations. With such safeguards in place, and much to Madison's chagrin, the Convention felt no qualms about quashing the veto on state laws.

The third and final mechanism for making states adhere to congressional resolutions was military force. According to the Virginia Plan, the new national legislature would have the right "to call forth the force of the Union agst. any member of the Union failing to fulfill its duty under the articles thereof." It was not a new idea. The amendment proposal Madison had helped write in 1781 and the recommendations Pelatiah Webster had published in 1783 asked for the same thing. No sooner had the Virginia delegation presented its resolutions than its members began to have second thoughts, however. They came to realize that a separate national government acting directly on individual citizens would not need the assistance of the states and hence would have no need to coerce them. The very next day after Randolph had read the resolutions, Mason observed that "punishment could not [in the nature of things be executed on] the States collectively, and therefore that such a Govt. was necessary as could directly operate on individuals, and would punish those only whose guilt required it." Madison had reached the same conclusion. The "more he reflected on the use of force," he said, "the more he doubted the practicability, the justice and the efficacy of it when applied to people collectively and not individually." Using force against a member-state "would look more like a declaration of war, than an infliction of punishment, and would probably be considered by the party attacked as a dissolution of all previous compacts by which it might be bound." Although the finished Constitution did give Congress the right to call out the militia "to execute the Laws of the Union," the convention's deliberations made clear that the new national government would not rest on such draconic means to administer its laws.[48]

Coercion was closely linked to revenue because it was the breakdown of the requisitions system that had provided much of the impetus for constitutional reform. The New Jersey Plan put the spotlight on this problem by stipulating that beyond import duties and a stamp tax, the national government would have to continue to resort to requisitions to raise money. Paterson and the other draftsmen of the plan were well aware of the problem with requisitions and provided for the right of the national government to collect taxes in states that failed to comply with them. But the supporters of the Virginia Plan were not impressed. They had now embraced the concept of separate governments and had no patience with requisitions or state involvement in the national revenue system. "There are but two modes, by which the end of a Genl. Govt. can be attained," Randolph remarked. The first was coercion of states; the second was legislation for individuals. "Coercion he pronounced to be *impracticable, expensive, cruel to individuals . . .* We must resort therefore to a national *Legislation over individuals.*" Mason questioned the practicality of the New Jersey Plan. "Will the militia march from one State to another, in order to collect the arrears of taxes from the delinquent members of the Republic?" he asked. As Madison had done, Mason also pointed out that such a "mixture of civil liberty and military execution" was incompatible with a republican system of government resting on the consent of the governed. "To punish the non-payment of taxes with death, was a severity not yet adopted by despotism itself: yet this unexampled cruelty would be mercy compared to a military collection of revenue, in which the bayonet could make no discrimination between the innocent and the guilty."[49]

V

During the months of June and July, the Convention had gradually come to an agreement on the questions of state representation and the organization of the new government. States would be represented in the Senate, state populations in the House of Representatives. There would be a tripartite national government capable of acting independently of the states and directly on individuals. But beyond general statements that the national government would inherit all "the Legislative Rights vested in Congress by the Confederation," along with an undefined grant "to legislate in all cases to which the separate States are incompetent, or in which the harmony of the United States may be interrupted by the exercise of individual Legislation," which had been made in the Virginia resolutions, there had been no sustained discussion about what the new government was expected to do, and what it would not be allowed to do. This would change when the Convention received the Committee of Detail's draft constitution on August 6 and had to confront the question about the extent of the powers to be invested in the new national government. In the course of the debate that followed over the next few weeks sectional interests came to the fore in discussions that revolved primarily around questions of Congress's power to tax and regulate commerce. These were deeply entwined issues, because commercial regulation often took the form of prohibitive taxes on imports and exports rather than outright bans on foreign ships and goods. The undisguised sectionalism evident in these discussions cast doubt on the existence of any shared sense of a larger national interest that could serve to balance the strong sectional concerns of the delegates. Yet strong sectional sentiments also forced the framers to conceptualize their union as a confederation of disparate states that could only remain united if they recognized the legitimacy of state and sectional identities and interests, and accepted the need for compromise.[50]

The convention had already come close to falling apart over the fear that large states would oppress small states. That debate produced some of the less edifying moments of the deliberations. Paterson at one point declared that New Jersey would rather "submit to a monarch, to a despot" than be governed by a coalition of large states. Gunning Bedford Jr. of Delaware threatened that unless the large states accepted equal representation of states in the Senate, the small states would "find some foreign ally of more honor and good faith, who will take them by the hand and do them justice." Outbursts like these led other delegates to question the idea that size determined state interests in any meaningful sense, however. The argument was presented in different versions, but at heart was the claim that the large states had such different economies that they were more likely to collide in the national councils than to collude to oppress the small states. Speaking of the past behavior of the three large states, Massachusetts, Pennsylvania, and Virginia, in the Continental Congress, Madison pointed out that "the Staple of Masts. was *fish*, of Pa. *flower*, of Va. *Tobo.* Was a Combination to be apprehended from the mere circumstance of equality of size? The journals of Congs. did not present any peculiar association of these States in the votes recorded." Once such arguments began to be made, the discussion soon turned to the familiar and long-standing tension between northern and southern states. The real conflict of interest in the United States, Alexander Hamilton said, was between "carrying & non-carrying States, which divide instead of uniting the largest States." "Carrying," in the language of the eighteenth century, referred to the shipping interest, which was strongest in New England, New York City, and Philadelphia. Returning to the theme of conflicting interests in the union, Madison on another occasion argued that conflicts of interests stemmed not from size but from "climate," that is, geography, and "principally from [the effects] of their having or not having slaves."[51]

The Convention debates thereafter came to be dominated by a conflict of interest not between small and large states but between the interests identified by Hamilton and Madison as running between the slave states of the South and the carrying states of the North that were dependent on international trade. During this debate, delegates were anything but coy in promoting the interests of their own states. In a typical intervention, Gouverneur Morris demanded guarantees for the "maritime" interests against free-trade legislation sponsored by southern states. South Carolina delegate Pierce Butler, meanwhile, explained that the "security the Southn. States want is that their negroes may not be taken from them which some gentlemen within or without doors, have a very good mind to do." This perception of fundamental sectional incompatibility as well as the confrontational style of debate came to shape the outcome of the Convention in important ways.[52]

Although it was composed of three northerners and two southerners, the Committee of Detail responsible for the first full draft of the Constitution had nevertheless assimilated southern fears that a northern-dominated Congress would betray the South's particular commercial interests. The committee's report thus proscribed Congress from taxing exports and from taxing, or otherwise interfering with, the slave trade. It also stipulated that Congress could only pass commercial legislation with the support of two-thirds of the members of both houses.[53]

As a bloc of staple-producing states, the South had an interest in free trade and cheap transportation. It was "the true interest of the S. States to have no regulation of commerce," noted South Carolina delegate Charles Cotesworth Pinckney at one point. Northern and middle states, in contrast, had extensive shipping interests that were threatened by international competition. Shipping was "the worst & most precarious kind of property and stood in need of public patronage," northerners argued. Such patronage would most likely take the form of navigation acts of the kind Britain had imposed on its colonies. These would raise shipping costs by forcing staple producers to ship their goods in American-flagged vessels. This inherent conflict of interest between North and South was usually defused by pointing to a sectional trade-off. The South and its slave economy could be safe from external attack and slave insurrection only with support from the North, especially from its naval strength. "A navy was essential to security, particularly to the S. States, and can only be had by a navigation act encouraging american bottoms [i.e., ships] & seamen," said Gouverneur Morris. It was a sign of the sectional tensions appearing in the convention that some southern delegates now denied the existence of this trade-off. "It had been said that the Southern States had the most need of naval protection," Maryland's John Francis Mercer observed. "The reverse was the case. Were it not for promoting the carrying trade of the Northn States, the Southn States could let their trade go in foreign bottoms, where it would not need our protection." Hugh Williamson of North Carolina feared no foreign invasion of the South, as "the sickliness of their climate for invaders would prevent their being made an object."[54]

During the debate over the Committee of Detail's report, delegates from the middle states tried to roll back some of the South's gains. They were only partially successful. The taxing of exports seemed to these delegates both proper and necessary. Morris argued that a tax on the export of lumber, livestock, and flour would put pressure on Britain to open the West Indies to American trade, because the islands could not survive without such imports. It was also "a necessary source of revenue." A coalition of southerners and New Englanders refused to budge, however. Because the "produce of different States is such as to prevent uniformity in such taxes," a duty on exports would be unjust and would therefore "engender incurable jealousies." The proscription against national export taxes was upheld by a vote of seven states to three, with only the small states of New Hampshire, New Jersey, and Delaware opposed to the measure.[55]

Luther Martin of Maryland next proposed to do away with the ban on interference with the slave trade. As could be expected, this was not well received by the delegations from the Lower South, whose constituents were dependent on the importation of enslaved Africans. The preservation of the slave trade was declared the sine qua non for the Carolinas and Georgia. Charles Pinckney made clear that "South Carolina can never receive the plan if it prohibits the slave trade." After an animated discussion, Morris moved that the clause on the slave trade and the ban on export taxes be referred to a committee along with the demand for a two-thirds majority for all navigation acts. "These things may form a bargain among the Northern & Southern States," he suggested. Just before the vote on Morris's motion was taken, Massachusetts's Nathaniel Gorham reminded the southern delegates that "the Eastern States had no motive to Union but a commercial one. They were able to protect themselves. They were not afraid of external danger, and did not need the aid of the Southn. States."[56]

Morris was right that an intersectional bargain could be found. Within two days the committee came back with a watered-down version of the Committee of Detail's stipulations. Congress would be permitted to legislate on the slave trade after the year 1800 and would be allowed to tax the importation of enslaved persons. Struck out was the section stating: "No navigation act shall be passed without the assent of two-thirds of the members present in each House." The ban on export duties was left to stand. In the ensuing debate the protection of the slave trade was extended to 1808 and the import duty on slaves set to a maximum of ten dollars per imported enslaved person. Some southern delegates made an effort to retain the qualified majority necessary to pass commercial legislation, but by now their compatriots were in a mellow mood. Charles Cotesworth Pinckney pointed to the northerners' "liberal conduct" on the slave question as sufficient cause to leave "the power of making commercial regulations" unfettered. Northern delegates meanwhile stressed that they could not agree to the Constitution unless they were "enabled to defend themselves against foreign regulations." Nathaniel Gorham asked, "If the Government is to be so fettered as to be unable to relieve the Eastern States what motive can they have to join in it, and thereby tie their own hands from measures which they could otherwise take for themselves?" The decision to strike out the demand for a qualified majority was accepted without objection.[57]

The South had thus successfully blocked the right of the national government to tax exports. They were also successful in defending their interests by shaping the rules of representation in the House of Representatives. The Virginia Plan had suggested that representation be calculated either according to "the Quotas of contribution" or to "the number of free inhabitants." The former was a reference to the manner of apportioning expenditures between the states under the Articles of Confederation. In 1783 Congress had accepted a committee proposal that contributions no longer be based on state wealth, which had been stipulated in the Articles, but on population. Under the new system, contributions would be "in proportion to the whole number of white and other free citizens and inhabitants, of every age, sex and condition, including those bound to servitude for a term of years, and three fifths of all other persons not comprehended in the foregoing description, except Indians, not paying taxes, in each state." In the convention, southerners and northerners disagreed on whether or not to include enslaved persons when calculating state populations for purposes of representation. After a long and tortuous process when the delegates tried to accommodate southern interests without making use of the objectionable term *slavery*, the convention finally adopted the three-fifths rule for apportioning both representatives in the lower House and direct taxes. The South was also successful in securing a fugitive-slave clause, which stipulated that escaped slaves could be apprehended and returned to slavery anywhere in the United States, and tacit agreement on the principle that the national government should keep its hands off the internal police of the states, including the matter of slavery's legality. By means of the three-fifths clause, the fugitive slave clause, the guarantee for the continuation of the international slave trade to 1808, and the proscription against national government interference with slavery in the states, the Constitution safeguarded the future of slavery in the United States.[58]

The debate on the powers of the national government drew attention to the fact that the exercise of federal powers, for example over trade and taxation, would produce different economic outcomes in different states. Convention delegates demonstrated a readiness to compromise, up to a point, but their readiness did not extend to core sectional interests. As the debate over representation had shown, delegates were even less prone to compromise on the question of their state's status as a separate body politic. In principle, the convention could have written the Constitution as a blueprint for a consolidated nation-state, providing for the dissolution of the existing states and the reconfiguration of the political geography of the United States. After all, the states had a recent and in many cases contingent history. During the debate on the Virginia Plan's provision for proportional representation, Nathaniel Gorham pointed out that Massachusetts was an amalgamation of three earlier colonies, and Connecticut and New Jersey of two. The opposite process had also appeared in the history of Britain's North American settlements. North and South Carolina had once been one colony, as had Pennsylvania and Delaware. At one point in the debate, Paterson suggested that "all State distinctions must be abolished, the whole must be thrown into a hotchpot, and when an equal division is made, then there may be fairly an equality of representation." Another delegate wished "that a map of the U.S. be spread out, that all the existing boundaries be erased, and that a new partition of the whole be made into 13 equal parts." But such proposals were hardly serious. Not even the nationalists in the Convention showed any interest in dissolving the existing states. To the contrary, Madison and his allies among the delegates held that representation had to be proportional to population precisely because the large states were anxious to retain their ability to defend and promote their particular interests and would not accept the bid to empower the national government unless they could also influence its actions.[59]

Contingent history or not, by 1787 all states, large and small, had become reified entities in the American political imagination. Citizens owed their primary allegiance to the state governments and supported the union as the means to protect the independence and interests of their states. No wonder therefore that the delegates to the Philadelphia Convention did not act like "a band of brothers" but like "political negociators" [sic] looking out for the best interests of their constituents. Delegates worked from the assumption that the states were different and that their interests were in potential conflict. "Each State like each individual had its peculiar habits usages and manners, which constitutes its happiness," Roger Sherman explained. And no state would "give to others a power over its happiness, any more than an individual would do, if he could avoid it." Had there not been a strong sense that the United States consisted not only of thirteen polities, but of thirteen polities with *distinct interests*, there would have been no bickering over the distribution of votes between the states and the sections. And there would have been no need for the three-fifths compromise that gave the southern states votes on the basis of both their free and their enslaved populations.[60]

An important, if sometimes overlooked, outcome of the Constitutional Convention was therefore the reconfirmation of the states as the principal political organization in the American federal union. The union was designed to preserve the states, not to replace them. Rather than a competitor to the states, the new national government was their creation and a powerful tool to realize interests they were too weak to effect on their own. The intellectual home to a powerful anti-statist ideology, the South would nonetheless benefit greatly from using the federal government to protect slavery, remove the Native American population, acquire land for cotton plantations, and promote American exports. But northerners also benefitted from the government's land policies that ensured that just like the planters of the South, they could reproduce their societies across the North American continent.

VI

The Constitutional Convention adjourned on September 17, 1787, and in a dramatic gesture, three of the delegates—Elbridge Gerry of Massachusetts, George Mason, and Edmund Randolph—refused to put their signatures to the finished Constitution. For Gerry and Mason the chief reason was fear that the convention had gone too far in creating a strong central government and had failed to safeguard basic civic rights and liberties. Their objections foreshadowed a widespread critique that would be directed against the Constitution when it became known to the people out of doors.

When the members of the convention approved of the Virginia resolutions, they also approved a ratification process, whereby their plan for a more perfect union would be accepted or rejected not by Congress or the states but by special conventions appointed by popular election, meaning the votes of free adult males. The Constitution was therefore forwarded to Congress with the recommendation that "it should afterwards be submitted to a Convention of Delegates, chosen in each State by the People thereof, under the Recommendation of its Legislature, for their Assent and Ratification." As Article VII of the Constitution made clear, ratification by nine states was required for it to take effect. Critics in Congress objected, claiming that the Constitutional Convention had exceeded its mandate and that the Articles of Confederation prevented Congress from approving the Constitution. Richard Henry Lee echoed the concerns of Gerry and Mason by proposing amendments for the protection of civic rights. But the majority favored immediate action and quickly agreed to submit the Constitution to the states with the request that they call ratifying conventions. Several of the states also acted with dispatch. Five states called conventions within a month. By the end of the year, five more had followed. South Carolina called its convention in January, and New York did so on February 1, 1788. Only Rhode Island chose to ignore the recommendation of Congress.[61]

The first of the ratifying conventions to assemble was Pennsylvania's, on November 20, 1787. North Carolina's, which began on July 21, 1788, was the last. From the perspective of the Federalists, the ratification process got off to a good start. Between December 7, 1787, and January 9, 1788, five states ratified the Constitution with little or no opposition. Only in Pennsylvania did the Antifederalists put up a determined fight. But their critique proved resilient, taking on life as the contest moved to other states. Thus, the objection that the Constitution lacked a bill of rights to ensure against the overreach of the new federal government and the demand that it be amended by a second constitutional convention came to resonate widely beyond Pennsylvania. Nonetheless, the Federalist majority in Pennsylvania held sway, and the state was among the first to ratify the new Constitution. Only with the Massachusetts convention did the march toward ratification begin to slow. Opposition to the Constitution was strong there, and compromise was required to secure adoption. Moderate Federalists proposed that the Constitution be adopted together with a series of amendments that would strengthen the rights of individuals and limit the federal government's powers over the states. This proposal won over enough Antifederalists to allow the ratification of the Constitution by a close vote of 187 to 168 on February 6, 1788. Ratification with recommended amendments would henceforth become the Federalists' strategy for placating the opposition, and with the exception of Maryland, every state that ratified the Constitution after Massachusetts also proposed amendments. The narrow vote in Massachusetts was followed by a setback in New Hampshire, where the Federalists escaped defeat only by accepting a four-month adjournment. Maryland, in April 1788, and South Carolina, in May, proved to be solidly Federalist, however, and in June 1788, New Hampshire became the ninth state to ratify the Constitution, thereby establishing the new government.

Without ratification by New York and Virginia, the future of the American union was nevertheless still in doubt. In Virginia, Federalists and Antifederalists were equally strong, whereas New York was overwhelmingly anti-Federalist. Both states came to ratification by narrow margins, Virginia by ten votes in June 1788, and New York by only three a month later. In both states the vote was influenced by the timing of the ratifying convention. Because they met relatively late in the process, after the nine ratifying votes were essentially secured, the convention delegates found themselves with a stark choice: to ratify the Constitution or leave the union. Under these circumstances ratification seemed the less bad choice. With New York and Virginia in favor, it mattered little that North Carolina and Rhode Island at first rejected the Constitution. Eventually, both states called new conventions and ratified in 1789 and 1790, respectively. Three years after the adjournment of the Philadelphia Convention, all of the thirteen original states had accepted the new compact.[62]

Within a few weeks after the Constitutional convention rose, sixty-one of the eighty newspapers then in operation in the United States had printed the Constitution in full, and the plan was also published as pamphlets and broadsides. The press frequently reported on the debates in the ratifying conventions, and the newspapers were also filled with essays and letters discussing the pros and cons of ratification. Even by twenty-first-century standards, the scope of the ratification debate is impressive. The modern critical edition of the public and private debates thus far published, the *Documentary History of the Ratification of the Constitution*, amounts to many thousand pages of print, collected in thirty-four volumes—and several additional volumes are projected. The supporters of the Constitution, who adopted the name of *Federalists*, controlled most of the newspapers and dominated the debate. Yet the voice of the opposition was distinctly heard both in print and ratifying conventions. Because of the bare-bones nature of the records from the Constitutional Convention, scholars have often turned to this debate to elucidate the meaning of the Constitution and the aspirations of its supporters.[63]

Federalists branded the critics of the Constitution *Antifederalists*, thus suggesting that they advocated disunion or smaller regional confederations. It mattered little that the vast majority of Antifederalist writers and politicians not only supported the American union but accepted the need for the Articles of Confederation to be reformed. Their real concern was that the Constitution had gone too far in creating a government with unlimited power to raise armies and taxes, regulate the militia, borrow money, and pass any law "deemed necessary and proper." The new federal government, Antifederalists feared, would assume all vital governmental powers and in the process would come to annihilate the states.

Because the new federal government proposed by the Constitution seemed to the Antifederalists incompatible with republican rule, the destruction of the states would mean the end of republican liberty in America. By creating a strong president eligible for reelection, a small House of Representatives with a ratio of only one representative for every thirty thousand inhabitants, and a small Senate with a six-year term, the convention had set up a government that would be un-responsive to the wishes of the common people and beyond the effective control of the citizens. As a result, it was destined to fall under the control of the rich and so-called wellborn, who would use the new government to oppress the people and to increase their own riches and prestige. Antifederalists found further evidence of such class bias in the Constitution's proscription against paper money and debt relief, and in its protection of the sanctity of contracts. Although the federal government would perhaps be able to act with energy against foreign nations, this ability would come at the price of a centralization of power that would eventually put an end to popular liberty.

The Antifederalists hoped to maintain a political union in which state sovereignty was less circumscribed and in which states and sections had a better chance to prevent the national government from acting in ways detrimental to their essential interests. To this end they proposed a number of structural amendments to safeguard the sovereignty of the states and to restrict the powers of the national government. In contrast to the early proposals by Mason and Lee, the Antifederalist amendments at their core did not aim to protect the civic rights of individuals as much as the sovereignty and rights of the states. They asked that federal officers take an oath not to violate the rights of the states; that the federal government be proscribed from interfering with state public finance, state taxation, or state militia regulations; and that no commercial treaty be approved that infringed on the powers and rights of the states. They wanted a two-term limit on the presidency, limits on the scope of federal court jurisdiction, and restrictions on Congress. The limits on Congress included a demand for a qualified majority to raise an army in peacetime and to enter into commercial agreements with foreign powers. Antifederalists also wished to prevent Congress from levying direct taxes or excises and from creating merchant monopolies.

The Federalists never accepted their opponents' analysis of the Constitution. They argued that the federal government rested on the principle of popular representation and that it would exercise its powers for the benefit of the people. They also refused to compromise on the specific clauses of the Constitution to which their opponents objected. To them, the far-ranging fiscal powers and the supremacy and general welfare clauses, as well as other powers invested in the federal government, were necessary if the new government were to perform its duties. However, the Federalist tried hard to assuage their opponents' fear that the states would be absorbed by the national government, by insisting that they, too, subscribed to the idea of a union in which two levels of government coexisted and divided up the task of governing roughly along the internal–external divide that had also been the hallmark of the Articles of Confederation. They presented the national government as a government of limited and enumerated powers and accepted that authority not explicitly delegated to Congress remained in the state governments and in the people.

The main theme in Federalist rhetoric was the contrast between the blessings of union and the horrors of disunion. No friends of the Constitution used it to better effect than Alexander Hamilton, John Jay, and James Madison, the authors of *The Federalist*, a work that remains the most famous exposition of the Constitution. *The Federalist* presented the American people with the choice not between alternative ways to reform the union, but between the Constitution and disunion. According to *The Federalist*, disunion would result in the creation of mutually antagonistic regional confederacies, which would build up their military strength and enter into alliances with Europe's great powers. War was bound to follow, and in its wake the political centralization and the decline of liberty that Antifederalists feared. Wars gave rise to standing armies, heavy taxes and large public debts, a trinity of evil that Madison once described as the bane of republics and the maker of monarchies. Adoption of the Constitution, in contrast, promised to secure the future of the union and thereby to banish war from the North American continent.[64]

The Federalist also urged the critics of the Constitution to accept that the American republic existed in a world of predatory monarchies. If the self-rule of the American people in their respective states was to be maintained, their national government had to be able to defend the independence and interests of the United States. Ultimately this defense rested on the ability to project military power, which required that unlimited authority over mobilization be granted to the federal government. If left to themselves, the states could mobilize sufficient resources to defend their interests only by exerting a heavy pressure on their citizens. In contrast, by joining forces they could establish enough strength to ward off hostile powers with a minimum imposition on the people. Thus, the Constitution promised the benefits of government at a nearly negligible cost.

The ratification debate is perhaps most famous for being the genesis of the Bill of Rights, the first ten amendments to the Constitution. It is often said that the Bill of Rights was the Antifederalists' lasting contribution to the Constitution and that its adoption was instrumental in turning erstwhile critics of the Constitution into reluctant supporters. Yet this reading is colored by the importance that the Bill of Rights took on in the twentieth century and ignores the contemporary reaction to the amendments from Antifederalists. The Bill of Rights was shepherded through Congress not by Antifederalists but by a Federalist, James Madison. The few Antifederalists in the Senate and House of Representatives consistently opposed him and derided his amendment proposals as a deception, calling them "a tub to the whale." This curious expression referred to the practice of sailors of the time, when troubled by a whale, to throw out a barrel, or "tub," to divert the creature's attention away from their ship.[65]

Madison surely understood what his critics were after. He admitted in private that his amendments were designed to minimize the effect on "the structure and stamina" of the federal government. During the ratification struggle, Antifederalists proposed roughly one hundred changes to the Constitution. Two-thirds of these addressed the structure of the union and aimed to retain power and sovereignty in the states. Madison virtually ignored these, and Congress included only three structural amendments in the proposal they sent to the states. Instead, Madison concentrated on procedural amendments to protect individual civic rights. Antifederalists had proposed around thirty of these, and Madison incorporated three-quarters of them in his draft Bill of Rights. In time these rights would become immensely important in American political life, but they did not address the principal Antifederalist objections to the Constitution. Senator William Grayson of Virginia, one of the few Antifederalists in the first Congress, remarked that "some gentlemen here from motives of policy have it in contemplation to effect amendments which shall effect [*sic*] personal liberty alone, leaving the great points of the Judiciary, direct taxation, &c. to stand as they are." Once the people's fears of unlimited government had been put to rest by a phony set of inconsequential amendments, the Federalists would "go on cooly [sic] sapping the independence of the state legislatures."[66]

In the very long run, the Antifederalists' dire warning that the Constitution created the conditions for a federal government with authority and power to make the states conform to national standards in their social, economic, and civic life did come true. By exempting the federal government from constitutional constraints when dealing with external affairs, such as war, international trade, and immigration, and by the strategy of "surrogacy," whereby creative interpretation allowed enumerated powers to be stretched "to achieve unenumerated policy goals," the president, the Congress, and the Supreme Court made the federal government all-encompassing. Yet this was largely a twentieth-century development, and it certainly did not spring ready-made from the Constitutional Convention. To the contrary, the framers of the Constitution envisaged the American union as a means to protect and promote the identity and interests of the member-states, not to destroy and replace them. And they expected that under the Constitution the states would continue to order their internal affairs in accordance to the wish of their citizens, as they had done under both British imperial rule and under the Articles of Confederation.[67]

Internal Police

The Residual Power of the States

No sooner had the Philadelphia Convention adjourned than Antifederalist critics warned that the Constitution's adoption was certain to mean the end of the states. The boundless legislative and judicial power of the new federal government, they said, would "annihilate the state governments, and swallow them up in the grand vortex of general empire." Soon, the idea that the Constitution intended for the "consolidation" of the thirteen American republics into "one entire government" became a staple of Antifederalist rhetoric. The claim first appeared in a broadside that sixteen members of the Pennsylvania assembly published on October 2, 1787, to explain their opposition to a ratifying convention. Under the new Constitution, they wrote, Pennsylvania would either be "annihilated" or else "dwindle into a mere corporation." Similar declarations followed in essays by leading Antifederalist writers like "Centinel" and "Brutus" later the same month. By the end of the year, two prominent Antifederalist tracts by the minority of the Pennsylvania ratifying convention and by "Federal Farmer" had also highlighted the fear of consolidation. Embedded among other objections and presented with less drama, a warning about the likely consolidation of the states also featured in public statements by the Constitution's nonsigners: George Mason, Edmund Randolph, and Elbridge Gerry.[1]

In the words of "Brutus," the great question facing the American union was "whether the thirteen United States should be reduced to one great republic, governed by one legislature, and under the direction of one executive and judicial [*sic*]; or whether they should continue thirteen confederated republics, under the direction and controul [*sic*] of a supreme federal head for certain defined national purposes only." Antifederalists came out strongly in support of the latter position as the only means to preserve the popular, or "democratic," nature of the American republics. According to eighteenth-century political theory, republics were governed by popular consent to the law but also by

Perfecting the Union. Max M. Edling, Oxford University Press (2021). © Oxford University Press.
DOI: 10.1093/oso/9780197534717.003.0004

popular participation in the law's administration. This fact placed strict limits on a republic's geographic and demographic size. Once the ratio of legislators to electors became too low, the electors would lose trust in their representatives and the legislators would no longer know the needs and mores of their constituents. The result would be legislation poorly suited to the wishes of the people and therefore lacking in popular legitimacy. Because such laws would not be administered by the people voluntarily, they would either be ineffective or be administered by government officers empowered to act independent of the popular will. With a ratio of only one representative for every 30,000 inhabitants, and no more than two senators for every state, it was in "the nature of things" that the federal government proposed by the Constitution would be "an *iron-handed despotism*, as nothing short of the supremacy of despotic sway could connect and govern these United States under one government."[2]

In the main the critics of the Constitution were staunch supporters of American union. The pejorative term *Antifederalist* that the Federalists coined to cast aspersions upon their objections to the Constitution is therefore both inaccurate and unfair. In fact, it followed from their support of the union that the majority of Antifederalists shared the Federalists' concerns about the flaws in the Articles of Confederation and the need for structural reform of the American compact of union. Their problem with the Constitution was that it distributed power between the states and the federal government in a dangerous manner. As the seceding Pennsylvania assemblymen made clear, had the Constitutional Convention only "extended their plan to the enabling the United States to regulate commerce, equalize the impost, collect it throughout the United States, and have the entire jurisdiction over maritime affairs, leaving the exercise of internal taxation to the separate states, we apprehend there would have been no objection to the plan of government." But instead of a limited and clearly delineated grant of power, the framers of the Constitution had saw fit to invest the federal government with unbounded fiscal powers and to provide for the limitless expansion of legislative and judicial power through the general welfare (Article I, section 8) and supremacy (Article VI) clauses.[3]

The Antifederalist position thus rested on the idea that *some* powers could be safely invested in the national government without endangering the republican form of government in the states, but that others could not. According to "Centinel," who drew on the teachings of Montesquieu, the only way to govern an extensive country on "democratic principles" was by forming "a confederation of a number of small republics, possessing all the powers of internal government, but united in the management of their foreign and general concerns." However, the broad grants of power in the Constitution, "Brutus" pointed out, meant that the actions of the national government could "affect the lives, the liberty, and property of every man in the United States" and that neither state constitutions and laws, nor their application in state courts, could offer any protection to the rights of the citizen. To correct this, Antifederalists sought a guarantee that "the sovereignty, freedom, and independency of the several states shall be retained, and every power, jurisdiction, and right which is not by this constitution expressly delegated to the United States in Congress assembled."[4]

In the pamphlet *Letters from the Federal Farmer to the Republican* can be found one of the few systematic discussions of the powers, jurisdictions, and rights that the Antifederalists wished for the states to retain. "Federal Farmer" argued that the American people had to choose between three different ways to organize their union. The first, which he called "the federal plan," meant continuing under the Articles of Confederation with the states acting as "the principal guardians of the peoples [*sic*] rights" and the exclusive regulator of "their internal police," with Congress subservient to the states and possessing only "advisory or recommendatory" rather than "coercive" powers. The second alternative, or the "compleat [*sic*] consolidating plan," was to "do away [with] the several state government, and form or consolidate all the states into one entire government, with one executive, one judiciary, and one legislature, consisting of senators and representatives collected from all parts of the union: In this case there would be a complete consolidation of the states." But "Federal Farmer" rejected both of these choices in favor of a plan for "partial consolidation," under which "we may consolidate the states as to certain national objects, and leave them severally distinct independent republics, as to internal police generally."[5]

Addressing Antifederalist objections, the Federalists always insisted that the far-ranging fiscal power, the supremacy and general welfare clauses, and other authority invested by the Constitution in the federal government were necessary if it were to perform its assigned duties. The strength of that persuasion is evident in their refusal to accommodate Antifederalist wishes for structural corrections of the Constitution in the first ten amendments, or Bill of Rights. Yet surprisingly, the Federalists readily conceded from the very start the general point on which their opponents insisted: that the American union ought to be organized as two distinct governments that divided the business of governing between themselves along the internal–external axis typical of early modern confederations or "federal republics." They strongly denied any intention of "annihilating" the states or that state annihilation would follow invariably from the Constitution's adoption. When offering their reassurances, Federalists employed the same term that their opponents used to describe the governmental powers that they believed ought to remain with the states in the American union, that is, the powers over *internal police.*[6]

On the evening of October 6, 1787, in one of the first public explications of the Constitution, James Wilson addressed "a very great concourse of people" in the Pennsylvania State House Yard. Subsequently published and very widely circulated, Wilson's speech explained how, in contrast to the state governments, the federal government was a government of limited and enumerated powers in which "everything which is not given, is reserved" by the people. This differed from the grant of power to the state governments, which had been invested "with every right and authority which [the people] did not in explicit terms reserve." Henceforth, the distinction between a central government of enumerated and limited powers and state governments of broad jurisdiction limited only by state constitutions and bills of rights would be a key element in the Federalist interpretation of the Constitution.[7]

Although Wilson did not explain precisely where the line demarcating the duties of the national government from the duties of the state governments would run, others soon did. Less than a fortnight after the State House Yard meeting, a pamphlet by another Philadelphian, Pelatiah Webster, summarily dismissed the idea "that the constitution proposed will *annihilate the state governments, or reduce them to mere corporations.*" To the contrary, Webster argued, nothing in the Constitution gave Congress or the federal judiciary the "power to interfere in the least in the internal police or government of any one state, when the interests of some other state, or strangers or, the union in general, are not concerned."[8]

Three weeks later, Webster again intervened in the debate on the Constitution with a pamphlet, this time in direct response to the first of the "Brutus" essays. In *The Weakness of Brutus Exposed*, Webster wrote that "the new Constitution leaves all the Thirteen States, complete republics, as it found them, but all confederated under the direction and controul [*sic*] of a federal head, for certain defined national purposes only, i.e. it leaves all the dignities, authorities, and internal police of each State in free, full, and perfect condition; unless when national purposes make the controul [*sic*] of them by the federal head, or authority, necessary to the general benefit." In a similar manner, his namesake Noah Webster attacked the dissenting minority of the Pennsylvania ratifying convention for "harp[ing] upon that clause of the New Constitution, which declares, that the laws of the United States, &c. shall be the supreme law of the land; when you know that the powers of the Congress are defined, to extend only to those matters which are in their nature and effects, *general*. You know, the Congress cannot meddle with the internal police of any State, or abridge its Sovereignty."[9]

Judging from these initial exchanges in the great debate over ratification, it appears that Federalists and Antifederalists were both committed to a federal union where two levels of government with distinctive roles coexisted. But acknowledging this fact does not take us very far in understanding how Americans of the founding generation imagined their union and what they wanted from the new constitution. Above all, it does not clarify what the national and the state governments were expected to do, or where precisely the line dividing their respective duties of government was supposed to run. Because the term was used so frequently by both Federalists and Antifederalists when speaking of the range of activities that the states would continue to perform also under the Constitution, recovering the meaning of the term *internal police* promises to shed light on these questions. Evidence of the centrality of the words *police* and *internal police* in American debates about the British Empire and the American union abounds. But pinpointing what the founding generation meant when they used the term is much more difficult. To find out the meaning of internal police it is necessary to go beyond both the American founding and the United States. Once the range of meanings open to the founding generation is established, it is possible to return to the Constitutional Convention to investigate how the convention distributed powers between the national government and the states.

I

The resistance of the American revolutionaries to the legislation of the British Parliament has so often been reduced to the slogan "No taxation without representation!" that the prominence of nonfiscal complaints among the colonists' lists of grievances has disappeared from view. Yet when in the late 1780s Noah Webster looked back at the protests of the 1760s and 1770s he recalled how the colonists' first act of resistance "was a declaration, or state of their claims as to the enjoyment of all the rights of British subjects, and particularly that of taxing themselves exclusively, and of regulating the internal police of the colonies." In one of the first histories of the Revolution, David Ramsay explained that the colonists had protested against Parliament because the imperial reforms introduced after the Seven Years' War were contrary to the long-standing British practice to regard the American "provinces as instruments of commerce" only. Previous to the war, Britain had not charged "herself with the care of their internal police or seeking a revenue from them; she contended herself with a monopoly of their trade."[10]

Webster was referring to the so-called Declarations and Resolves of the First Continental Congress, dated October 14, 1774, a document that did not in fact use the term *internal police* but the related "internal *polity*." In the declaration, the Continental Congress claimed that the colonies had the right to "a free and exclusive power of legislation in their several provincial legislatures . . . in all cases of taxation and internal polity," subject only to the royal veto. When the Continental Congress took up arms against the mother country eight months later, the justification was Parliament's attempt to not only tax but to alter and change "the constitution and internal police" of several colonies. Soon after, Congress addressed the British people with the complaint that absent American representation in Parliament, the "regulation of our internal Police" by a distant imperial legislature "must be always inconvenient, and frequently oppressive, working our wrong, without yielding any possible Advantage to you."[11]

In their opposition to Parliament, the colonists' claimed an exclusive right of "taxing themselves" and regulating their internal police in accordance with the British constitution, which they argued invested different and distinctive powers in the imperial and the colonial governments. From the Virginia legislature's petitions to the King and Parliament in December 1764, to Congress's address to the inhabitants in Great Britain in June 1775, Americans insisted that as transplanted Britons they possessed the "ancient and inestimable Right of being governed by such Laws respecting their internal Polity and Taxation as are de-rived from their own Consent." They willingly submitted to the Navigation Acts and other trade regulations adopted prior to 1763 and "cheerfully consent[ed] to the Operation of such Acts of the *British* Parliament, as shall be restrained to the Regulation of our external Commerce, for the Purpose of securing the com-mercial Advantages of the whole Empire to the Mother Country, and the com-mercial Benefits of its respective Members," but they refused to accept either "internal or external" taxation aimed to raise revenue or any interference with the internal police of the colonies without the consent of the colonial assemblies.[12]

The many reconciliation plans that aimed to defuse the imperial crisis before the outbreak of armed hostilities also used the term *internal police* to demarcate the authority that the colonies in their capacity as distinctive bodies politic re-served to themselves. In his 1774 plan of union, for example, Joseph Galloway proposed that a "British and American legislature, for regulating the administra-tion of the general affairs of America" be set up, but that "each colony shall retain its present constitution, and powers of regulating and governing its own internal police, in all cases what[*so*]ever." The second article of New Jersey minister Jacob Green's "Plan of an American Compact with Great-Britain" similarly stated that "Parliament shall not intermeddle with the internal police of the colonies: Let Britain provide for her own internal government, and the colonies for theirs."[13]

Once the Declaration of independence had turned the colonies into "free and independent states" many of them hastened to adopt protections against out-side interference with the regulation of their internal police. The declarations of rights of Pennsylvania, Delaware, Vermont, and "New Ireland," the latter a fanciful state-building project in present-day Maine promoted by the aptly named Alexander McNutt, gave prominent place to the people's "sole, exclusive and Inherent Right of governing and regulating the internal Police" of their own state. The second article of the declarations of Maryland and North Carolina consisted in a similarly worded passage.[14]

After independence, American politicians faced the question which powers to invest in Congress and which to reserve to the states. Unsolicited proposals for American union as well as the early drafts of the Articles of Confederation varied considerably in their recommendations about representation and voting. But all agreed on the need for a basic division of power between a central government entrusted with foreign affairs, on the one hand, and state governments entrusted with the duty to regulate domestic matters, on the other. A draft version of the Articles of Confederation, for example, proposed that "Each State reserves to itself the sole and exclusive regulation and government of its internal police, in all matters that shall not interfere with the articles of this Confederation." In the end, the Articles of Confederation were silent about internal police powers. The reason for this was Congress's gradual acceptance of the principle that the national government was a government of explicitly enumerated powers only. This understanding removed the need to reserve specific powers to the states, which risked being counterproductive. Thomas Burke, the principal ideologue of a narrowly confined central government in Congress at the time, moved an amendment that "all sovereign Power was in the States separately, and that particular acts of it, which should be expressly enumerated, would be exercised in conjunction, and not otherwise; but that in all things else each State would Exercise all the rights and powers of sovereignty, uncontrolled." A more elegant and economic version became the second Article of Confederation, which stated that "Each state retains its sovereignty, freedom and independence, and every Power, Jurisdiction and right, which is not by this confederation expressly delegated to the United States, in Congress assembled."[15]

II

If the term *internal police* played a key role in capturing American perceptions of how to distribute authority between the different levels of government in the British Empire and, later on, in the American union, the meaning of the term is frustratingly elusive. Quite possibly, this vagueness only recommended its use to contemporaries. Sufficiently well understood to be bandied about in debates, *internal police* still had an elastic and imprecise meaning. Perhaps no one came closer to the truth than Alexander Hamilton, who once said that the term had "no definite meaning."[16]

The limited scholarship on the conceptual history of *police* bears out Hamilton's assertion. Although an American doctrine of "police powers" developed in the second half of the nineteenth century, the principal trait of the concept of *police* in the eighteenth century is its refusal to be pinned down and defined. Neither eighteenth-century police legislation nor legal commentary ever managed to proceed beyond unsystematic enumerations of police powers. William Blackstone's *Commentaries on the Laws of England* is probably the most prominent example of this practice. It is certainly the legal tract most widely read by Americans in the founding period. Blackstone defined "the public *po-lice* and *oeconomy*" as "the due regulation and domestic order of the kingdom; whereby the individuals of the state, like members of a well-governed family, are bound to conform their general behaviour to the rules of propriety, good neighbourhood, and good manners; and to be decent, industrious, and inoffensive in their respective stations." He then turned to an enumeration of offenses against the "public police" in a highly eclectic list lacking in any apparent system or logic, ranging from prohibitions against bigamy, "Egyptians," that is, Roma, disorderly "bawdy houses" and unlicensed lotteries, eavesdropping, idling, and extravagant dress. In the American context, William Novak has collected similar eclectic lists of police legislation and ordinances passed by antebellum states and cities, dealing with everything from lotteries, dogs, and stock jobbing to commercial transactions, health, labor relations, idlers, trades, roads, and fraud.[17]

A word search of *internal police* in late eighteenth-century British pamphlets on social, economic, and political issues reveals that a broad range of regulations fitted under this rubric, such as local taxation, poor relief and poor laws, the preservation and improvement of public roads, wage regulations and labor contracts, and the establishment of hospitals; restrictions on felling pitch- and tar pines and on exporting hats, rules for the recovery of debt, the regulation of naturalization, censorship of literary works, the establishment of markets and market houses, and general questions of law and order of the sort we associate with police business today. The term is less frequent in American prints. Before the adoption of the Articles of Confederation, only five imprints had the word *police* in the title. There are no more than thirteen such titles before 1800. Of these, five were either in, or translated from, French. The only title in English that predates the adoption of the Constitution was a remonstrance by the unrecognized State of Vermont against Congress's alleged interferences in its internal police. Only one of these tracts was actually devoted to the topic of police, a reprint of Patrick Colquhoun's 1796 *Treatise on the Police of the Metropolis*, which dealt with the City of London. American pamphlets, books, and broadsides show no trace of a public discourse on internal police on par with what can be found in eighteenth-century Britain and continental Europe in this period.[18]

Yet the frequent appearance of the term *internal police* in American newspapers of the 1780s belies this conclusion and indicates that Americans in fact tapped into European discourses and used the term frequently to describe a broad array of phenomena. *Police* was used to describe civilization and progress, or their absence, when writers discussed the past or faraway places, such as France under Louis XIII, the Aztec Empire, China, the port of Ha-Tien, and the rapid development of British North America from a barren wilderness to a space of "cities, towns, villages—laws, order, police—agriculture, arts, manufactures." There were reports about the police of Paris and the new police force established in Dublin in 1786. Such use of police in the more familiar context of law and order was also employed to applaud the City of Rotterdam in the Netherlands for putting an end to robberies by rounding up vagrants, incarcerating them in houses of correction, and expelling them from the country. The police of Charleston and Philadelphia were criticized and contrasted with the police regulations in Paris, where the "property and the person are as safe in the night as in the day." *Police* was also frequently used in more general discussions about the well-ordered city, and both Boston and Philadelphia newspapers carried articles criticizing existing regulations of internal police in their cities.[19]

The discourse on the well-ordered city often focused on disturbances and inconveniencies that appear petty and insignificant. One Boston newspaper complained that "boys" endangered the lives of citizens by "continually firing about the streets" homemade guns manufactured from bellows' noses. A Philadelphia paper carried an article warning that the careless disposal of watermelon rinds on smooth brick pavements constituted a danger to limb and, possibly, life. Watermelons brought into the city were as dangerous as loads of cannonballs "that were soon to be played off against us by an enemy." No doubt the intent was partly humorous. But warnings about the dangers of homemade guns and watermelon rinds draw attention to the fact that cities were places where large numbers of people congregated and engaged in commerce and exchange. Such spaces required government regulation to prevent dangers to life and limb from disease and negligence, to buildings from fire, and to property from robberies and fraud.[20]

City and town governments paved and lighted streets, provided public water pumps and sewers, controlled weights and measures, inspected buildings, and signs, designated and maintained marketplaces, constricted dangerous or nuisance trades and goods to out-of-the-way locations, offered poor relief, and prevented and prosecuted crimes against persons and property. City police regulations ranged from instructions how to re-package meat and pork to directions to water dusty summer streets. When the new office of High Constable was created in Philadelphia in 1787, this officer was charged with examining "all vagrants, beggars, and such others as fall under the description of idle and disorderly persons" and to carry them before city authorities; with preventing swine from running free in the city; and with giving notice to the city authorities of all "nuisances, obstructions, and impediments in the streets, lanes and alleys" to have them removed and the guilty parties prosecuted. The pressing problems that arose from managing a large population in a restricted space meant that the most extensive discussions about the nature and benefits of police in late eighteenth-century America revolved around the government of cities and towns.[21]

Nevertheless, city regulation did not exhaust the meaning of police in American newspapers. The term was used to describe state government regulations to ensure a steady supply of, and stable prices for, provisions. One author spoke of the promotion of agriculture as "the first object relative to internal police, after securing commutative justice." If legislatures were "the guardians of their country's welfare, agriculture . . . merits their most laboured attention." Governments could promote manufactures and the liberal arts by incorporation acts, patents, and rewards, or, like Spain, they could adopt a "system of internal policy and taxation" averse to the development of "industry and manufactures." In this context the word *industry* referred to "industriousness," and the establishment of manufactures promised not only to increase wealth but to banish idleness and poverty, thus bringing about the well-ordered society. Dutch *rasphuizen* were praised and the creation of a similar workhouse in Philadelphia employing women and children would, one author suggested, "take away from all but the very old and disabled the plea of a want of work, which is every day made in our streets; it will have a good effect in aiding our police to preserve decency and peace, by imposing on those who are now idle and disorderly, a sort of necessity to work, or leave the city." Trade, other newspaper items said, should be regulated so that exports were balanced by imports, "otherwise it will disturb their internal police, and render almost every member of the community in some degree uncomfortable." Public finance in the form of loan offices, paper money, and taxation were other aspects of American police. Although no newspaper article mentioned police in the context of road construction in America, an extract from William Robertson's *History of the Americas* praised the Aztecs' method of conveying information by public couriers along their highways as "a refinement in police not introduced into any kingdom of Europe at that period."[22]

III

When British writers such as Blackstone wrote about *police* they employed a term that was relatively new in Anglophone reflections on society. Police and its alternate *policy* entered English from the French language and by the middle of the eighteenth century the word had several identifiable meanings, such as the "regulation and control of a community; the maintenance of law and order, provision of public amenities"; and the "public regulation or control of trade in a particular product." The modern meaning, in contrast, became common only in the nineteenth century when constabularies were set up to oversee and implement police regulations.[23]

But if the term arrived in England from France, its continental development owed much to a German discourse about *Polizei*. The handful of investigations of the intellectual history of police in existence have focused on national genealogies despite the evident transnational nature of eighteenth-century police discourse. One example of the European flow of ideas can be found in Adam Smith's Glasgow lectures on jurisprudence, where Smith cited Jakob Friedrich von Bielfeld's *Institutions politiques*. The *Institutions* was an early political science textbook written in French, but von Bielfeld was a Prussian administrator educated in Leiden in the Netherlands. Another prominent Scottish writer to use the term *policy* was James Steuart, who had become acquainted with German *Statswissenschaft* during his exile in Tübingen. Although not much is known about the transnational exchange of ideas about police in the eighteenth century, it is possible to identify four discourses that likely influenced American understandings of the term either directly or indirectly: a French discourse about city regulation; German *Kameralistik*; natural law conceptions of the "ends of government"; and early British explorations of political economy.[24]

In France the term *police* figured in a distinctive discourse concerned with city regulation, starting with Nicolas Delamare's multi-volume work *Traité de la police* (1705–1738), which collected all historic regulations for the city of Paris. The aim of this French branch of knowledge was the creation of the *ville policée*, or the well-ordered city, an urban space that was clean, safe, and civilized. Delamare intended to treat the task of police in eleven books, dealing with religion, mores (*mœurs*), public health, food supply (*vivres*), public ways or space (*voirie*), public safety, liberal arts and sciences, commerce, manufacture and mechanical arts, domestic servants, and the poor. Each book was further subdivided. The treatment of mores, for examples, had sections on luxury, banquets, spectacles, games, prostitution, blasphemy, and fortune tellers and sorcerers. Although he only lived to complete the first five books, Delamare's plan gives an indication of both the breadth and diversity of *police*. French "police science" presented governmental control of society and people as a prerequisite for, rather than a threat to, life, liberty, and the pursuit of happiness, and as the mark of a modern and civilized society. Thus, in the *Encyclopédie* of Diderot and d'Alembert, *sauvages* were defined as "peuples barbares qui vivent sans lois, sans police, sans religion, & qui n'ont point d'habitation fixe."[25]

The French literature on city regulation is reflected in English-language dictionaries. Samuel Johnson's *Dictionary of the English Language* (1755) both noted the French origin of the word *police* and defined it as "the regulation and government of a city or country, so far as regards the inhabitants." Three-quarters of a century later, Noah Webster's *American Dictionary of the English Language* (1828) instead pointed to the word's Latin and Greek roots but still defined *police* as "the government of a city or town; the administration of the laws and regulations of a city or incorporated town or borough; as the *police* of London, of New York or Boston." But Webster also defined *police* as "the internal regulation and government of a kingdom or state." This second definition is closer to the use of the term found in the German practical body of knowledge called "cameralism" (*Kameralistik* or *Kameralwissenschaft*), which was concerned with the management of states rather than cities and was the intellectual forebear of German political economy. *Polizei* was a central part of cameralism and addressed the economic aspect of governing. In an influential textbook from 1756, Johann Heinrich Gottlob von Justi explained that "*Polizei* concerns itself with nothing but the maintenance and increase of the entire property of the state through good internal organisation, lending the republic all inner power and strength of which it is capable according to its condition. To this end, it seeks to cultivate the lands, improve the state of subsistence, and maintain discipline in the common weal."[26]

In the course of addressing the proper functions of government, eighteenth-century treatises on natural law and jurisprudence also made frequent use of the terms *police* and *policy*. The second volume of Jean-Jacques Burlamaqui's textbook, which dealt with "the principles of politic law," defined "policy," *politique* in the French original, as "that knowledge or ability by which a sovereign provides for the preservation, security, prosperity, and glory of the nation he governs." In this sense, the term was closely related to what Emer de Vattel's even better-known *Law of Nations* defined as the three "objects of good government." Despite its standing as a milestone in the history of international law, book I of *The Law of Nations* was devoted to "nations considered in themselves," and the bulk of this book to the objects of good government. According to natural law, nations were under obligation to preserve and perfect themselves and their members. It therefore comes as no surprise that one object of good government was the defense of the nation, a topic closely linked to the reminder of Vattel's work on international law. But the first object of good government that Vattel identified was to provide for "the Necessities of the Nation" and the second was "to procure the true Happiness of a Nation." Under these rubrics, Vattel listed a striking number of areas of social and economic life open to government intervention. In the five chapters that discussed how to provide for the necessities of the nation, he addressed demography, agriculture, commerce, public ways and tolls, and money and exchange. His three chapters on how to procure the happiness of the nation were even more diverse, covering education, the arts and sciences, "freedom of philosophical discussion," the love of virtue and abhorrence of vice, patriotism, piety and religion, and justice and "polity," that is, regulations prescribing "whatever will best contribute to the public safety, utility and convenience."[27]

Drawing on French and German writers, police also became a key concept among the pioneers of political economy in Britain. Malachy Postlethwayt's *Britain's Commercial Interest Explained and Improved; In a Series of Dissertations on Several Important Branches of Her Trade and Police* (1757) may have been the first English tract to employ police in the sense of Justi and other German *Kameralisten.* Postlethwayt, who was certainly familiar with French writings on political economy, addressed how Britain could improve its agriculture, commerce, and manufactures to generate plenty and thereby strength. A decade later, James Steuart published his *Inquiry into the Principles of Political Oeconomy,* whose indebtedness to German *Kameralwissenschaft* is revealed by the subtitle: *An Essay on the Science of Domestic Policy in Free Nations.* It was a broad-ranging work that addressed "many questions of great importance to society" such as

> how far population can be increased usefully, by multiplying marriages, and by dividing lands: how far the swelling of capitals, cities and towns tends to depopulate a country: how far the progress of luxury brings distress upon the poor industrious man: how far restrictions laid upon the corn trade, tend to promote an ample supply of subsistence in all our markets: how far the increase of public debts tends to involve us in a general bankruptcy: how far the abolition of paper currency would have the effect of reducing the price of all commodities: how far a tax tend to enhance their value: and how far the diminution of duties is an essential requisite for securing the liberty, and promoting the prosperity and happiness of a people.

A concern with the property and plenty of the state is present also in Blackstone, who argued in his chapter on the King's prerogative in *Commentaries on the Laws of England* that the monarch had the right to regulate the "oeconomy" or "domestic polity" of the realm by establishing markets, issuing legal tender, and fixing weights and measures.[28]

But it was Adam Smith who offered the most detailed and systematic account of the meaning of *police* and its place in the well-governed state. Smith's course of lectures on moral philosophy, which he delivered at Glasgow University starting in 1752, was divided into four parts: natural theology, ethics, justice, and expediency. The lectures on ethics would become Smith's *Theory of Moral Sentiment.* The third and fourth parts of the course have survived only as student notes. They show that under the headings of justice and expediency, Smith treated the four "Ends of Government," namely security of property, police, revenue, and "Arms, Law of Nations, etc." According to Smith's protégé John Millar, the lectures on police, revenue, and arms dealt with "those political regulations which are founded, not upon the principle of *justice,* but that of *expediency,* and which are calculated to increase the riches, the power, and the prosperity of a State." Eventually, Smith's reflections on police, revenue, and arms would be published in 1776 as *An Inquiry into the Nature and Causes of the Wealth of Nations.*[29]

In *Lectures on Jurisprudence*, Smith remarked that the first object of "every system of government is to maintain justice." Justice meant safeguarding the property rights of all members of society. "When this end, which we may call the internal peace, or peace within doors, is secured, the government will next be desirous of promoting the opulence of the state. This produces what we call police. Whatever regulations are made with respect to the trade, commerce, agriculture, manufactures of the country are considered as belonging to the police." Smith's claim that governments sought to promote opulence echoed Justi and the German *Kameralisten*, Vattel's three "objects of good government," and von Bielfeld's five "*objets de la politique*," which included both that "*Il faut établir dans l'Etat une bonne & exacte police*" and that "*Il faut faire fleurir l'Etat & le rendre opulent.*" It is noteworthy that Smith was very dismissive of that branch of police regulations devoted to the preservation of the "cleanlyness of the roads, streets, etc." and the prevention of "the bad effects of corrupting and putrifying substances." Smith used the French word *net[t]eté* (neatness) to describe such regulations and made a direct reference to the police of Paris. But he also said that the topic was "too mean to be considered in a general discourse of this kind," and he dismissed in a matter of minutes a subject to which Delamare had devoted the better part of a lifetime.[30]

Among the powers of police that Smith discussed when he turned his attention to the "opulence of a state" were taxes on production and consumption, and on imports and exports; trade monopolies; government subsidies of exportation; export bans; control over coinage; the fixing of weights and measures; laws regulating descent and entail; the status of labor—free or unfree—and labor contracts; transportation and communications; and the creation of staple and market towns. It is an extensive list with far-ranging implications, which gave the government the ability to set prices, shape patterns of production and consumption, and distribute wealth among the members of society. As with German *Kameralwissenschaft*, the writings of natural law thinkers, and the political economy of Steuart, the most striking aspect of Smith's lectures is the sheer breadth of the topics covered by the term *police*.[31]

At present it is not possible to say how European and British uses of the term *police* travelled across the Atlantic in the 1770s and 1780s. American students of law and moral philosophy were familiar with Burlamaqui and Vattel; even more had read Blackstone. Those with an interest in commerce and political economy knew Postlethwayt's writings, some no doubt had come across Steuart's *Principles of Political Economy* and Smith's *Wealth of Nations*, although neither had an American imprint by 1787. The term also appears frequently in Hume's *Essays and Treatises on Several Subjects* (1753), which circulated in North

America. Yet the precise trajectory of the concept may not matter much. None of the European writers surveyed here invented the term *police* and no one defined it. Instead, they employed a term already in circulation. From what is known about the flow of information in the Atlantic basin it is obvious that North America was an important cell in this circulatory system. The frequency of the word *police* in American newspapers in the 1780s, and the different contexts in which the term appeared there, confirm as much. Hence, it seems reasonable to conclude that informed Americans, just like informed Europeans, used the term *police* to designate a range of government activities intended to create a specific socioeconomic outcome: the refined, well-ordered, and opulent society.[32]

IV

The record of the Constitutional Convention is as devoid of definitions of the terms *police* and *internal police* as are late eighteenth-century law treatises and tracts on political economy. Yet when the convention came to address the question where to best draw the line between the powers to be invested in the new national government and the powers that ought to remain in the states, delegates fell back on these commonly used terms. The demarcation line was an ongoing concern but the question how to distribute power and duties between the two levels of government in the American union came to the fore on two occasions in the convention: when delegates confronted James Madison's veto proposal in mid-July 1787 and when they debated the powers that were to be invested in the new federal government in late August.[33]

Preparing for the upcoming convention in Philadelphia, Madison outlined his belief in the need for a reformed national government possessing not only its "present federal powers" but also "complete authority in all cases which require uniformity," which to Madison meant commercial regulation, taxation of imports and exports, and rules of naturalization. Still, something more was needed for the American union to work. Madison proposed that Congress be equipped with "a negative in all cases whatsoever on the legislative acts of the States, as heretofore exercised by the Kingly prerogative." In other words, he meant to correct the flaws in the American republican system of government by reintroducing a key mechanism of British imperial rule in America, the royal veto. In popular systems of government such as the American republics, Madison argued, majorities had free rein to abuse their power to the detriment of the interest of both minorities and the other members of the union. But Madison believed that the new national government would be sufficiently distant and neutral to put the good of the whole, such as the right of minorities, before local interest.[34]

Madison's vision of good government required vigilant oversight of state legislation by the national government and, potentially, interference with the internal government of the states. This was an idea that American political leaders
had consistently and forcefully resisted for over two decades. Nevertheless,
Madison explained in a postconvention letter to Thomas Jefferson, he was convinced that the "mutability" and "injustice" of state legislation had "contributed
more to that uneasiness which produced the convention, and prepared the
public mind for a general reform, than those which accrued to our national character and interest from the inadequacy of the Confederation to its immediate
objects." However, Madison's views were hardly representative of the convention as a whole, although the early days of the proceedings saw some remarkably
open-ended statements about the nature of the American union. On the second
day, Edmund Randolph moved that the tepid wording of the Virginia Plan's first
resolution to correct and enlarge the Articles of Confederation be scrapped and
replaced by a bold declaration that "an union of the States, merely fœderal, will
not accomplish the objects proposed by the articles of confederation." But he
immediately recanted. Another delegate proposed that the existing states be
abolished and that borders be redrawn to create completely new states of equal
size. As late as June 29, Madison said that self-preservation suggested that the
"true policy of the small States . . . lies in promoting those principles & that form
of Govt. which will most approximate the States to the condition of Counties."[35]

But soon positions hardened and the political imagination contracted. At first
delegates of the so-called small states insisted that the American union would
continue a confederation of sovereign states. They were content when the convention accepted the principle of equal state representation in the Senate on
July 16, the so-called Connecticut Compromise. From this moment, large state
delegates began to temper their nationalist or "consolidationist" inclinations.
Madison was no exception. Within three days of the vote on equal representation in the Senate, he questioned popular election of the president with an
openly sectionalist argument. Because suffrage was broader and the free population was larger in the North than in the South, a popular election would give the
northern states more votes. "The substitution of electors" appointed by the state
legislatures, and proportionate in number to total state population, "obviated
this difficulty and seemed on the whole to be liable to the fewest objections."
The inclination of the convention's nationalists and states' rights advocates alike
to protect the identity and privileges of the states as distinctive bodies politic
would eventually doom Madison's negative on state laws.[36]

Yet from Madison's perspective things began smoothly enough. A diluted
version of the veto "to negative all laws passed by the several States, contravening
in the opinion of the National Legislature the articles of Union" sailed through
the convention with no opposition or comment on May 31. It formed part of the

Virginia Plan's sixth resolution, which also included the recommendation that the new national legislature inherit "the Legislative Rights vested in Congress by the Confederation" in addition to a broad power "to legislate in all cases to which the separate States are incompetent, or in which the harmony of the United States may be interrupted by the exercise of individual Legislation."[37]

On June 8, Charles Pinckney, seconded by Madison, moved that the sixth resolution of the Virginia plan be amended to give the national assembly the authority "to negative all laws which to them shall appear improper," that is, a more sweeping power. The motion was voted down seven to three, but the delegations of the heavy-weight states Massachusetts, Pennsylvania, and Virginia all voted in favor. Madison later replaced his speech supporting the motion in his convention notes with a new text. But evidence from other note takers shows that Madison believed it was impossible to draw a "precise Line" between the jurisdiction of "the State Governments and the General Government." In other words, at this point in the convention, Madison was arguing for the creation of a relatively unfettered national government that would possess considerable discretion in interpreting the limits of its legitimate authority. Some of the arguments against the June 8 motion presaged objections that would be raised when the veto came up for debate again in July. Hugh Williamson disliked "giving a power that might restrain the States from regulating their internal police." Elbridge Gerry, too, was against a general veto power that would "enslave the States" but he supported the proscription of enumerated state actions such as the issuing of "paper money and similar measures."[38]

The convention began debating the sixth resolution of the Virginia Plan on July 17. The delegates were now forced to consider the difficult matter of where to draw the line between the authority invested in the national legislature and the authority to be retained in the state assemblies. The convention voted on four motions, including Madison's negative on state laws, and the outcomes suggest that by this stage the delegates had come to think of the American union as a compact that created a limited central government with enumerated powers and also proscribed certain state actions that threatened to sabotage orderly interstate and international relations. Interestingly, several of the delegates who are conventionally described as nationalists, such as Gouverneur Morris and James Wilson, spoke against Madison's veto.

The proceedings began with Roger Sherman's motion to amend the Virginia Plan's proposal that Congress should have the right to legislate in all cases affecting the interests of the American union. Sherman wished to add the restriction that Congress was "not to interfere with the government of the individual States in any matters of internal police which respect the government of such States only, and wherein the general welfare of the United States is not concerned." Wilson seconded this motion "as better expressing the general principle," but in an important intervention Morris turned against it. "The internal police," he said, "as it would be called & understood by the States *ought* to be infringed in many cases, as in the case of paper money & other tricks by which Citizens of other States may be affected." The majority of the convention sided with Morris and Sherman's motion was rejected eight to two with only Connecticut and Maryland voting in favor.[39]

Seconded by Morris, Gunning Bedford next moved an addition to the original resolution that would give Congress a broad right "to legislate in all cases for the general interests of the Union." Edmund Randolph, who as Governor of Virginia had presented the Virginia Plan to the convention, called this "a formidable idea indeed" because it involved "the power of violating all the laws and constitutions of the States, and of intermeddling with their police." Randolph appears to have been the only delegate to speak in opposition to Bedford's motion, which passed six to four. Apart from Connecticut, the states of Virginia, South Carolina, and Georgia voted against the measure—an indication that southern delegates had begun to fear for the future of slavery from an all-powerful Congress.[40]

No note taker apart from Madison recorded the debate on July 17. He was understandably more focused on the debate on his veto proposal, which followed on the adoption of Bedford's motion, than on the other matters of the day. Morris was the first to oppose Madison's negative, calling it a power likely "to be terrible to the States." Sherman next dismissed it as "unnecessary." Luther Martin said it was "improper & inadmissible." Madison's spirited defense fell on deaf ears and only Pinckney spoke up in support. As the discussion continued, Morris declared he was growing ever more opposed to the veto, which "would disgust all the States. A law that ought to be negatived will be set aside in the Judiciary departmt. And if that security should fail; may be repeald by a Nationl. law." Sherman agreed. A state law that was contrary to the compact of union would automatically be considered invalid and inoperative. The veto was struck out after the convention voted seven states to three against, with Massachusetts and North Carolina the only delegations to join Virginia in favor.[41]

Before the convention finished with the sixth resolution and moved on to a discussion of the executive, Martin, a small states man who would go on to become a virulent Antifederalist, moved what would become the Constitution's supremacy clause. Despite the enormous importance it would later take on, the clause seems to have been altogether uncontroversial to the convention delegates at this stage. There was no debate and not a single word is recorded to have been spoken in opposition. In late August, Pinckney made an attempt to reintroduce Madison's veto proposal. But at this stage the convention refused to even commit his motion. Responding to Pinckney, George Mason declared the proposal unpractical, whereas John Rutledge repeated Morris's point about state objections with greater force, asking "will any State ever agree to be bound hand

& foot in this manner. It is worse than making mere corporations of them whose bye laws would not be subject to this shackle."[42]

The votes on July 17 show that a clear majority of the convention was unhappy with the idea of giving the national government free rein to interfere with state legislation. Although Sherman's motion was voted down, there is nothing to suggest that a majority of the delegates wished to give Congress extensive internal police powers. Nevertheless, the majority of the delegates *did* wish to prohibit *some* state actions that would have a negative impact on the rights of out-of-state citizens and foreign nationals. Their concern with interstate and international relations also explains their wholesale support for the supremacy clause. However, at this point the convention did not proceed to flesh out the enumerated powers they wished to lodge in the national government. That work would begin only a few weeks later.

On August 6, the Committee of Detail reported a draft constitution in twenty-three articles. Article VII of the draft contained an enumeration of powers that were to be invested in the national legislature and ended with a precursor to the "necessary and proper" clause that gives Congress the power "to make all Laws which shall be necessary and proper for carrying into Execution the foregoing Powers, and all other Powers vested by this Constitution in the Government of the United States, or in any Department or Officer thereof" (Article I, section 8). Articles XII and XIII of the draft had restrictions on the states. The convention debated and amended Article VII between August 16 and 23, and Articles XII and XIII on August 28. A few days into the discussion, two lists of "additional powers" to be added to the seventh article were proposed by Madison and Pinckney and referred to committee. In the following days, as the convention worked its way through the Committee of Detail's report, other delegates on occasion moved for additional powers to be added to the national government. Finally, a concerted attempt to add more powers to Congress came in the very last days of the convention in response to the draft constitution that was reported by the Committee of Style. The record of debates in this late stage of the convention is meager and provide limited insight into the reasons behind decisions. But it does give information about the powers that delegates wished to invest in, or withhold from, Congress. The finished Constitution, the lists by Madison and Pinckney, and other proposals to amend the Committee of Detail report form a catalogue of governmental powers that either were, or conceivably could have been, invested in the new national legislature.[43]

The taxonomy of the ends of government that Adam Smith presented in his *Lectures on Jurisprudence* can be used to analyze the catalogue of governmental powers that the Constitutional Convention either invested in, or withheld from, Congress, and the powers it withheld from the states. Using Smith's taxonomy, which is representative of late eighteenth-century political thought on the ends

of government, makes it possible to assess the Constitution against the benchmark of a sophisticated contemporary understanding of the duties of government, rather than against a universal and abstract concept of the state. In Smith's
scheme, governmental powers can be classified as belonging to one of four
categories: justice (which to Smith above all meant the security of property);
police; revenue; and international relations. Classifying the powers of the national government and the states according to these four categories clarifies how
the framers envisioned the line separating their respective spheres of authority.
Tables 3.1 to 3.3 present the powers granted to or withheld from Congress and
the states by the finished Constitution along with rejected proposals in italics. As
noted, in addition to the powers listed in Table 3.1, the Constitution also gives
Congress a blanket authority "to make all Laws which shall be necessary and
proper" for carrying the powers vested in the federal government into execution,
a clause that was widely criticized by Antifederalists for introducing an unlimited national government that would "annihilate" the states.

   Table 3.1 shows that the powers vested in the national government were
mainly such that would allow it to deal effectively with foreign nations and interstate relations. Congress had the authority to declare war and attendant powers,
that is, the power to raise and maintain armies and navies, to punish offences on
the high seas and against the law of nations, to establish rules of naturalization,
and so on. In addition to this, the national executive was empowered with the
right to make treaties with European and American Indian nations with Senate
approval, and the national courts were granted jurisdiction over cases involving
foreign nationals. Table 3.2 shows that there were hardly any restrictions on the
national legislature with respect to powers over the military and international
relations. In contrast, Table 3.3 shows that the states were stripped of powers
over foreign affairs and defense. The revenue class reveals the same pattern of
investing next to unlimited powers in the national legislature. But the restrictions
on state authority over fiscal legislation were limited, amounting only to a proscription on levying import and export duties. Taken together, these tables show
that apart from the right to tax, the Constitution does not represent a major redistribution of the authority between the states and the union put in place by the
Articles of Confederation.[44]

   The question of Congress's police powers is more complex. The convention
invested the national legislature with some police powers but rejected other
proposals. Clearly, the Constitution meant for the federal government to regulate
some aspect of American police. It was responsible for maintaining a common
market by regulating interstate commerce, the value of coin, and weights and
measures. It was also responsible for foreign trade and so-called Indian trade.
Finally, it was given responsibility over the flow of information by managing
the post office. Turning to the police power proposals that were rejected, they

Table 3.1 **Powers invested in US Congress**

Justice	Revenue
To punish counterfeiting US securities and coins.	To impose taxes, duties, imposts, and excises
To create federal courts inferior to the Supreme Court	To borrow money
To determine punishment for treason against US	
To determine if officeholders can accept emolument, office, or title from a foreign state	

Police	International relations
To regulate commerce	To define and punish
a) with foreign nations	a) Piracies
b) with Indian nations	b) felonies on the high seas
c) between the states	c) offenses against the law of nations
To establish a uniform rule of bankruptcy	To create federal courts inferior to the Supreme Court
To coin money and determine the value of coins	To declare war
To fix standards for weights and measures	To make rules governing captures on land and water
To establish post offices and post roads	To provide and maintain a navy
To promote the progress of science and useful arts by awarding copyrights and patents	To make rules for the government of land and naval forces
To grant charters of incorporation in cases where the public good may require them, and the authority of a single State may be incompetent†	To provide for calling forth the militia
To establish a university†	To govern the militia when called forth in the service of the US
To encourage, by proper premiums and provisions, the advancement of useful knowledge and discoveries†	To provide for organizing, arming, and disciplining the militia
	To exercise exclusive jurisdiction within the ten-mile square and in other federal territories
	To establish a uniform rule of naturalization.

(*continued*)

Table 3.1 **Continued**

To establish seminaries for the promotion of literature and the arts and sciences[††]	To prescribe the manner in which the public acts, records, and judicial proceedings of the states shall be proved, in order to their obtaining faith and credit in other states, and the effects thereof
To establish public institutions, rewards and immunities for the promotion of agriculture, commerce, trades, and manufactures[††]	
To pass sumptuary laws (Farrand, *Records* II, 337*)	To admit new states into the Union
To emit bills of credit (Farrand, *Records* II, 303*)	To dispose of and make rules and regulations for the territories of the US
To cut canals where deemed necessary (Farrand, *Records* II, 611*)	To guarantee a republican form of government to all states in the Union and protect them from invasion and rebellion
To negative state laws interfering with the interests and harmony of the Union (Farrand, *Records* II, 382*)	To determine punishment for treason against US
	To dispose of the unappropriated lands of the United States[†]
	To institute temporary governments for the new states arising on the unappropriated lands of the U.S.[†]
	To regulate affairs with the Indians as well within as without the limits of the U.S.[†]

Notes: Powers in italics represent proposals that were rejected by the convention.

[†] Power proposed by Madison on August 18, not on Pinckney's list.

[††] Power proposed by Pinckney on August 18. Pinckney listed almost every item that appeared on Madison's list.

[*] Max Farrand, ed., *The Records of the Federal Convention of 1787*, 4 vols. (New Haven, CT: Yale University Press, 1966).

show that a minority in the Constitutional Convention could and did envision a national government playing a more active role in shaping American domestic developments. But the fact that the proposals were rejected shows that this vision was not shared by the majority. Had Madison and Pinckney's wish to grant Congress the power to create federal charitable and trading corporations, Franklin's wish to give the federal government authority to cut canals, and Mason's that it would have the right to pass sumptuary laws, together with other proposals made, been adopted, the national government might have become a force to be reckoned with also in the regulation of America's internal police.

On August 20, Morris, seconded by Pinckney, moved to refer to the Committee of Detail a proposal for a Council of State to assist the executive

Table 3.2 **Powers withheld from US Congress**

Justice	Revenue
To suspend habeas corpus, unless in cases of rebellion or invasion	To impose a direct tax unless proportional to population
To pass bills of attainder	*To impose direct taxes prior to a state's failure to comply with congressional requisitions* (Farrand, *Records* II, 353–54*)
To pass ex post facto law	To tax exports from any state
	To tax vessels in interstate trade
	To draw money from the Treasury without appropriations made by law
	To disown US debt contracted prior to the adoption of the Constitution
	To neglect payment of the public debt[†]

Police	International relations
To restrict the migration or importation of persons into states before 1808	To form new states by division or junction of existing states without consent of the state legislature or legislatures
To give preference to any port over others by means of commercial or revenue laws	*To maintain standing troops in time of peace beyond a stipulated number* (Farrand, *Records* II, 323*)
To grant titles of nobility	
To interfere with the liberty of the press (Farrand, *Records* II, 617–18*)	
To pass navigation acts without two-thirds majority of Congress (Farrand, *Records* II, 183*)	
To interfere with the governments of individual states in matters which respect only their internal police (Farrand, *Records* II, 367*)	

Notes: Powers in italics represent proposals that were rejected by the convention.

[†] Power proposed by Pinckney on August 18. Pinckney listed almost every item that appeared on Madison's list.

* Max Farrand, ed., *The Records of the Federal Convention of 1787*, 4 vols. (New Haven, CT: Yale University Press, 1966).

power. The motion amounted to a blueprint for executive departments and it constitutes another failed attempt to create a national government with more extensive powers over domestic affairs than what the Constitution allowed. The proposed Council would consist of a Council secretary, the Chief Justice, and

Table 3.3 **Powers withheld from the state legislatures**

Justice	Revenue
To pass bills of attainder	To tax imports and exports without the
To pass ex post facto laws	consent of Congress
To pass laws impairing the obligation of	To levy tonnage duties without the
contracts	consent of Congress
To nullify the US Constitution, laws or	
treaties	

Police	International Relations
To coin money	To enter into treaty, alliance, or
To emit bills of credit	confederation
To make anything but gold and silver coin	To enter into any agreement or compact
legal tender	with another state
To grant titles of nobility	To enter into any agreement or compact
To abrogate the rights and privileges of	with a foreign power
citizenship for out-of-state citizens	To grant letters of marque and reprisal
of the US	To keep troops in time of peace without
To shield out-of-state fugitives from	the consent of Congress
justice from extradition	To keep ships of war in time of peace
To discharge out-of-state fugitives from	without the consent of Congress
service or labor from their service	To engage in war unless invaded

five secretaries responsible for domestic affairs, commerce and finance, foreign affairs, war, and the marine. The first of these executive secretaries is of particular interest to a discussion of national police powers, for the proposal specified that the duties of the Secretary of Domestic Affairs would be "to attend to matters of general police, the state of agriculture and manufactures, the opening of roads and navigations, and the facilitating of communications through the United States." It also said that the secretary should "from time to time recommend such measures and establishments as may tend to promote those objects." The convention never acted on the motion, however. Although the Constitution speaks of the "principal Officer[s]" of "executive Departments" that were to be created by Congress, it does not enumerate either departments or secretaryships.[45]

Nevertheless, the idea of a Secretary of Domestic Affairs did not die in the Constitutional convention. When the first Congress debated the creation of executive departments on May 19, 1789, Delaware representative John Vining moved that in addition to departments of finance, war, and foreign affairs there should also be a "home department." Although on a later date he is reported to have spoken of a department of "domestic affairs," the name he chose was most likely not coincidental. In Britain, the Southern and the Northern Departments were reorganized in 1782 into the Home Department and the Foreign Office. Despite its name, one responsibility of Britain's new Home Department was colonial affairs. The federal territories—the colonies of the United States—appears in fact to have been foremost on Vining's mind, indicating that the department he envisaged had a more limited remit than the Secretary of Domestic Affairs proposed in the Constitutional Convention. Vining argued that the "territorial possessions of the United States and the domestic affairs, would be objects of the greatest magnitude," second only to finance in importance. When representatives countered that the duties of a prospective Secretary of the Home Department could be divided among other secretaries and that a separate department was expensive and unwarranted, Vining shot back "by enumerating a number of objects which could not come within the management of either department [i.e., Treasury and War], such as the numerous and increasing objects of a territorial nature, and the extensive correspondence between the federal government and its western dependencies. He also mentioned the propriety of instituting this office for the authentication of public instruments of every kind." But Vining lost his battle for a Home Department and, just like his critics had suggested, the duties that would have fallen to the Home Secretary were distributed between the departments of the Treasury, War, and State. It was not until the Mexican Cession increased the workload of the Treasury Department to breaking point that Congress in 1849 decided to create the Department of the Interior.[46]

The failure of Morris, Pinckney, and Vining to garner support for a department of domestic affairs is a further indication that the idea of national government regulation of social and economic life left a majority of American statesmen cold. The police powers that were indeed granted to Congress by the Constitution was to a large extent already invested in the national government by the Articles of Confederation. This is true of the authority to coin money, to fix weights and measures, and to establish post offices and post roads. The articles also granted Congress the right to regulate trade with Indian nations "not members of any of the states." A substantial new power given to Congress by the Constitution was the right to regulate trade with foreign powers, which in the articles were circumscribed by the states' power to decide over imports, exports, and duties. Strengthening the national government's ability to pass navigation acts in order to secure commercial treaties was one of the primary reasons for calling the Constitutional Convention. That southerners voiced fears of high duties give the lie to Madison's assertion in *Federalist* 45 that the right to regulate commerce was "an addition" to the new compact of union "which few oppose, and from which no apprehensions are entertained." Nevertheless, there was never any suggestion that such authority belonged to the class of powers that were labeled *internal* police.[47]

The Constitution did introduce new proscriptions on state actions that curtailed the power of state legislatures and courts over the states' internal police in important respects. The states were banned from issuing paper money, from making anything but gold and silver coin legal tender, from impairing the obligations of contracts, and from passing ex post facto laws. Historians have traditionally interpreted the paper money ban as an attempt to redistribute wealth from "ordinary people" to the elite. But on closer inspection, the contemporary discussions about paper money tend to address the danger that state bills of credit might defraud out-of-state and foreign creditors, thereby negatively affecting relations between the states and between the union and other nations. Madison's understanding of the prohibition is a good case in point. Discussing paper money in his famous preconvention "Vices" memorandum, he asked if citizens and assemblymen in Rhode Island "in estimating the policy of paper money, ever considered or cared in what light the measure would be viewed in France or Holland; or even in Massts or Connect.?" After the convention, Madison made the same point in *Federalist* 44, when he wrote that should the states be permitted to issue paper money, "the subjects of foreign powers might suffer from the same cause, and hence the Union be discredited and embroiled by the indiscretion of a single member." Two other delegates, Roger Sherman and Oliver Ellsworth, extended this argument to a discussion of restrictions on state police legislation more broadly, explaining that "the restraint on the legislatures of the several states respecting emitting bills of credit, making anything but money a legal tender in payment of debts, or impairing the obligation of contracts by ex post facto laws, was thought necessary as a security to commerce, in which the interest of foreigners, as well as of the citizens of different states, may be affected."[48]

Perhaps the clearest evidence that the majority of delegates never believed that Congress ought to intervene in the internal police of the states beyond a limited list of proscribed state actions comes from the very last moments of the Constitutional Convention. When the Committee of Style submitted its draft constitution to the convention on September 10, the department of domestic affairs and most of the national police powers proposed by Madison and Pinckney had been excised. There was no right to grant charters of incorporation, to establish a university and other institutions of learning, or to provide for "public institutions, rewards and immunities for the promotion of agriculture, commerce, trades, and manufactures." As the convention went over the draft, on September 14 Franklin moved that in addition to the right to establish post roads, Congress should also be empowered to cut canals. This prompted Madison to reintroduce his proposal that Congress be given the right "to grant charters of incorporation where the interest of the U.S. might require & legislative provisions of individual States may be incompetent."[49]

What was said in the convention on that September day cannot be established with any certitude. The official journal from the last few days is particularly sketchy, and the published version of the journal filled in the blanks with information provided by Madison. But according to Madison's notes, opponents responded to the motions by arguing that national canal works would stoke the fires of sectionalism and that a general authority to grant charters of incorporation would awaken fears of national "mercantile monopolies" and banks that would give rise to factions and endless party struggle in the national assembly. Franklin's motion was voted down eight states to three. The fact that the states voting in favor—Pennsylvania, Virginia, and Georgia—all had much to gain from improved communications with the western hinterland only confirmed the opposition's point about sectional interests. Unwilling to grant a right to incorporate canal companies, the convention naturally refused a general right of incorporation. Madison and Pinckney next moved to insert the right to establish a nondenominational university in the text of the Constitution. Sherman later recollected that "it was thought sufficient that this power should be exercised by the States in their separate capacity" and it, too, was voted down six states to four. There was no appetite for a national government active in promoting communications, the economy, or education.[50]

V

When the Constitutional Convention adjourned and presented its labors to the American public, a vocal minority expressed fear that the Constitution meant the end of the states. The New York writer "Brutus" complained that "the legislature of the United States are vested with the great and uncontroulable powers, of laying and collecting taxes, duties, imposts, and excises; of regulating trade, raising and supporting armies, organizing, arming, and disciplining the militia, instituting courts, and other general powers." As a result, the states would "dwindle away." Against the backdrop of the great "ends" of eighteenth-century governments outlined by Adam Smith and other writers, "Brutus's" concerns are understandable. By investing the national government with powers over the military, the revenue, and diplomacy independently of the states, the sovereignty of the states was undoubtedly circumscribed. French diplomats posted in America perceived this clearly. The consul in New York City, Antoine de Laforêt, reported to Paris that "nothing remains to the states of their individual independence but their Judicial powers, the right to make their laws for inspection and police, and to attend to the details of their internal administration. Congress will no longer need their consent to any of its operations." Louis Guillaume Otto, the French chargé d'affaires, likewise concluded that henceforth, the state legislatures would be limited "to regulating their internal police; they will resemble corporations rather than Sovereign assemblies."[51]

Yet for all the Antifederalists' fears, the truly significant change in the American union that was brought about by the transition from the Articles of Confederation to the Constitution was an expansion of national government means rather than national government ends. There is therefore a good deal of truth in Sherman's claim that the powers delegated to Congress by the Constitution were basically "the same as Congress have under the articles of Confederation with this difference, that they will have authority to carry into effect, what they now have a right to require to be done by the States." It was a change of immense importance, but it did not entail a broadening of the remit of the national government beyond intraunion and international affairs. Hamilton said as much in *The Federalist* when he brushed aside fears that the national government might interfere in the internal concerns of the states by asserting that the "regulation of the mere domestic police of a State" held no attraction to ambitious statesmen. "Commerce, finance, negociation [i.e., diplomacy] and war seem to comprehend all the objects, which have charms for minds governed by that passion," he wrote. The administration of "private justice" or the "supervision of agriculture," in contrast, "would contribute nothing to the dignity, to the importance, or to the splendour of the national government."[52]

Other Federalists were less disdainful of police regulations and private justice. But they, too, made clear that it was the states and not Congress that would regulate internal police and that they had no wish to see the national government crowd out the states in this domain. Like Hamilton, they envisioned a union in which the division of labor between the states and the national government would be relatively clear-cut. An unsentimental description of that division was presented by a writer styling himself "A Virginian":

> I will admit, that by this Constitution, the several States will be abridged of some of their powers; but of no more than are necessary to make a strong federal government. Sufficient still remains with the State Legislatures to preserve the quiet, liberty, and welfare, of their citizens. To them is left the whole domestic government of the States; they may still regulate the rules of property, the rights of persons, every thing that relates to their internal police, and whatever effects neither foreign affairs nor the rights of the other states.[53]

The view expressed by this anonymous writer did not differ significantly from that of another Virginian, the prominent Antifederalist "Federal Farmer," widely believed to have been Richard Henry Lee. Like "Brutus," "Federal Farmer" worried that national government "powers to lay and collect internal taxes, to form the militia, to make bankrupt laws, and to decide on appeals, questions arising on the internal laws of the respective states" would undermine state sovereignty. Nevertheless, he supported the creation of a tripartite national government entrusted with "external objects." These included "all foreign concerns, commerce, imposts, all causes arising on the seas, peace and war, and Indian affairs," which could "be lodged no where else, with any propriety, but in this government." The national government should also possess power over several "internal objects," such as the authority "to regulate trade between the states, weights and measures, the coin or current monies, post-offices, naturalization, &c.," that would not materially affect the "internal police" of the states.[54]

In the thousands of pages that make up the record of the ratification debate, the most complete statement of the range of things that state governments *"must or may do"* under the Constitution was made by the Philadelphia merchant Tench Coxe in his "Freeman" essays. These essays originated in Coxe's wish "to demonstrate that the *proposed federal Constitution* does not provide for the exigencies of civil Society, and the execution of domestic government" and therefore was no threat to the existence and power of the states. The second essay, in particular, was devoted to a long enumeration of the powers that were retained by the states. They involved the right to appoint officers of the militia; to regulate religion and religious bodies; to determine the qualifications of electors in federal elections; to regulate the law of descent and to forbid entails; and to regulate and administer the criminal law. It was also left to the states "to determine all the innumerable disputes about property lying within their respective territories between their own citizens, such as titles and boundaries of lands, debts by assumption, note, bond, or account, mercantile contracts, &c." But this was not all. Coxe ended with a long list of police powers to be exercised by the state governments:

> The several states can create corporations civil and religious; prohibit or impose duties on the importation of slaves into their own ports; establish seminaries of learning; erect boroughs, cities, and counties; promote and establish manufactures; open roads; clear rivers; cut canals; regulate descents and marriages; license taverns; alter the criminal law; constitute new courts and offices; establish ferries; erect public buildings; sell, lease, and appropriate the proceeds and rents of *their lands*, and of every other species of *state property*; establish poor houses, hospitals, and houses of employment; regulate the police; and many other things of the utmost importance to the happiness of their respective citizens. In short, besides the particulars enumerated, every thing of a domestic nature must or can be done by them.[55]

Federalist supporters of the Constitution thus agreed with their Antifederalist opponents that the state assemblies rather than the national legislature would regulate internal police. They postulated that by harnessing the powers listed by Coxe, the states much more than Congress would shape the future society and economy of America. In this they were proven right. Far from being annihilated by the Constitution, the states would continue to be the central source of political power in the early republic. As William Novak has so forcefully argued, rather than a laissez-faire society where government intervention in social and economic affairs was shunned, well beyond the Civil War the central aim of American government was the realization of the "well-regulated society." Yet the "locus of authority" of this nineteenth-century governmental regime, Novak writes, was not the federal government, but "State and Local Government." In the nineteenth century, the states, not the federal government, employed their powers over police and the rules of property—often by delegating supervisory authority to cities, towns, and county courts—to promote the "opulence of the state" that had been the subject of Adam Smith's Glasgow lectures, and the well-ordered society that was the concern of French police science and Anglo-American common law.[56]

4

Legislation

Implementing the Constitution

The representatives and senators elected to the first federal Congress took their good time to arrive in New York City. In a bid to remain the capital of the American union, the city had contracted Pierre L'Enfant to redesign City Hall on the corner of Wall Street and Nassau Street into an elegant, if modestly sized, legislative building that was renamed Federal Hall. Here the new Congress was set to convene on March 4, 1789. But as had often been the case with the old Congress, neither chamber had reached a quorum when the day arrived. Somewhat inauspiciously, the House of Representatives did so only four weeks later, on All Fools' Day. The Senate required yet another week to reach its minimum number of twelve senators. By early April, Congress could at long last begin to count the electoral votes for president and soon after inform George Washington that to nobody's surprise, he had been unanimously elected the first president of the United States.[1]

Washington was inaugurated on April 30. The Chancellor of New York State, Robert Livingston, administered the oath of office on the second-story balcony of Federal Hall. His cry of "Long live George Washington, President of the United States," was reportedly answered with cheers from the crowd assembled below and by a thirteen-gun salute. The president then retired to the Senate Chamber to deliver the first ever inaugural address, a performance that the surly William Maclay, Senator for Pennsylvania, described as singularly uninspiring. Washington's address noted that the new Constitution instructed the executive to recommend "necessary and expedient" measures for the consideration of Congress. He therefore suggested that the legislature contemplate constitutional amendments to still the disquiet that had been so much in evidence in state conventions and print discourse during the recent ratification struggle. But Washington otherwise refrained from any "recommendation of particular measures" and instead passed the buck to the assembled legislators, expressing his

Perfecting the Union. Max M. Edling, Oxford University Press (2021). © Oxford University Press.
DOI: 10.1093/oso/9780197534717.003.0005

faith in "the talents, the rectitude, and the patriotism" of the representatives and senators in audience. His only hint about the business facing the new Congress was an opaque reference to the Constitution, "which in defining your powers, designates the objects to which your attention is to be given."[2]

The reference to "the Great Constitutional Charter" indicates that Washington believed that the first Congress would strive to realize an agenda that had been formulated by the Philadelphia convention. In this he was far from alone. The previous summer, James Iredell had said that "the first session of Congress" would put in execution "every power contained in the Constitution." Samuel Osgood, who would become postmaster general under Washington, simply described the first Congress as "a second convention." The composition of the federal government meant that Congress could seamlessly continue the work of the Convention. Knowledge of the past proceedings in Philadelphia, which had taken place behind closed doors, was widespread in all branches of the new government. Nine representatives and ten senators in the first Congress had been members of the Constitutional Convention. In the executive branch, the president, treasury secretary, and attorney general had also been at the convention, as had three of the six justices on the Supreme Court. Although opposition to the Constitution from so-called Antifederalists had been strong in many of the states, the first Congress was controlled by men who had favored the Constitution. With 49 of 59 representatives and 20 of 22 senators supporting the Constitution, effective opposition to the Federalists' political program was ruled out.[3]

The Constitutional Convention was summoned to amend the Articles of Confederation so as to "render the federal constitution adequate to the exigencies of government and the preservation of the Union." Although the inadequacies were not spelled out, years of reform attempts in the Confederation Congress demonstrate that even if the flaws in the articles were considered to be serious, they were relatively few in number. These flaws prevented Congress from regulating commerce, from raising revenue to pay the running costs of government and charges on the public debt, and from administering the western lands. In order to address these shortcomings, the convention exceeded its mandate and replaced the articles with a completely new Constitution that created a tripartite national government capable of acting directly on the citizens and inhabitants of the United States independent of the state governments. Yet the record of the convention suggests that the majority of delegates did not envisage any dramatic broadening of the remit of the national government beyond the management of international and interstate affairs. The brief report that conveyed the finished Constitution to Congress instead presented the new compact of union as the answer to a long-standing desire among "the friends of our country . . . that the power of making war, peace and treaties, that of levying money and regulating commerce, and the correspondent executive and judicial authorities should be fully and effectually vested in the general government of the Union."[4]

Preparing to accept the presidency in January 1789, Washington expected that the new government would pursue a narrow agenda of reforming the public finances in order "to extricate my country from the embarrassments in which it is entangled, through want of credit; and to establish, a general system of [commercial] policy, which, if pursued will insure permanent felicity to the Commonwealth." James Madison, who had been the leading light in the Constitutional convention, also expected questions of commerce and revenue to require "our first attention, and our united exertions" in Congress. He explicitly linked the question of revenue to the ability of the government to resume payments on the debt and thereby to restore public credit. Referring to the United States' debt obligations, Madison's first speech in the House of Representatives declared that "the union, by the establishment of a more effective government having recovered from the state of imbecility, that heretofore prevented a performance of its duty, ought, in its first act, to revive those principles of honor and honesty that have too long lain dormant." A few weeks later he claimed that the Constitution's origins lay in the need to retaliate against British commercial discrimination.[5]

Debate on measures that would become the impost, tonnage, and collection acts in fact came to dominate the House agenda for its first three months. Later, the first Congress would tackle the restructuring of the national debt and vote to incorporate a national bank. At first sight, the regulation of commerce and the reform of the public finances may seem like highly technical questions unlikely to cause much political passion. Yet over the course of the Congress these issues came to generate disagreement that would grow into an organized opposition to administration policies from within the ranks of former Federalist sympathizers in Congress. Having worked closely to secure the adoption of the Constitution, Madison and Alexander Hamilton fell out over its application. As treasury secretary, Hamilton's financial and fiscal policies included the restructuring of the national debt, the creation of the Bank of the United States, and appeasement toward Britain. Madison believed that Hamilton's program enhanced the power of the federal government to the point where it threatened to overpower the states. He also wished the United States to stand up to British commercial discrimination.

Scholarship on the first and subsequent Congresses during the Washington administration has concentrated on the unfolding of the events that began with the dissolution of the Hamilton-Madison alliance and ended with the formation of political parties in the legislative assembly. There are good reasons for this. Hamilton and Thomas Jefferson, Madison's mentor, have been cast as the original exponents of two competing visions of the destiny of the United States, which have remained in tension over the course of American history. Nevertheless, this focus has fostered a one-sided view of the early Congresses as primarily a site for ideological conflict and party formation. Few scholars have taken an interest in the main activity of this political institution: the enactment of legislation.

For those familiar with the literature on "the Age of Federalism"—that is, the presidencies of Washington and John Adams—this may sound like an exaggerated, perhaps even false, claim. It is true that there are many studies of specific acts of legislation and that every survey of the period highlights the major legislative achievements of at least the first Congress, such as the adoption of the Bill of Rights, the funding and assumption of the national debt, the creation of the Bank of the United States, the establishment of the federal judiciary, and the decision to locate the capital on the Potomac River. What is missing is rather a *systematic* analysis of the total body of legislation adopted by the early Congresses, an analysis that places landmark legislation alongside the more mundane actions of the legislature. This chapter aims to provide such a systematic study by means of a quantitative analysis of the legislation of Congress under Washington.[6]

The purpose is not to supplant but rather to complement existing scholarship on the early Congress and its role in the federal government. It is obvious that no political history of the early United States can ignore the milestone acts just listed, and it would be absurd to claim that all laws are equally salient. Few historians would argue that the construction of a lighthouse on Portland Head mattered as much to the nation's development as did the incorporation of the Bank of the United States. Because a quantitative analysis cannot measure the relative significance of laws either in terms of contemporary controversy or long-term significance, it is ill-equipped to capture the dramatic turning-points in political development that often structure historical narratives. But such weakness is also a strength. For although much is learnt about politics from controversy and adversity, the majority of actions undertaken by any political institution consists of routine tasks that give rise to limited or no contention. A single-minded focus on ideological clashes and party formation will direct attention away from the day-to-day operations that form an equally important part of the history of the early federal government.

To understand the legislative activities of Congress, the federal legislature cannot be understood in isolation from the state governments. The men who wrote the Constitution expected that the national legislature would do some things, the state legislatures other things. To find out if the Constitution realized their idea of a division of labor between the two governments, it is necessary to study the activity of state legislatures alongside the activity of Congress. To reach a provisional answer to this question it is not necessary to investigate the legislative output of all of the eleven states that made up the union when the first Congress convened in 1789, or of all of the sixteen united states of America in existence when the fourth Congress adjourned, however. If the Constitution established a division of labor whereby the national government looked after external matters, and the state governments took care of their own internal affairs, a clearly discernable pattern of legislation ought to be present in every single one of the state legislatures in the union, albeit with some local variation. In this chapter Congress will be compared to the assembly of the Commonwealth of Pennsylvania, a state that shared both its capital and its capitol with the national government from 1791 to 1800.[7]

A quantitative analysis of congressional and state legislation in the 1790s faces significant methodological challenges. To discover patterns in legislative output requires classification of individual acts. Such class categories can either be analytical or already inscribed in the sources. Because historians of the early United States have "been remarkably inattentive to the legislature," as William Novak points out, there have been no quantitative analysis of legislation in the early United States at either federal or state level. The situation is different in European historiography, where the state has always appeared a decisive force in the shaping of society and therefore a legitimate object of study. In England before the union with Scotland in 1707, and in Britain from 1707, Parliament was the core governmental institution in the centuries that followed the Glorious Revolution and the parliamentary statute an essential governmental instrument. In the early 1990s, a group of British historians led by Julian Hoppit and Joanna Innes collected and classified the approximately 13,600 acts passed by Parliament between 1688 and 1800, together with several thousand failed legislative attempts. Dealing with such numbers over an extended time-period required a classification schema that could be easily imposed on the legislative record, often only on the basis of the statute title. The only classification used by Parliament in the eighteenth century was the distinction between public and private acts, a distinction of limited analytical value. Because Hoppit and his collaborators were interested in the "purposes of legislation," they instead developed analytical categories that took into account "the subject matter of acts and failed initiatives." The result was a classification schema made up of ten main categories, divided into 31 subcategories, which were further subdivided into 177 particular categories.[8]

Applying the same categories to the record of the first four congresses and the Pennsylvania assembly makes it possible to compare the actions of the American and British legislative assemblies, thereby highlighting specificities about the early federal government that stand out less clearly when Congress is investigated on its own. Using Parliament as a reference point has the added advantage of making possible an assessment of the early federal government's actions against the benchmark of an actual eighteenth-century state, rather than

against the benchmark of an ahistorical concept of the state taken from the social sciences. Britain is a relevant point of comparison because it was both the
nation out of which independent America sprang, and an unusually successful
eighteenth-century state. In the eyes of Britons and foreigners alike, the British
eighteenth-century state appeared to be more resourceful and more efficient
than any of its competitors.[9]

Historians have written much about Britain's ability to engage in frequent and
costly wars and to dictate the rules of international commerce thanks to its powerful *fiscal-military state*: a war machine singularly effective in raising revenue
from loans and taxation to be spent on soldiers, warships, and foreign subsidies.
Less prominent in the literature is the concept of Britain's *reactive state*, a term
coined by historians of Parliament. The concept points to Parliament's role in
reacting, or responding, to demands by individuals and small interest groups for
legislation aimed to enable economic and social projects that were typically personal or local, rather than national, in scope. The process involved a systematic
and often radical redefinition of different types of property rights by Parliament,
and the "reactive state" was to that extent a constitutive as much as a reactive
governmental institution. In the long eighteenth century, Parliament was primarily concerned with meeting demands for landed property regulation, improved
transportation, and the promotion of agriculture by means of enclosure. Much
more than a cog in Britain's war machine, Parliament was an institution that
allowed the landed nobility and gentry to promote their material interests. In
terms of the volume of legislation, the reactive state outdistanced the fiscal-
military state by a long stretch.[10]

The British *reactive* and *fiscal-military state* provide two analytical concepts
that can be fruitfully used to discuss the nature of the early federal government.
The concepts also have a bearing on the question that has been running though
this book. Did the Constitution aim to create a government that would manage
international and interstate affairs only, or did it aim to create a national government that would also be active in managing domestic affairs? Britain's reactive state was concerned with domestic economic regulation and promotion,
broadly construed. The raison d'être of the British fiscal-military state, in contrast, was to provide for the security of the nation and its overseas possessions
and to promote British interests relative to other nations, including the regulation of international trade.

A comparison of the legislative output of the American and the British
legislatures has to be sensitive to the considerable geopolitical and socioeconomic differences between the United States and Britain in the late eighteenth
century. The United States was a young, peripheral, and weak nation removed
from European great power politics, whereas Britain, despite the loss of the
thirteen colonies, remained arguably the most powerful state in the world and

carried great weight in the European balance of power. Economic differences also abounded. Agriculture dominated in both nations but there was great disparity in the distribution of wealth, the supply and price of farmland, the predominant labor regimes, and the nature of property rights—freehold in America, leasehold in Britain. Geographic dissimilarities were equally pronounced. England was a compact and densely populated nation. With only half the population of England, the United States was almost eighteen times its size. Nevertheless, comparing the legislative assemblies of Britain, the United States, and Pennsylvania allows for a comparison between the bisected American state and a mature unitary state. This comparison is likely to illuminate how the Constitution effected the distribution of political authority in the American federal republic.

I

England's Glorious Revolution was followed by a dramatic upsurge in parliamentary activity. In the two centuries before 1688, Parliament passed around 2,700 acts. Between 1688 and 1800, it passed more than 13,600 acts and turned down some 5,600 legislative proposals. The volume of legislation increased gradually as the eighteenth century progressed. Between 1689 and 1714 (i.e., before the accession of George I), Parliament passed around 45 acts every year. In the 1790s, the annual average had jumped to 275 acts. The growth in legislation was caused by the constitutional changes following the events of 1688. In the seventeenth century, the monarch and the courts regulated and governed society. In the eighteenth century, Parliament became the principal institution of the British government and the Act of Parliament became the principal instrument of government.[11]

Parliament's rise in importance was a boon to the social classes that elected it—that is, the landowning gentry and, to a lesser extent, the merchant class. These groups made use of parliamentary legislation to meet the demands of a changing society. The vast majority of legislation in the eighteenth century originated with individuals and small groups seeking the authority of an Act of Parliament to further their specific and local interests. Most legislative activity can be described as economic and domestic in nature, directly or indirectly concerned with wealth and income. An Act of Parliament bestowed authority on local bodies of diverse kinds: turnpike trusts, poor law authorities, charities, improvement commissioners, and the like, and the central government did not pursue national policy as much as it invested local bodies with the power to do so. This defused a long-standing tension between the center and the localities, as Parliament became a resource rather than a threat or competitor to local power magnates. "For many within the upper echelons of society, the expansion of legislation was central to their financial hopes and commercial aspirations," Hoppit writes. "Without the changes that followed 1689 we might doubt whether estate settlements could so readily have been altered, turnpikes built and fields enclosed."[12]

Hoppit found that between 1688 and 1800 Parliamentary legislation belonged overwhelmingly to the categories *personal legislation, communications,* and *the economy* (see Table 4.1 for classes of legislation). *Personal legislation* refers to private matters, primarily estate and inheritance legislation. Laws pertaining to *the economy* were primarily concerned with enclosures. In the period from 1688 to 1714, slightly more than three-fifths of all acts fell in these three categories. In the four decades between 1760 and 1800, the figure rose to just above 70 percent of the total. The relative importance of the three categories shifted over time, however. In the period to 1714, close to half the total number of acts belonged in the personal class. The economy and communications accounted for only 7.7 and 5.1 percent, respectively, of total legislation in these years. Both were dwarfed by financial legislation, which made up 13.9 percent of the total. In the period from 1760 to 1800, however, personal legislation had fallen from half to less than a fifth of all acts, whereas the economy and communications had jumped to, respectively, 30.9 and 21.6 percent. Communications legislation increased sharply in the middle, and economic regulation toward the end, of the century. Thus, it is evident that Parliament's interest in promoting the economy and transportation began in earnest only in the second half of the eighteenth century.[13]

Legislation in all three categories had bearing on private income and wealth accumulation. In the *personal* category, the laws were predominantly estate acts. Put simply, these were a means to free landed property from restrictions imposed by legal settlements. Settlements were introduced to protect the interests of the landowner's family at the expense of the individual landowner, primarily to preserve the property intact for coming generations. But settlements also distributed family property among a broader circle of family members beyond the estate holder and his heir, for instance by providing annual incomes for younger sons and dowries for daughters. Essentially, a settlement made the landholder a tenant for life rather than a freehold property owner and could impose extensive restrictions on the use of the property. Cutting down trees, draining peat bogs, and opening mines, for example, could all be proscribed in legal settlements. In particular, the sale of the property, in whole or in part, was not permitted. An estate act removed these restrictions and transformed the estate into property that could be developed, mortgaged, or sold. One study reports that of the 3,500 estate acts passed between 1660 and 1830, more than half authorized the sale of property and close to three-quarters the sale, lease, or exchange of

Table 4.1 **British, US, and Pennsylvania legislation by category (percentage)**

	British acts, 1789–1797	US statutes, 1789–1797	PA acts, 1790–1797
Personal	16.6	16.3	13.4
Government	2.4	24.4	27.8
Finance	11.5	32.2	17.2
Law and order	2.3	7.5	4.6
Religion	2.4	—	0.4
Armed services	4.0	9.5	2.2
Social issues	5.5	0.8	8.8
Economy	31.0	1.8	13.7
Communications	24.2	7.5	11.9
Miscellaneous	0.2	—	—

Note: US laws includes both public and private statutes as well as the five international treaties and the nine treaties with American Indian nations ratified in this period.

Source: UK: Julian Hoppit et al., "Parliamentary Acts, 1660–1800," Excel file in author's possession. US: *The Public Statutes at Large of the United States of America* (Boston: Charles C. Little and James Brown, 1845–), I, 23–519; VI, 1–30; VII, 1–60; VIII, 116–56. PA: *Acts of the General Assembly of the Commonwealth of Pennsylvania, Passed at a Session which was Begun and Held at the City of Philadelphia on Tuesday, the Seventh Day of December, in the Year One Thousand Seven Hundred and Ninety, and of the Independence of the United States of America, the Fifteenth* (Philadelphia: Hall and Sellers, 1791); *Acts of the General Assembly of the Commonwealth of Pennsylvania, Passed at a Session which was Begun and Held at the City of Philadelphia on Tuesday, the Twenty-Third Day of August, in the Year One Thousand Seven Hundred and Ninety-One, and of the Independence of the United States of America, the Sixteenth* (Philadelphia: Hall and Sellers, 1791); *Acts of the General Assembly of the Commonwealth of Pennsylvania, Passed at a Session which was Begun and Held at the City of Philadelphia on Tuesday, the Sixth Day of December, in the Year One Thousand Seven Hundred and Ninety-One, and of the Independence of the United States of America, the Sixteenth* (Philadelphia: Hall and Sellers, 1792); *Acts of the General Assembly of the Commonwealth of Pennsylvania, Passed at a Session which was Begun and Held at the City of Philadelphia on Tuesday, the Fourth Day of December, in the Year One Thousand Seven Hundred and Ninety-Two, and of the Independence of the United States of America, the Seventeenth* (Philadelphia: Hall and Sellers, 1793); *Acts of the General Assembly of the Commonwealth of Pennsylvania, Passed at a Session which was Begun and Held at the City of Philadelphia on Tuesday, the Twenty-Seventh Day of August, in the Year One Thousand Seven Hundred and Ninety-Three, and of the Independence of the United States of America, the Eighteenth* (Philadelphia: Hall and Sellers, 1793); *Acts of the General Assembly of the Commonwealth of Pennsylvania, Passed at a Session which was Begun and Held at the City of Philadelphia on Tuesday, the Third Day of December, in the Year One Thousand Seven Hundred and Ninety-Three, and of the Independence of the United States of America, the Eighteenth* (Philadelphia: Hall and Sellers, 1794); *Acts of the General Assembly of the Commonwealth of Pennsylvania, Passed at a Session which was Begun and Held at the City of Philadelphia on Monday, the First Day of September, in the Year One Thousand Seven Hundred and Ninety-Four, and of the Independence of the United States of America, the Nineteenth* (Philadelphia: Hall and Sellers, 1794); *Acts of the General Assembly of the Commonwealth of Pennsylvania, Passed at a Session which was Begun and Held at the City of Philadelphia on Tuesday, the Second Day of December, in the Year One Thousand Seven Hundred and Ninety-Four, and of the Independence of the United States of America, the Nineteenth* (Philadelphia: Hall and Sellers,1795); *Acts of the General Assembly of the Commonwealth of Pennsylvania, Passed at a Session which was Begun and Held at the City of Philadelphia on Tuesday, the First Day of December, in the Year One Thousand Seven Hundred and Ninety-Five, and of the Independence of the United States of America, the Twentieth* (Philadelphia: Hall and Sellers,1796); *Acts of the General Assembly of the Commonwealth of Pennsylvania, Passed at a Session which was Begun and Held at the City of Philadelphia on Tuesday, the Sixth Day of December, in the Year One Thousand Seven Hundred and Ninety-Six, and of the Independence of the United States of America, the Twenty-First* (Philadelphia: Hall and Sellers,1797).

property. Estate acts could therefore allow property holders to take advantage of opportunities brought about by economic change.[14]

Economic legislation was heavily dominated by enclosure acts. Hoppit reports that for the whole of the period 1660 to 1800, around 70 percent of economic legislation consisted of such legislation. In the middle years of the 1790s that figure was 75 percent. The enclosure movement began in earnest in the 1750s and the rise of enclosure acts explains why economic legislation rose so sharply in the second half of the eighteenth century. Typically, enclosure allowed for the consolidation of strips of open field into compact farms or for the privatization of land previously held in common. Economic historians debate the effect this had on agricultural productivity, whereas social historians have been much more concerned with the social upheaval and dispossession of the rural poor that followed in the wake of the enclosure movement. The second most important subcategory of economic legislation was the regulation of external trade, which amounted to about 16 percent in this period. Next in size was the regulation of internal trade. These were measures that eighteenth-century commentators placed under the rubric of internal police regulations, dealing with weights and measures, consumption, and middlemen, for example. Hoppit and the other investigators also counted laws promoting agricultural production and manufactures as economic legislation, although such statutes were few in number.[15]

Turnpike acts were by far the most common type of legislation affecting communications. Over the 1660 to 1800 period, almost three-quarters of communications acts either incorporated new turnpike trusts or extended already existing corporation charters. Other acts were concerned with bridge construction, canal and river improvements, and harbor developments. By the middle of the 1790s turnpike acts accounted for a little over 60 percent, and legislation incorporating canal companies or regulating canals for slightly more than a fifth, of total communications legislation. A turnpike act gave a trust the right to build or improve a road and to charge users of the road a fee. Fees were intended to cover road repair and maintenance only, because turnpike trusts were prohibited from turning a profit from road management. Economic historians have nevertheless shown that there were very significant indirect profits to be made from road construction, which made it worthwhile to petition for incorporation of a turnpike trust. Trusts were normally made up of property owners who owned the land on which the road ran and there is a strong correlation between the construction of turnpikes and the rise in the value of land and the income from landed estates located within easy reach of turnpike roads. Corporations chartered for the purpose of bridge building had a similar composition, whereas legislation for river improvements and canals were often backed by manufacturing and mining corporations. Both bridges and improved water communications generated the same advantages to investors as turnpike trusts did.[16]

In the course of the seventeenth century all English colonies in America acquired representative assemblies, and during the eighteenth century the North American colonial assemblies took on several of the features of the British Parliament. Like Parliament, the assemblies passed a growing number of laws per session, reflecting "their developing ability to handle the legislative needs of their constituents." There are therefore indications that the same trend toward "demand-led" legislation that can be observed in the mother country also existed in the colonies. In North America rapid demographic, geographic, and economic growth generated demands from the population for more and better provisions for defense, mediums of exchange, American Indian relations, and transportation; for adjudication between competing interest groups; and for the creation of more accessible governmental institutions and officers, such as county courts and justices of the peace. When local government at town and county level could no longer meet these demands, the colonists turned to their assemblies for assistance.[17]

The American Revolution enhanced the colonial assemblies' ability to respond to constituency demands. The collapse of the empire that resulted from the refusal of the American colonists to go along with Britain's far-ranging reforms created a vacuum that was soon filled by the new states. Although the colonists had vehemently opposed Parliament's legislation over the colonies, they were not averse to government as such. In fact, historians have argued that they wanted more, not less, government intervention in social and economic affairs, but that they wanted governments that were under their own control. With independence the Privy Council's power to review and overrule colonial legislation and Parliament's contested right to legislate for the colonists were terminated. As a consequence, the obstacles to the assemblies' ability to legislate on economic and social matters were removed.[18]

The revolutionary transformation of government that turned colonial dependencies into sovereign states, and which privileged the legislature over the executive in the new state constitutions, meant that there were few restrictions on the actions that could be undertaken by the state assemblies after the Revolution. This development laid the foundation for the nineteenth-century regulatory regime that has been so carefully mapped in Novak's *The People's Welfare*. As Novak shows, the notion that antebellum United States was stateless laissez-faire society where government intervention in social and economic affairs was shunned is incorrect. At state and local level, government was busy bringing about the well-ordered and opulent society.[19]

In the Continental Congress the Revolution produced an anomalous central government that was a hybrid between a legislature and a diplomatic congress with executive functions, "formed to coordinate rather than direct the exertions of the states, and with primary responsibility for deliberating on war, peace, treaties, and alliances." The deliberations in the Constitutional Convention and the initial business of the first Congress suggest that the federal government was designed to manage a similarly limited agenda emanating from the after-effects of the War of Independence. Yet a legitimate claim to an almost unlimited right to legislate could be based on the broad grant to Congress to "promote the general Welfare" found in the Constitution's preamble, and in the "necessary and proper" clause of Article I, Section 8. Such, at least, were the fears voiced by the Antifederalist critics of the Constitution in the struggle over ratification. Given the trend witnessed in both the British Parliament and the American eighteenth-century legislatures before independence, it seems at least conceivable that the new federal government would be eager to try its hand at social and economic reform. However, the legislative agenda of the national assembly turned out to be much narrower as Congress under Washington pursued a course that left social and economic regulation largely alone.[20]

II

Even a casual glance at the legislative output of the early Congress indicates that it was a different institution from the British Parliament. The volume of legislation was considerably lower. Whereas the annual average of Parliament was around 275 acts in the 1790s, the first four Congresses managed less than 400 in eight years. Instinctively, one is led to believe that the business of setting up a new government—dealing with everything from the judiciary to the revenue system—was vastly more time consuming than the routine matters facing Parliament. But this explanation does not stand up to closer scrutiny. The average number of statutes enacted by each Congress stayed at less than a hundred up to the War of 1812. Between the War of 1812 and the Civil War the average hovered at 150, still very much below Parliament's output in the 1790s. It was not until the Harding administration that congressional output remained consistently above 500 statutes per Congress. It is much more likely that the United States differed from Britain because the vast mass of legislation that kept Parliament busy in the final decade of the eighteenth century simply was not on the agenda of Congress.[21]

A comparison of the main classes of legislation adopted by Congress during the Washington administration and by Parliament in the corresponding time period supports this assumption (see Table 4.1). The first four Congresses passed 319 public and 66 private statutes. In addition to this, the Senate ratified five international treaties and nine treaties with American Indian nations. Congressional legislation belonged overwhelmingly in the classes *government* and *finance*, which together accounted for 56.6 percent of total legislation. The former category includes legislation concerned with the executive and legislative branches of the national government, with local government, and with *the colonies*, which in the US context has been interpreted as legislation related to the federal territories. In the classification of Parliamentary statutes, the *finance* category includes not only public finance but also private financial measures such as laws on banking and money. Congress's ventures into private finance were limited to only three statutes governing insolvent debtors, however. Almost all financial legislation concerned appropriations, taxation, and debt management, including the creation of the Bank of the United States. These were areas where Parliament was relatively inactive in the 1790s, and indeed in the last four decades of the eighteenth century generally. Conversely, Congress did little to regulate the economy or promote transportation. Less than one statute in ten belonged to these classes whereas in Britain they dominated Parliament's agenda, accounting for 55.2 percent of the total number of acts passed in the 1789–1797 period.[22]

The record of Congress and Parliament converge only in the area of *personal legislation*. About a sixth of all acts passed in both assemblies fall in this category. But beyond a superficial similarity, it is once again the differences that stand out. Parliament passed estate acts, naturalization acts, and a smattering of acts granting name changes and divorces. Congress, in contrast, passed laws granting relief to merchants, on the one hand, and compensation for goods supplied and services rendered during the War of Independence, on the other. In fact, there was virtually no overlap between the activities of the two legislatures in the category of *personal legislation*. The handful of US statutes dealing with landed property all concerned land grants in the Northwest Territory, located on the extreme geographical periphery of the United States.

The categories *social issues*, *the economy*, and *communications* made up more than three-fifths of the total legislation in Parliament. Enclosure acts and the incorporation of turnpike and canal companies were by far the most common types of laws passed. In contrast, apart from running the post office, Congress hardly made any attempt to directly promote the economy or transportation. The only social issue–related legislation were a naturalization act and an act regulating quarantines. Economic legislation was restricted to one act each addressing the exchange rate of a Danish coin, the fisheries, and the slave trade, and to two acts prohibiting the exportation of arms and ammunition. The *communications* category, finally, was by far the largest of the three. There were seven acts regulating the post office and post roads, fifteen acts for the construction of lighthouses and the placement of buoys, and eight acts adjusting the shipping register, issuing passports for US ships, and governing the coastal trade. With the exception of the post office legislation, which dealt with the relationship between the states of the American union, the common denominator of all legislation in these three categories is plain to see: they all regulated relations between the United States and the outside world, by dealing with immigrants, international commerce, and shipping.[23]

The pattern of congressional legislation reveals a national assembly confined to a very narrow remit. It is indeed striking that so many of the classes that historians of Parliament needed to categorize British eighteenth-century legislation do not apply to the legislative output of Congress. No laws passed in the period from 1789 to 1797 fit categories such as: *banks, lenders; law of property; rivers; canals; bridges, ferries, and tunnels; roads, general;* or *roads, specific,* for example. Nor were there any estate acts or enclosure acts. Only a small trickle of laws had anything do to with landed property. The reason for this is obvious. Property titles were held under state governments and were governed by state laws and regulated by state courts. The federal government and the federal courts had little to do with private property in land. Once the sale of lands in the Northwest Territory began this would change, but only for people who bought land and settled in the federal territories.[24]

In contrast to political historians of early America, political scientists working in the subfield of American Political Development have taken more of an interest in the substance of legislation, often in an attempt to better understand party behavior, polarization, and leadership in Congress. Ira Katznelson and John Lapinski have developed a detailed coding schema to allow for the classification of US legislation over time, and Lapinski has applied it to the period after 1877. Table 4.2 presents the legislation of Congress under Washington coded according to the Katznelson-Lapinski classification schema. Because it adheres quite closely to the structure of legislation of the modern Congress, the schema can be used to compare the activities of the early Congress to that of the twentieth-century Congress.[25]

The many gaps in the legislative activity of the early Congress is the most striking feature of Table 4.2. The first four Congresses passed 94 acts that can be classed as dealing with international relations and 131 that can be classed as dealing with domestic affairs. But the vast majority of acts in the latter category concerned federal matters, appropriations, and taxation. Once these laws are subtracted the total number of domestic affairs laws falls to a modest 38. Half of these dealt with monetary matters (i.e., the mint and the valuation of foreign coin), and with military pensions. The seven acts in the *economic regulation* class concerned bankruptcy (three) and patents and copyrights (four). The virtual absence of activity in the tier 2 areas of *agriculture and food, planning and resources,* and *social policy* is of course significant. It would be a mistake to explain this difference by pointing to the obvious differences between the late eighteenth-century warfare state and the late twentieth-century welfare state, however. Although it would be a gross exaggeration to label them welfare states,

Table 4.2 **US legislation 1789–1797 by modern policy categories.**

Tier 1	Tier 2	Tier 3	# Acts
Sovereignty	Liberty	*Loyalty & expression*	1
		Religion	
		Privacy	
	Membership and nation	*Commemorations & national culture*	1
		Immigration & naturalization	2
	Civil rights	African Americans	
		Native Americans	
		Other minority groups	
		Women	
		Voting rights	
	Boundaries	*Frontier settlement*	3
		Indian removal & compensation	18*
		State admission/union composition	3
		Territories & colonies	10
Organization & scope	Government organization	*Congressional organization, administration & personnel*	14
		Executive organization, administration & personnel	26
		Impeachment & misconduct	
		Judicial organization, administration & personnel	24
	Representation	*Census & apportionment*	4
		Elections	1
		Groups & interests	
	Constitutional amendments	Federalism & terms of office	
		Political participation & rights	
		Other	

(*continued*)

Table 4.2 **Continued**

Tier 1	Tier 2	Tier 3	# Acts
International relations	Defense	Air force organization & deployment	
		Army organization & deployment	12
		Conscription & enlistment	
		Militias	7
		Naval organization & deployment	3
		General military organization	
		Military installations	4
		Civil & homeland defense	
	Geopolitics	*Diplomacy & intelligence*	6**
		Foreign aid	
		International organizations	
	International political economy	*Maritime*	25
		Trade & tariffs	37
		Economic international organizations	
Domestic affairs	Agriculture & food	Agricultural technology	
		Farmers & farming support	
		Fishing & livestock	
	Planning & resources	Corporatism	
		Environment	
		Infrastructure & public works	
		National resources	
		Social knowledge	
		Post Office	6
		Transportation	
		Wage & price controls	
		Interstate compacts & federalism	21
		Urban, rural & regional development	

Table 4.2 **Continued**

Tier 1	Tier 2	Tier 3	# Acts
	Political economy	*Appropriations*	36
		Omnibus legislation	
		Business & capital markets	
		Fiscal & taxation	36
		Labor markets and unions	1
		Monetary	10
		Economic regulation	7
	Social policy	Children & youth	
		Crime	4
		Disaster	
		Education	
		Handicapped & disabilities	
		Civilian health	1
		Housing	
		Military pensions, benefits, & civilian compensation	9
		Public-works employment	
		Social regulation	
		Social insurance	
District of Columbia			1
Housekeeping			1
Quasi-private			2

Notes: The table excludes all private acts but includes nine Indian treaties and five international treaties. One act continued earlier legislation passed to regulate "maritime" matters, "trade and tariffs," and "Federalism" and has been counted as three statutes (An act to continue in force for a limited time the acts therein mentioned. (Obsolete.) March 2, 1795, ch. 38, *US Statutes at Large* I, 425). One act continued earlier legislation passed to regulate "appropriations" and "trade and tariffs" and has been counted as two statutes (An act to continue in force, for a limited time, the acts therein mentioned, May 30, 1796, ch. 43, *US Statutes at Large* I, 488). All acts with the word *appropriations* in the title, and acts that make clear that the purpose was to appropriate money to meet specific costs, have been classed as "appropriations" regardless of the use of appropriations, for example military, treaties, or government. Acts dealing with the Bank of the United States have been coded as "fiscal & taxation" rather than "monetary." The three acts classed as "economic regulation" are legislation regulating bankruptcies. The single act coded as "labor markets and unions" addressed sailors. "Monetary" legislation refers to coinage and the value of foreign coins in the United States.

* Includes nine Indian treaties.

** Includes five international treaties.

Sources: US statutes and treaties, see sources cited in Table 4.1.; Ira Katznelson and John S. Lapinski, "The Substance of Representation: Studying Policy Content and Legislative Behavior," in *The Macropolitics of Congress*, ed. John S. Lapinski and E. Scott Adler (Princeton, NJ: Princeton University Press, 2011), Table 4.1, 114–15.

the late eighteenth-century "reactive state" in both Britain and Pennsylvania were nevertheless active in many of the areas that the federal government left alone.

Table 4.3 provides yet another analysis of the pattern of congressional legislation under the Washington administration. Rather than comparing the output to that of Parliament or applying modern policy categories, it identifies legislation as belonging in one of three jurisdictional spaces in an attempt to highlight *where*, in spatial terms, Congress was most active: in the heartland of the American union made up of the original thirteen, by 1797 sixteen, republics; in the western borderlands of the trans-Appalachian national domain that was organized as federal territories; or in the Atlantic world of diplomatic and commercial interaction with European nations. Because the many statutes concerned with the internal operations of government were not geographically determined, they have been allocated to a residual class of *government* legislation.

Invariably, there is a certain arbitrariness to all classification attempts, including Table 4.3. The army did not guard only the Indian frontier but was posted in coastal forts. Appropriations were made for many specific outlays, such as defense and diplomacy. Customs duties were intended to raise revenue but also to protect domestic manufactures. Nevertheless, placed alongside the comparison

Table 4.3 **US legislation and treaties by jurisdictional space**

Heartland (117)	Atlantic (87)
Federal-state relations (27)	*Customs duties* (32)
Judiciary (25)	*Trade regulations; shipping; fisheries* (20)
Debt and BUS (23)	*Lighthouses, etc.* (16)
Excise (11)	*Diplomacy* (12)
Pensions (9)	*Navy* (3)
Post Office (7)	*Naturalization* (2)
Mint (6)	*Coastal defense* (2)
Patents, copyright (4)	
Insolvent individuals (3)	
Other (2)	
Borderlands (52)	**Government (77)**
Army (19)	*Salaries, compensation* (28)
Indian Affairs (17)	*Appropriations* (26)
Land sales and grants (10)	*Seat of government; Congress* (13)
Organization of territorial government (4)	*Central executive departments* (6)
State land cessions (2)	*Other* (4)

Note: The table excludes private acts but includes international and American Indian treaties.

Source: See Table 4.1.

with the British Parliament presented in Table 4.1, Table 4.3 sheds additional light on the major focus of the legislative activities of Congress under the Washington administration. The first thing to note is that Congress passed more laws to govern the thirteen republics than to govern the western territories or to regulate international relations. Nevertheless, legislation pertaining to the borderlands and the Atlantic combined was more frequent than legislation governing the heartland.[26]

Contrary to first impressions, the long list of acts in the *heartland* category in fact bears out the conclusion that the federal government did very little to directly shape society or the economy by means of legislation. The most common type of legislation in this category was statutes governing intraunion relations between the federal government and the states, such as federal government assent to state laws, the settlement of accounts between the federal government and the states, and the addition of two stripes and two stars to the national flag. These laws had to do with the American union rather than the internal affairs of the states. This is true also of legislation relative to the post office, the mint, and patents and copyrights. On average six laws per Congress were passed to organize and reorganize the judiciary. But these acts were primarily administrative in nature, creating circuit courts and determining fees for example. Congress also passed many laws to regulate the national debt and, starting in earnest with the third Congress, to implement a program of internal taxation. Although this legislation had consequences for manufactures, private credit, and the consumption of households, they were enacted to generate revenue rather than to regulate or promote the economy. Pensions were paid to soldiers of the War of Independence and their widows and children. The three laws that specified the terms of imprisonment for debt were of a highly specific and limited nature and did not amount to an attempt to introduce a national law of bankruptcy.[27]

The overall picture that emerges from the analysis of the legislative output of the first Congress is that of a federal government concerned with the management of the common domain in the West, relations to the outside world, primarily in the sphere of foreign commerce and coastal navigation, and interstate relations. As previous chapters have argued, the Constitution created a federal government designed to deal with international relations, including commerce, intraunion affairs, and the management of the West, including so-called Indian diplomacy. The record of congressional legislation supports this conclusion. In addition to such concerns, it also fell to the federal government to employ the customs service, the federal judiciary, the post office, the Mint, and the Patent Acts to maintain the common market and customs union created by the American union. The federal government undoubtedly had an indirect impact on the economic fortunes of most American households in the 1790s due to its commercial policies, western land management, and fiscal and financial legislation. But the early Congresses were not involved with the direct regulation of the domestic economy in the manner of the British legislature. Congress neither redefined nor redistributed landed property. Apart from the creation of the Bank of the United States, it incorporated no business companies. It did not invest in, initiate, or manage any internal improvement projects within state borders. Although there were designated postal roads, there were no federal turnpikes or canals. Nor did Congress tamper with the religious establishments or the internal police of the states.[28]

III

The comparison between British and American legislation in the 1790s shows that Congress had different priorities than Parliament. In particular, the American national legislature was not involved in the routine business of regulating private property, promoting communications, and enclosing land, the activities that preoccupied Parliament. Nor is there any indication that congressmen tried their hand at what contemporaries called internal police regulation. Congressional inaction in such fields raises the bigger question about the nature of the early American state and its relation to society. As Novak's polemical intervention suggests, it has long been customary to describe early America as a virtually stateless society, a social condition that many historians believe lasted to the Civil War, or possibly even to the days of the New Deal. Yet just as Novak argues, this is a misconception brought about by what Louis Hartz long ago called a "disproportionate degree of attention" to national matters in an era when in fact "by far the greatest amount of governmental activity in economic life was initiated not by the national government but by the state governments." Above all this is true of almost everything that eighteenth-century governments did in the domestic sphere. For this reason, Thomas Jefferson insisted in his first annual message to Congress that it was the states, rather than the national government, which had the "principal care of our persons, our property, and our reputation, constituting the great field of human concerns."[29]

Hartz made his observation in a book analyzing economic policy in Pennsylvania between the Revolution and the Civil War. The Commonwealth of Pennsylvania adopted a new state constitution in September 1790 in response to the reorganization of the American union under the federal constitution of 1787. From that point and throughout the 1790s, the Pennsylvania General Assembly began its major session in December and met on occasion for an extra session in August or September. The ten sessions between December 1790 and April 1797 adopted a total of 454 acts and resolutions, a figure that comes fairly close to the 373 statutes adopted and the 14 treaties ratified by Congress between 1789 and 1797.[30]

The legislation passed by the first session of the General Assembly under the new Constitution at first look appears strikingly similar to that of the early Congress. No less than 55 percent of the laws adopted concerned government and finance, exactly the same figure as in the first four Congresses. In the *finance* category half the acts dealt with the public debt, and close to a quarter with taxation. All acts addressed public, none private, finance. Personal legislation accounted for 18.1 percent, which corresponds closely to the figure of 16.8 percent of federal laws. As was the case with Congress, the Pennsylvania assembly legislated primarily to offer relief to soldiers and suppliers who had served the commonwealth during the War of Independence. And just as in Congress, there was very limited legislative activity in the areas of social, economic, and communications regulation. One in five laws adopted by the Pennsylvania assembly dealt with such matters, compared to one in ten of the laws adopted by the early congresses. A cursory investigation therefore suggests that similarities rather than differences characterize the Pennsylvania and the national legislatures. But such a conclusion would be premature. Closer inspection reveals the 1790–1791 winter session to be an anomaly when Pennsylvania was dealing with the fallout from the War of Independence and with the changes in the American union and in the organization of the commonwealth caused by the adoption of the federal and state constitutions. Over the next six years, a different pattern of legislation emerged (see Tables 4.1 and 4.4).

Table 4.4 **Some major types of Pennsylvania legislation, 1790–1797.**

Election districts	54
Incorporation boroughs & counties	35
Landed property	23
Dams, permission to construct	21
Canals & river transportation	21
Bridges & ferries	12
Roads	13
Health & community	23
Poor law & poverty	11
Education	6
Inspection of goods	5
Total	224

Sources: See Table 1, PA.

The share of personal, government, and finance legislation of the General Assembly's total legislative output dropped off over time. In the final two sessions studied (i.e., the sessions beginning in December 1795 and December 1796), these classes accounted for 45.3 percent of the total, compared to 73.3 percent in the 1790–1791 session. Instead, legislation pertaining to social issues, the economy, and communications grew. In 1790–1791, 20 percent of all legislation belonged in these categories. For 1795–1797, the figure is 46.3 percent. Although the latter figure still falls short of the share of such legislation in the overall legislative output of Parliament, where it accounted for 60.7 percent of total output, the trend is for the activity of the Pennsylvania General Assembly to resemble the British Parliament more and Congress less. Even if the General Assembly did not pass either estate or enclosure acts, it shared with Parliament the impulse to promote the economy and reform society in accordance with the wishes of its constituents.

Beginning in the late colonial period, the Pennsylvania electorate placed increasing demands on the assembly to provide law courts and justices of the peace to manage local government, and more representatives to the assembly to represent electors in the legislature. In a society where the state took on an increasing role in economic intervention and social regulation, influence over the government became more important. Although some historians have claimed that the Pennsylvania constitution of 1790 represents a conservative and anti-democratic turn in the politics of the state, it is clear that the assembly continued to respond to local demands also under the new constitution. Around 42 percent of legislation in the *government* category consisted of laws establishing or altering election districts, highlighting the fact that a major impediment preventing electors from exercising their right to vote was their geographic distance to the polling place. Another significant subclass of legislation in this category was the many incorporation acts that created counties and boroughs. No less than thirteen counties and twenty-three boroughs were incorporated between 1790 and 1797, accounting for close to 30 percent of the total number of *government* laws. In other words, more than 70 percent of *government* legislation aimed at establishing working local governments, on the one hand, and to give outlying communities a voice in the assembly, on the other. This record is in marked contrast to both Parliament and Congress. The British Reform Act was adopted only in 1832 and in Congress *government* legislation was dominated by salaries and compensation, and the location and workings of the legislature.[31]

Whereas Congress passed only public finance legislation, save for the three statutes dealing with the imprisonment of insolvent debtors, 13 of the 78 finance acts passed by the General Assembly between 1790 and 1797 concerned private finance. Five of them addressed the problem of bankruptcy and debtors. A single act prohibiting private lotteries is a typical example of the exercise of eighteenth-century police powers. But the assembly also incorporated a bank (the Bank of Pennsylvania, 1793) and two insurance companies (the Insurance Company of North America, 1794 and the Insurance Company of the State of Pennsylvania, 1794). The incorporation of private business companies was a new phenomenon. In the entire colonial period only a single business venture was chartered by the Pennsylvania legislature. But from the 1790s, the assembly incorporated several companies every year. The actions of the General Assembly in fact represent the beginnings of a broad trend in the early United States of state legislatures making increasing use of their power of incorporation. Between 1790 and 1860 more than 2,300 business charters were granted in Pennsylvania alone, although the share of the banking and insurance sectors was less than a fifth of the total.[32]

The first Pennsylvania assembly to meet under the Constitution of 1790 spent little time on internal improvements, but it did enact a general law that outlined a broad commitment to the improvement of roads and waterways and appropriated money, partly from the sale of the Commonwealth's appreciated federal bonds, to build twenty-five designated roads and to build and improve nineteen designated waterways. The state also reserved £5,000 annually from the interest Pennsylvania received on its US 3-percent bonds for the maintenance of roads. On the back of this act, subsequent assemblies passed a large number of specific laws for the construction of roads, canals, and bridges, and to declare rivers public highways. Once more the actions of the General Assembly in this respect heralded a broad nineteenth-century trend in American political and economic life, although the so-called transportation revolution took off in earnest only a few decades into the next century. It should be noted that many of the statutes passed in the 1790s, and in later periods, never resulted in the construction of roads or the improvement of waterways. The legislation that was passed in the 1790s is a reliable guide to the aspirations and remit of the state legislature. But on its own it cannot be used to determine the state's impact on society and the economy.[33]

Nine acts were passed to declare various waterways public highways, thereby allowing for the legal removal of any natural or artificial obstructions to the passage of boats and rafts. The purpose was to facilitate riverine transportation, but because of the frequency of dams along the creeks of Pennsylvania, these laws impacted on the private property rights of dam owners. The General Assembly was therefore careful to stipulate that the locks and slopes, which would be constructed to make transportation by rafts and boats across mill dams possible, would not damage the operations of existing waterworks. Transportation of livestock and goods was also the prime rationale behind the surveying and construction of roads. Many of the laws were for rather limited improvements and made appropriations for sums of only a few hundred or at most a couple of thousand dollars. But the assembly also incorporated four turnpike companies: the Philadelphia and Lancaster Turnpike Road Company (1792), the Lancaster and Susquehanna Turnpike Road Company (1794), the Lancaster, Elizabethtown, Middletown and Harrisburg Turnpike Road Company (1796), and the Gap Newport and Wilmington Turnpike Road Company (1796). The construction of these roads was a major undertaking that went far beyond what local governments could achieve with their limited resources. The actions of the Pennsylvania assembly should be seen in the wider context of a huge increase in the incorporation of transportation companies in the early United States. According to one calculation 10,800 transportation corporations were formed between 1790 and 1860 under special acts of incorporation. The real number is higher because from the middle of the nineteenth century, many states passed general incorporation acts that made the special act redundant. A little over two-fifths of the transportation corporations were turnpike companies. Bridge companies accounted for slightly more than 12 percent and canal and navigation companies for slightly less than 13 percent of the total. In the decades after 1790, before the advent of the railroad, these figures would have been significantly higher.[34]

Legislation providing for the creation of ferries, bridges, and canals and for the clearing of waterways were other means by which the General Assembly promoted communications but also created property rights. Between 1790 and 1797 four acts gave individuals a monopoly on the operation of ferries where busy roads crossed rivers. In a similar manner, three acts granted individuals or partnerships the right to erect toll bridges. These rights were granted in perpetuity and could be willed to descendants or assigned to third parties. Larger construction works were beyond the means of individuals and required a different response from the legislature. The Pennsylvania assembly incorporated two bridge companies to build stone bridges over the Lehigh River at Northampton and over the Delaware River at Easton. Other bridge-building initiatives originated in the counties but were supported by the assembly by granting permission for lotteries to raise additional money. The Pennsylvania assembly also launched four navigation companies in the early and middle years of the 1790s. The Schuylkill and Susquehanna Navigation Company (1791) and the Delaware and Schuylkill Canal Company (1792) were intended to construct a waterway between Philadelphia and the Susquehanna River; the Conewago Canal Company (1793) was chartered to create a waterway that would bypass Conewago Falls and allow for riverine transportation up the Susquehanna; and the Brandywine Canal Company (1793) was intended to make possible water transportation to the point where Brandywine Creek intersected with the Lancaster turnpike. The legislative program was based on the optimistic but flawed notion that existing rivers could be made navigable. Real improvements of water transportation had to await the canal era that began with the construction of the Eerie Canal in the late 1810s.[35]

The scale of these prospective communications undertakings is striking. The Susquehanna and Schuylkill companies were to be capitalized at $400,000 and the Brandywine company at $300,000. In a separate act, the Susquehanna Company was granted the right to raise an additional $400,000 to meet construction costs. The Conewago Falls Company was entitled to hold property not exceeding $1 million. Slightly smaller, the turnpike companies were capitalized at sums from $50,000 to $300,000. In an age where businesses and individual fortunes were small, these corporate bodies represent significant concentrations of capital. With shares costing $300 a piece, investment in transportation companies was restricted to individuals with wealth or access to credit. Although turnpike companies would turn out to be notoriously unprofitable, the assembly tried to make initial investment attractive by providing for a minimum 6 percent dividend and holding out the prospect of 15 to 20 percent profits on capital invested in road and bridge companies.[36]

Most Pennsylvania legislation dealing with social issues fit under the rubric of internal police regulations of the kind that would bring about a well-ordered society. As the use of the term *internal police* in late eighteenth-century American newspapers show, such police regulations were most frequent in cities. It therefore comes as no surprise that the concentration and growth of population and the increase in commercial transactions in Philadelphia spurred the Pennsylvania assembly to pass measures to impose and maintain order in the city. Much internal police legislation concerned mundane matters such as the direction, paving and lightning of streets; the repair of wharfs; the organization of the night watch; fire regulations; the creation and regulation of market places; and prohibitions against prostitution, gambling, and "disorderly sports and dissipation." William Novak has shown that Americans in the early national and antebellum period generally expected their governments to provide such regulation. In cities this expectation was present already in the colonial era. Other police legislation dealt with poor relief and orphans. The Pennsylvania assembly also supported Dickinson College and the Pittsburgh and Washington academies, and it created the University of Pennsylvania by merging two existing educational institutions. The assemblymen's broader interest in education and social mores led to specific legislation for the Library Company and a general incorporation act to facilitate the establishment of religious, charitable, and educational societies. In the aftermath of a deadly yellow fever epidemic, the assembly also passed several laws that created and reformed a health office in Philadelphia and introduced routines to prevent European immigrants from bringing contagious diseases into the city.[37]

Although the vast majority of police legislation appearing on the Pennsylvania statute books concern Philadelphia, indirectly the General Assembly also shaped the regulation of internal police outside city limits. Returning to the *government* category of legislation, the principal purpose of incorporating a borough was to invest the local community with police powers. As Novak points out, "in contrast to the modern ideal of the state as a centralized bureaucracy, the [ideal of the] well-regulated society emphasized local control and autonomy." He is correct to stress that local autonomy was considered essential to the realization of the well-regulated society, but at least in Pennsylvania such local control and autonomy was always exercised under the supervision of the state government. Incorporation acts defined the geographic boundaries of the borough and gave resident freeholders and "house-keepers" the right to elect local government officers and supervisors of streets and highways, who were responsible for looking after borough affairs. Like all incorporation acts, incorporation made the borough a legal person that could own land and buildings and could sue and be sued in courts. Boroughs could also levy taxes on the inhabitants to meet the costs of road maintenance and other items of expenditure.[38]

Boroughs were incorporated for the purpose of "regulating the buildings, preventing nuisances and encroachments on the commons, squares, streets, lanes and alleys of the same." Most Pennsylvania incorporation acts used the incorporation of Reading, Berks County, in 1783, as the template for the "powers, jurisdictions, exclusions, authorities and privileges" of newly incorporated boroughs and for the "qualifications, restrictions, penalties, fines and forfeitures" that limited such boroughs and their inhabitants. The Reading act ran to twenty-three pages and contained very detailed instructions about the police regulations that the burgesses and other officers were expected to oversee. It addressed what to do about such diverse matters as clay and shavings thrown into the street, oversized doorsteps, the unhygienic disposal of rotting carcasses and excrement, storage of gunpowder in houses and dwellings, and "foul or nauseous liquor" coming from distillers, soap-boilers, and tallow-chandlers. In addition to the power to regulate the police of the borough, incorporation acts also had economic implications because they typically gave boroughs the right to hold two markets per week and two annual two-day fairs. Boroughs were required to appoint a clerk of the market, who had "the assize of bread, wine, beer, wood, coals, hay, corn, and other provisions, brought for the use of the inhabitants."[39]

Although social regulation and communications had economic consequences, in their classification of legislation, Hoppit and colleagues treat economic legislation as a separate category. In the case of Pennsylvania, roughly half the economic legislation concerned the regulation of real estate in the form of land. In table 4.1 many of these laws have been classed as economic land lease legislation although they might just as well have been classed as property law legislation in the law and order category. Regardless of this, the Pennsylvania laws were different from Parliament's legislation in the same period because the practice of holding land in fee simple in Pennsylvania meant that there was no need for estate acts. Christopher Pearl explains that a main concern of the state's landowners was instead to ensure that they had clear and undisputed title to their property. The state constitution of 1776 responded to this request by establishing a Register's Office for the Probate of Wills and Granting Letters of Administration and an Office for the Recording of Deeds. Five years later, the government created a new court, the Board of Property, that would arbitrate land disputes, and a Public Land Office, which "surveyed land, developed standard forms, gathered pre-existing land documents, and housed all land records for easy access." The concern of the landholders is reflected in the fact that the most common economic legislation in the early and mid-1790s regulated boundaries and land claims. But the assembly also passed the occasional act dealing with land improvements.[40]

The second most important group of laws in the *economy* category was the twenty-one acts authorizing individuals to erect dams. Such authorization was necessary because dams were a potential infringement of transportation on rivers and waterways that the assembly had declared public highways. It was rare for these acts to spell out the type of mills or waterworks that the dams would power and they therefore give no indication about the economic activities that the lawmakers wished to promote. A final and smaller group of acts in the *economy* category, finally, belongs to an important branch of police regulation: the inspection of the quality and price of goods produced in the state. The Pennsylvania assembly passed five such acts related to things like auctions, the assize of bread and the quality of gunpowder and exported flour.

IV

The legislative record of the first Congresses shows that under the Washington administration the federal legislature concentrated on building new governmental institutions and managing the public finances. It also acted to harmonize relations within the American union and to organize the western domain, and it passed legislation addressing naturalization, international commerce, and coastal navigation. Apart from the reform of the public debt and the incorporation of the Bank of the United States, which certainly were major reforms with far-reaching consequences, the first Congress did next to nothing to promote the domestic economy or to regulate society. It created the post office and a common market, which involved regulating the coin and the weights and measures of the nation. But with these exceptions Congress left the wide field of

internal police regulation alone. It passed no legislation to promote transportation projects, it redistributed no land, and it incorporated no business ventures
other than the Bank of the United States—a joint private–public venture. This
inaction is best explained by the fact that the duties of the federal government lay
elsewhere than in economic and social regulation. The laws passed by the early
Congresses show that the principal concerns of the national government were
to manage the common domain in the West; relations with the outside world,
primarily in the sphere of foreign commerce; and interstate relations between
members of the American union. The federal republic and the federal government were created to provide security to the American states from both external
threats and civil war, and to promote the material interests of their citizens in the
trans-Appalachian West and in the Atlantic marketplace.

To understand the nature and function of the early American union it is important to recognize that the relatively narrow set of activities of the federal
government was not typical of eighteenth-century states. Providing national security and looking after the national interests were certainly among the most
important tasks of the British government. But Members of Parliament spent far
more time promoting the domestic economy by incorporating transportation
companies and other businesses ventures, liberating landed estates from legal
restrictions on sale and development, and turning common land into private
property. In the American system of government such tasks were not neglected,
but they fell to the state governments rather than to Congress. The record of the
Pennsylvania assembly shows a legislature with an agenda quite similar to that of
Parliament, especially once the significant differences in the geography, demography, and economy of Pennsylvania and Great Britain are taken into account.

The limited scope of the investigation cautions against making too sweeping
conclusions. Only eight years of federal legislation have been studied, only
one state assembly scrutinized. It goes without saying that Congress under the
Washington administration may not be representative of Congress in the nineteenth century, and that Pennsylvania may not be representative of all the other
states in the union. Conclusions about the respective roles of Congress and the
state assemblies in the early American union can therefore only be tentative
at this stage. Nevertheless, as an invitation to further discussion, it is possible
to use the two concepts of the British eighteenth-century state introduced by
historians of Parliament to propose that whereas the fiscal-military and the reactive state were merged in the same government in Britain, in the United States
they existed at different levels of the federal structure. Congress was central to
the American fiscal-military state. The General Assembly of Pennsylvania was
central to the American reactive state.[41]

Contemporary writers who commented on the nature of the federal government would have been quite comfortable with this description of the early

United States. In his *Lectures on Law*, James Wilson described the General Assembly of Pennsylvania as "vested with every power necessary for a branch of the legislature of a free state" whereas Congress was a legislature of only "enumerated powers." These enumerated powers, said Wilson, were confined to foreign affairs and commerce, relations between the members of the union, and Indian diplomacy. The domestic duties of the federal government, in contrast, were essentially reduced to the creation and supervision of the common market, or customs union, the management of the national post office, and the promotion of arts and sciences by granting copyrights and patents. Wilson was a Federalist. On the other side of the party divide, St. George Tucker argued in his law lectures that governmental power could be divided into internal power, "or such as are to be exercised among the citizens of a state, within the state itself," and external power, "or such as may be exercised towards foreign nations, or different and independent states." "These powers," Tucker continued, "which in all great empires, and monarchies, and even in smaller states, are generally united in one and the same man, or body of men, according to the system adopted by the states of the American confederacy, are . . . separated from each other; the former branch, being with some exceptions, confided to the state-governments, the latter to the federal government."[42]

Conclusion

Toward a New Understanding of the Founding

Today the original engrossed copy of the Constitution is exhibited alongside the Declaration of Independence and the first ten amendments to the Constitution in the Rotunda for the Charters of Freedom in the National Archives Building. Every year, millions of Americans visit the rotunda to view it and to reflect on their nation's origins and values. There can be no doubt that the Constitution is cherished by the American people. A Pew Research Center poll from the turn of the millennium asked Americans about the reasons for US success in the twentieth century. "Our Constitution" came out the top scorer with 85 percent of respondents saying it was a "major reason" for American success. In comparison, "God's will" scored no more than 64 percent, "our geographic isolation" a mere 53 percent, and "good luck"—perhaps not surprisingly—a measly 25 percent. Belief in the Constitution's importance is not necessarily matched by knowledge of its content, however. Polls show that the share of the population that can correctly name all three branches of the federal government fluctuates between a quarter and a third.[1]

The discrepancy between the status and the knowledge of the Constitution among the American people has been of concern to educators at least since the 1930s. Such concerns were much in evidence at the time of the bicentennial. To encourage study of the document, the Commission on the Bicentennial of the United States Constitution distributed millions of copies of the Constitution to the American public. Commission member Phyllis Schlafly expressed her delight "that General Mills is going to put vignettes about the Constitution on 100 million cereal boxes; that McDonalds is printing 16 million tray liners that will carry educational quizzes; and that there are going to be 59 million milk cartons with vignettes about the Constitution." Others were less impressed. Corporate America's enthusiastic response to the bicentennial inspired

Perfecting the Union. Max M. Edling, Oxford University Press (2021). © Oxford University Press.
DOI: 10.1093/oso/9780197534717.003.0006

political cartoonist Garry Trudeau to suggest that the text of the Constitution be pasted to a cereal box for a "mighty fine breakfast reading! And whole-grain goodness to boot!" Two centuries and a third after the Philadelphia Convention it is fair to say that despite compulsory civics classes in school, the Constitution remains a document celebrated by all, yet read and understood by a select few.[2]

Explanations of the Constitution aimed for popular consumption tend to emphasise its importance to the creation of civic rights and representative democracy. The interpretation offered by the National Archives is a case in point: "Written in 1787, the Constitution established an ingenious practical system of government that derives its power from 'We the People of the United States' and promotes the welfare of all its citizens." This rather vacuous and seemingly uncontroversial assertion contains two statements that are worth a closer look. First, it suggests that in 1787 there was a single American people from whom all political power sprang. Second, it implies that the framers hoped that the Constitution would realize a universal national citizenship. Both claims are highly questionable. Such misconceptions are not confined to the United States. Across the Atlantic, the 220th anniversary of the Constitution prompted the normally sober-minded *Guardian* newspaper to publish a leader under the title "In praise of . . . the US constitution [*sic*]," presenting the document as "one of those texts that transformed the history of the world. From its stirring preamble promising to 'secure the blessings of liberty to ourselves and our posterity' to its specification of a separation of power between president, congress and courts, the document founded a modern democratic republic." But if the idea that the Constitution's principal purpose was to introduce a democratic form of government for a consolidated American republic is common, it is also deeply problematic.[3]

In contrast to the popular view, this book has employed a Unionist perspective to argue that the Constitution was not in fact designed as the fundamental law of the American republic with the aim to introduce a system of liberal democracy. Rather, it was an instrument that renewed the compact of union between thirteen American republics and provided a form of government for their common national government. As such, it offered an organizational solution to the security concerns of the newly independent American states. Early modern legal and political theorists were well aware that confederation allowed weak states to maintain their independence by joining in union to manage relations with the outside world from a position of strength. Equally important, the act of confederation transformed the immediate international environment by turning neighboring states from potential enemies into sister states in a common union or peace pact.

When the "more perfect union" of the Constitution was substituted for the less perfect union of the Articles of Confederation, the United States was transformed in very fundamental ways. The Constitution based the new national government on an act of popular sovereignty and gave it both the authority and the capacity to act independently of the states by legislating directly on the individual citizens and inhabitants of the United States, and by implementing its legislation by means of national administrative departments and courts. The Constitution also added important new powers over taxation and commercial regulation to Congress and created a powerful executive invested with many of the powers wielded by the monarch in Old World kingdoms and empires. Yet the primary function of the American federal union did not change with the adoption of the Constitution. The union was still meant to deal first and foremost with international affairs, including foreign trade and Indian diplomacy, and with interstate affairs, including arbitration between member-states and the management of the customs union and the western lands.

Contemporary critics of the Constitution, the so-called Antifederalists, did not agree that the reform was limited. To them, the new national government represented a centralization of power so extensive that the state governments would be rendered politically irrelevant by a consolidated nation-state, thereby ending the American experiment in republican government. Modern historians have listened to this critique and it has shaped their assessment of the framers' aspirations, leading to erroneous conclusions about the nature of the Constitution. The Constitution's Antifederalist critics insisted that a republican system of government could only be preserved if the states retained the authority and right to regulate their own *internal police*. They believed that the states ought to control a whole range of government regulations that served to create and maintain the well-ordered, refined, and opulent polity. Most of the Constitution's framers and supporters never challenged this idea, however. To the contrary, they agreed with their critics that the states, rather than the national government, ought to be responsible for the promotion of infrastructural developments, what contemporaries called "internal improvements," for the incorporation of business, educational, and eleemosynary corporations, for the regulation of religion and morality, and for the definition and upholding of property and civic rights.

In fact, the Constitution's adoption did not lead to consolidation. State laws and local bylaws, state and local regulations, touched the lives of citizens and inhabitants in the early United States far more often and far more directly than the actions of the federal government did. As a consequence, the political order that emerged from the American founding was not shaped by national laws and institutions as much as it was shaped and upheld by the states, the counties, the cities, and the townships. A history of the founding that takes into account only developments at the national level of government will therefore prove to be partial at best and seriously flawed at worst.

The framers' promise that the Constitution would maintain the division of labor between the national government and the states was honored by the Washington administration. The legislative agenda of the first four Congresses was dominated by foreign affairs, international commerce, the federal territories in the trans-Appalachian West, Indian diplomacy and trade, and relations between the member-states in the union. Apart from the post office hardly any laws were adopted to regulate social and economic relations within the thirteen republics. In contrast, in the 1790s the Commonwealth of Pennsylvania was busy passing social and economic legislation that created boroughs; declared public highways; incorporated banks and insurance companies; laid out and funded turnpikes, canals, and bridges; and regulated landed property. In late eighteenth-century European consolidated states like Britain, foreign and domestic policy was formulated by the central government. But in the early United States these tasks were divided between the national government and the states. The arrangement may strike a modern observer as odd, but it reflects early modern ideas about federal unions.

Interpreting the Constitution as a renewed compact of union has important implications for founding historiography. Most obviously, it invites us to assess the significance of the Constitution against the record of US international, rather than domestic, history. If the framers did not seek to create a national government by the elite, of the elite, for the elite, the failure of such a government to materialize does not signal the failure of the Constitution. Instead, scholars have to turn to the national government's interactions with European maritime powers in the Atlantic marketplace and with American Indian nations, European colonial governments, and European American settler migrants in the western borderlands to correctly assess the impact of the Constitution. But a Unionist interpretation also challenges students of the founding to explain social, economic, political, and legal change in the age of the American Revolution without reference to the Constitution as the explanans.

I

The reform of the American union took place in the eleventh hour. After a year-long struggle over ratification, the Constitution was adopted and elections held to a new Congress that would convene in early March 1789. To this Congress was left the task of turning the paragraphs of the Constitution into governmental institutions and policies that could address the union's problems. Only when these were in place would the Constitution truly be "adequate to the exigencies of the union" and the promise of the framers and the Federalists be fulfilled. Within a few months after the first Congress convened events took place that would culminate in the turmoil of the French Revolution. This social and political upheaval soon spilled over in international wars of great magnitude and global scope that would last for close to a quarter-century. The European wars came to impose severe strains also on the United States and made the trials of the critical period look like nothing more than a trial run. Had the states not confirmed their intent to remain in union and had they not transferred essential powers to a new central government, it is more than likely that the bands of union would have snapped.

Initially the Wars of the French Revolution proved a boon to the American economy. United States neutrality allowed the nation's merchants to engross more and more of the Atlantic trade and the war created rising demand for American agricultural products. The federal government, too, benefitted from the growing volume of trade, which translated into increasing income from customs duties, its major source of income. But the European war also represented serious threats. The major belligerents Britain and France both thought the Atlantic decisive to the war's outcome, and both nations interfered with American trade on repeated occasions between 1792 and 1815. International trade, in many ways the lifeblood of the American economy, therefore threatened to drag the United States into international war, which eventually happened in the summer of 1812. Having to steer a neutral course through global war meant that the federal government was not free to pursue a domestically formulated agenda. Instead, for the first quarter-century of its existence, the new government had to respond to events and processes that originated outside the nation's borders and over which it had next to no control.

When assessing the federal government's record in the troubled decade after the meeting of the first federal Congress it is helpful to start with the related policy areas of foreign affairs, the management of the western lands, and payments on the public debt, all of which had caused difficulties in the 1780s. Despite the tensions of the European war the government's record in all these fields had improved considerably a few years after the first Congress met. In President George Washington's seventh annual message, from December 1795, he told the members of Congress that "I have never met you at any period, when more than at present, the situation of our public affairs has afforded just cause for mutual congratulations." With the benefit of hindsight it is clear that this moment was only the calm before the storm. Later in the decade, Washington's Federalist party would have to deal with domestic and international crises growing out of deteriorating relations with revolutionary France. Nevertheless, there was reason to present 1795 as a year when the government had scored some remarkable successes and as a moment to take stock of what the federal government had achieved since 1789.[4]

Washington began by drawing attention to the pacification of the Indians in the Ohio country and to the recently concluded Treaty of Greenville. To the nations in the northwest, and indeed to North American Indians in general, the Army's victory at the Battle of Fallen Timber and the subsequent treaty signed at Greenville were the opening stages of a tragedy. To the United States, on the other hand, it meant that one of the most serious impediments to western expansion—an expansion pursued as eagerly by Federalists as by their Republican opponents, although by different means and driven by different visions of the region's future—had been removed. In addition to success in the Ohio country, where the government had concentrated its resources, in 1795 peace had also been secured with the powerful Indian nations in the Old Southwest.

The pacification of the Native Americans opened the door for the expansion of European American settlements in the vast Northwest Territory. In the train of the soldiers came federal surveyors and land offices followed by settlers. The Treaty of Greenville forced the door open but it was only one of many Native American land cessions in the period. In the decade from 1791 to 1800, the Senate ratified eleven treaties with Indian nations, seven of which involved the alienation of land. The United States thereby acquired 18,500 square miles in return for payments of $200,000. At a price of less than two cents an acre this was considerably below what white settlers had to pay for public land. Once the Jeffersonians came to power, the federal government would intensify the transfer of land from Americans Indians to the United States. The period 1801 to 1810 saw the government acquire 153,400 square miles by means of 33 land sessions, an area roughly the size of New England, New York, and Pennsylvania combined. Always frugal, Jefferson and Madison paid no more than $400,000 for this land, or considerably less than half a cent per acre. Transferring sovereignty of the land to the federal government was the first step toward peopling the national domain with European Americans. It was followed by the sale of public lands to white settlers. In the first decade of the nineteenth century, 3.2 million acres were sold by the government, much more would be sold in ensuing decades. Between 1790 and 1800 the European American and African American population in the trans-Appalachian West grew from 110,000 to 375,000. Of the total population growth recorded in the United States in this decade, a full 20 percent took place in the region west of the mountains.[5]

Of no less importance to the future development of the trans-Appalachian West was the conclusion of negotiations between the United States and European powers with colonial possessions in North America. From the court of Madrid, Washington reported, news had arrived that the American envoy,

Thomas Pinckney, was about to sign a treaty "securing amicably, very essential interests of the United States." Although the existence of a new treaty with Britain had been widely known for months, the president also took the opportunity to disclose officially that John Jay had concluded "a Treaty of Amity, Commerce and Navigation" with the former mother country. Pinckney's Treaty reopened the Mississippi River to American trade, thereby bringing to an end the long-standing conflict between the United States and Spain that began in 1784 when the river was closed, and thus provided for the realization of the full economic potential of the West. Jay's Treaty was of no less importance to the future of the West, as Britain at last agreed to evacuate the Great Lakes military posts it had occupied in breach of the 1783 peace treaty. Because these posts controlled the fur trade and the transport routes in the Old Northwest they held the key to the subjection of the Indian nations living there. Without American possession of the posts, the Treaty of Greenville would have been little more than a dead letter. "This interesting summary of our affairs," Washington concluded,

> with respect to foreign powers between whom and the United States controversies have subsisted, and with regard also to those of our Indian neighbours, with whom we have been in a state of enmity or misunderstanding, opens a wide field for consoling and gratifying reflections. If by prudence and moderation on every side, the extinguishment of all the causes of external discord, which have heretofore menaced our tranquillity [sic], on terms compatible with our national rights and honor, shall be the happy result; how firm and how precious a foundation will have been laid for accelerating, maturing and establishing the prosperity of our country.

The United States' standing among its European peers did indeed improve in the 1790s as a result of the adoption of the Constitution. Before 1787 foreign observers sometimes questioned to what extent the thirteen united states could even be considered a nation. In 1778, France asked that the state governments ratify the treaties of alliance and of amity and commerce separately rather than as a union. With the Articles of Confederation not yet ratified, France could hardly have done otherwise. But even after Britain had formally recognized American independence British politicians still insisted that diplomatic agreements "must be made with the states separately," because "no treaty can be made with the American states that can be binding on the whole of them." With a federal government in sole command over foreign policy and with a new Constitution that emphatically stated that "all Treaties made, or which shall be made, under the Authority of the United States, shall be the supreme Law of the Land; and the Judges of every state shall be bound thereby, any Thing in the Constitution or

Laws of any State to the Contrary notwithstanding" (Article VI), foreign powers were willing to enter into agreements with the United States. Prior to 1789, the United States had treated with governments which in the context of international commerce and North American power politics were relatively light-weight states, such as Sweden, Prussia, and Morocco. In the 1790s and 1800s, the Barbary powers continued to figure prominently in the nation's diplomacy, but treaties and conventions were also signed with Britain, France, and Spain, European great powers that were also major players on the North American continent and in the Atlantic marketplace.[6]

Although Washington was grateful that the nation had avoided involvement in the European war, his message made a reference to a recent demonstration of US military power in western Pennsylvania. A large expeditionary force had put down the so-called Whiskey Rebellion, a protest against the federal excise on distilled spirits, and restored order in the region. "The misled have abandoned their errors, and pay the respect to our Constitution and laws which is due from good citizens to the public authorities of the society," as Washington phrased it. Respect for the Constitution and federal laws had been achieved by a volunteer army of over 10,000 men. At roughly the same size as the Continental army that laid siege to Yorktown in the final stages of the War of Independence, this was an enormous undertaking for the government at the time. Its overwhelming response to the rebellion shows the administration's determination to exert its sovereignty in the interior regions of the continent and to ensure that taxes levied on the citizens were duly collected.

The taxes collected by the Unites States went primarily to payments on the public debt. In his message, Washington spoke of a process that had begun a year earlier when he had asked Congress to adopt "a definite plan" for the final redemption of the debt. Such a plan should place "credit on grounds which can not be disturbed," as well as "prevent that progressive accumulation of debt which must ultimately endanger all governments." Washington could put the debt on the congressional agenda thanks to the government's rapidly increasing revenue. In what must have been a surprising development to contemporaries, the federal government went from the verge of bankruptcy to flush in the span of a few years after the adoption of the Constitution. In 1789 the first Congress promptly created a customs service, and customs revenue would provide the mainstay of the government's income for more than a century. From small beginnings it rose from $3.2 million in 1792 to $5.6 million in 1795. When Jefferson became president, customs duties brought in more than $10 million per year.[7]

Up to 1795, the government made payments on the interest but not on the principal of its debt, which then stood at close to $80 million. But that year Congress adopted a plan than that would set the three principal loans that made up the Revolutionary War debt on the road to extinction. Under this plan the foreign debt was paid off in 1808, the so-called 6 percent debt in 1819, and the so-called deferred 6 percent debt in 1824. As these dates suggest, repayment was a prolonged process and the honor of finally liquidating the Revolutionary debt fell to the Jeffersonians rather than the Federalists. But the plan of debt redemption was adopted midway through the Age of Federalism.

It would be a mistake to reduce the Federalists' management of the public debt to a plan for its redemption. Rather, their principal achievement was the restoration of public credit, which made possible renewed borrowing. During Hamilton's tenure at the Treasury Department, the government borrowed to finance Indian wars and the expedition against the whiskey rebels, but it never had to finance a war with a European power. Washington's successor John Adams was less fortunate and had to contract new loans to pay for the naval build-up during the Quasi War with France. But it was the Jeffersonians, and statesmen in the Jeffersonian tradition, who made by far the greatest use of the government's ability to borrow. Public credit allowed the United States to purchase Louisiana. Public credit also allowed the United States to embark on its second war for independence against Britain in 1812. Loans paid for land acquired from Spain in 1819 and for compensation for territory and claims of Texas after the annexation of the state by the United States. Loans also paid for the invasion of Mexico in 1846. Tax revenue and loans, finally, paid for compensation to American Indians for land, for Indian wars, and for Indian removal.[8]

The considerable achievements that Washington listed had been brought about by a federal government that to a modern observer looks slimmed down to its bare bones. The three central executive departments in Philadelphia were few in number and small in size. The field services they oversaw were on a scale to match. Only the army, navy, and, later on, the post office counted its personnel in the thousands. Other services employed a few dozen or at most a couple of hundred staff. Yet despite its small size the federal government was essential to the development of the United States. In the short run, the clearest evidence of the successful reform of the American union is that the rebuilt ship of state managed to sail unharmed, if not altogether untroubled, through the storm of the French Revolution and the ensuing quarter-century of worldwide war. This period brought down kings and empires on both sides of the Atlantic, and it placed great stress on the union, particularly during the War of 1812. But the fabric of the union held. The decades that followed on the Constitution's adoption were also a time of territorial expansion. At first the federal government organized the national domain in the territories by setting up and policing an Indian frontier and transferring land from Americans Indians to white settlers. Later on it would expand the nation's domain over the North American continent, first in 1804, then in 1819, 1845, 1848, 1853, and, finally, in 1867.

The Philadelphia convention did not solve the tension that resulted from conflicting sectional interests. To the contrary, the Constitution facilitated the articulation of sectional interests through the representation of the states in the Senate and the guarantee to protect state interests, such as the preservation of slavery. Sectionalism would be the great scourge to the American union after the pressing matters of international weakness had been resolved. By 1861, state interests had trumped the desire for union. Yet in the seven decades that preceded the Civil War, the Constitution provided the institutional basis on which the nation would grow in territory, population, and riches. That legacy provided the foundation that propelled the United States to world power status after the era of Reconstruction. In the long run, therefore, the framers of the Constitution demonstrated that republics were not forever destined to weakness and instability but that by means of federal union they could become powerful even to the point of world domination.

II

The Unionist interpretation of the Constitution places the American founding in a story of territorial and commercial expansion and the making of empire. It is a perspective shift that will appear new and exciting to many scholars. But it may seem to have little to offer those invested in established meta-narratives about America's transition to liberal democracy and a market economy. The existence of political and economic modernization processes in nineteenth-century America appears incontestable. The Unionist perspective does not question the existence of these processes, only that the Constitution triggered and drove them. It downplays the transformative role of national political institutions and policies, and instead points to state and local levels of government as crucial institutions in promoting development. Perhaps counterintuitively, the focus on the union and international relations thereby in fact allows for fresh perspectives also on established modernization narratives by helping to rectify what Jack Greene has called the long "neglect of the states as the areas in which most governance, most public life, and the domestic life of most Americans were primarily centered."[9]

William Novak has demonstrated that in nineteenth-century America, state and local governments were the real "loci of authority." It follows that political and economic modernization are best studied at state level. In the 1940s, the so-called Commonwealth school of economic history did this with great success. Louis Hartz's work on Pennsylvania and Mary Handlin and Oscar Handlin's work on Massachusetts showed how the American economy was shaped by state legislation, not least by a multitude of incorporation acts. John Brooke has

argued that the study of state driven economic development need not be a consensus history with a singular focus on institutions. Government is a means to
an end, and social groups vie to control it. And it can be made to serve a range of
ends ultimately determined by those in control. Thus, legislation and policy can
be used to further either equality or greater inequality, for example. Nor does
a state-centered political history have to be insular. Emulation and harmoni-
zation of governmental institutions and policies between the American states
were central to economic and political development in the period between the
Constitution and the Civil War, as were political alliances and party organizations that cut across state boundaries. National histories of the United States can
therefore still be written. But the peculiarities of the federal system mean that
such national histories should take the form of an aggregate history of development in the constituent parts of the American union, which should pay careful
attention to the differences, interactions, and tensions between the states.[10]

But the Unionist interpretation points not only to an alternative approach
to the study of change. It also invites scholars to reconsider the transformative
nature of the American founding. This is of particular relevance to our understanding of political modernization—that is, our democratization narratives.
The idea that the founding was a major historical turning point is deeply in-
grained in both American historiography and American national identity. How
could it be otherwise? The Declaration of Independence and the Constitution
created a new nation, and the documents are framed in a language of innovation
and improvement. Nevertheless, historians have long debated how to correctly
characterize the American Revolution and some have questioned its transformative power. The bone of contention that the Ideological historians fought over in
the 1970s and 1980s, for example, revolved around the question if the American
founding was or was not a new beginning. Was it, in John Pocock's memorable
words, "the first political act of revolutionary enlightenment" or "the last great
act of the Renaissance"? The Unionist interpretation suggests that this is not an
absolute question. The American founding combines change, even dramatic
change, in some areas of political, economic, and social life, with an attempt to
protect and preserve colonial life forms in other areas.[11]

Suffrage requirements can serve to illustrate how a rhetoric of change some-
times disguised an underlying reality of continuity. In the Constitutional
Convention delegates disagreed on whether the federal legislature should be
elected by "the people" or by the states. In the ratification debates, the "popular"
House of Representatives was often contrasted with the "aristocratic" Senate.
Reading such claims and counterclaims it is only natural to conclude that the
House of Representatives was *democratically* elected, and that this mode of elec-
tion signaled a new departure. But what exactly did a democratic election of the
House of Representatives mean? The limits of the federal electorate were set

by the states rather than Congress. The Constitution gives the right to vote for members of the US House of Representatives to anyone with "the Qualifications requisite for electors in the most numerous Branch of the State Legislature" (Article I, section 2). The extent to which the House of Representatives was *democratic* can therefore only be answered by looking at suffrage requirements in the states. In Virginia, the most populous state at the time of the founding, the state Declaration of Rights used seemingly universal language to grant "all men, having sufficient evidence of permanent common interest with, and attachment to, the community . . . the right of suffrage" (Section VI). But the Virginia Constitution, in contrast, said only that "the right of suffrage in the election of members for both Houses [of the Virginia legislature] shall remain as exercised at present." Because that right was restricted to freeholders, the law ruled out persons who fell short of a property requirement, no matter how extensive their "common interest with, and attachment to, the community." Furthermore, because the common law of Virginia did not recognize married women as property holders, most adult women were also excluded from the right to vote. And, finally, because a 1723 act determining that "no free negroe, mulattoe, or Indian whatsoever, shall hereafter have any vote at the election of burgesses" was still in effect after the Revolution, a person had to be classed as "white" to be an elector. Suffrage rights is but one example of a general principle. Questions of political change and continuity in the period of the founding can only be answered by studying the multiple legalities of early America, and the action and inaction of different governmental institutions in the multi-layered federal republic.[12]

The implications of such a decentered approach to the study of political change and continuity in the American founding can be further illustrated by a brief analysis of rights in the age of the American Revolution. Although the history of rights hardly exhausts the meaning of the founding, the many state declarations of rights, the so-called federal bill of rights, and the famous statements of political principles in documents like the Declaration of Independence, have nonetheless always been central to the interpretation of the American Revolution as a landmark event on the path to liberal democracy. As with attempts to define the federal electorate, an investigation of American rights needs to move well beyond the Constitution and the national level of politics. This does not mean that national developments are completely irrelevant to the story, however. To begin with, the Constitution is not entirely silent on the matter of rights. Article I, section 9 guaranteed habeas corpus and prohibited bills of attainder and ex post facto laws, and Article III guaranteed trial by jury in criminal cases and prohibited corruption of blood for treason. The proscriptions in Article I, section 10 against making paper money legal tender, impairing the obligations of contracts, and passing bills of attainder and ex post facto laws offered protection against the actions of state governments. In Article IV the framers inserted a comity clause. The same article also safeguarded the property rights of slave owners and masters to the labor of slaves and servants by promising that "No Person held to Service or Labour in one State, under the Laws thereof, escaping into another, shall in Consequence of any Law or Regulation therein, be discharged from such Service or Labour, but shall be delivered up on the Claim of the Party to whom such Service or Labour may be due" (Article IV, section 2). But the most significant impact of the Constitution on the civic rights of Americans came two sections later where the framers declared that "The United States shall guarantee to every State in this Union a Republican Form of Government" (Article IV, section 4). For in 1787, the word *republic* implied a social fabric that distributed the rights and obligations of citizens and inhabitants in a particular way.[13]

The early modern republic was conceptualized as a political association in which citizens governed themselves free from outside interference. In their capacity as citizens, propertied white adult males were equipped with equal rights. But a republican citizen was also invariably constructed as a *kyrios*, a head of household who governed a retinue of dependents. This had an immediate impact on the structuring of the American social order. If the republic made possible the collective self-government of the citizens, the republic also made possible the autarky and autonomy of the *oikos*, or household, the fundamental socioeconomic element that made up the political association that was the republic. In fact, the stability and survival of the republic was perceived to depend fundamentally on the well-being of the households that formed its constituent parts. As late as the middle of the 1850s, an essay in the *Southern Quarterly Review* remarked that "the discipline of the family is that which renders the work of government easy. When that discipline is perfect, the reign of order and virtue in the state is established." The well-being of the households, in turn, could only be guaranteed by maintaining a certain distribution of rights and obligations that served as the foundation of household government.[14]

When the concept of *rights* is mentioned in the context of the American Revolution, thoughts go immediately to the words of the Declaration of Independence that "all Men are created equal" and are "endowed" with "certain unalienable Rights," among them the right to "Life, Liberty, and the Pursuit of Happiness." But the Declaration refers to but a small part of the landscape of rights in early America. American jurists tended to follow the English jurisprudent William Blackstone in classifying rights as either "absolute" or "relative." Absolute rights restricted the authority of the state over the subject or citizen. As such they were of course important and they are the kind of rights typically associated with modern liberal democracy. But to the majority of Americans living in the founding era they were hardly the most important rights. As Carole Shammas has pointed out, "most inhabitants of early America had no direct access to the state; the household head mediated between his dependents, whether children, wife, servants, slaves, or wards, and formal government bodies." What mattered to these inhabitants of early America were relative or "social" rights.[15]

To Blackstone and American legal writers, relative rights were "posterior to the formation of states and societies" and arose when free individuals joined in a political association, or "state." Relative rights always entailed duties, which meant that one person's right was another person's duty. Writing about a monarchical society with an established church, a large military, and a hereditary aristocracy, Blackstone spent much time on so-called public relative rights. American writers did not. Their truncated discussion of rights instead focused on what Blackstone called the "*private* oeconomical relations" of individuals, that is, the rights and duties of the master and servant, husband and wife, parent and child, and guardian and ward. Blackstone's choice of terminology is important. The term *oeconomical* in this context referred to an old meaning of the word *economy*, which referred to things pertaining to the management of the household.[16]

Among American writers, St. George Tucker, professor of law and police at the College of William and Mary, provided what is perhaps the most lucid treatment of rights in the founding period. Tucker, who published an edited version of Blackstone with extensive commentaries on Virginia and US law, followed Blackstone in classing rights as "absolute" and "social." Absolute rights were rights that the individual held in the state of nature. Social rights were those that individuals held in the social state, that is, after they had associated in a state. Such rights were partly residual absolute rights and partly rights that arose from an individual's relationship to other members of society. In addition to these rights, Tucker also spoke of "civic" rights, which "appertain[ed] to man as a citizen or subject," and "political" rights, which were inherent in political offices.[17]

Tucker claimed that "all free persons"—a category that included foreigners, women, children, servants, free blacks, and "ideots and lunatics"—had social rights. The only persons in Virginia stripped of all social rights were the enslaved. But in words that sound alien to standard accounts of the American Revolution as an event ushering in a modern liberal rights regime, Tucker said that "social rights are not unfrequently unequal." In other words, all persons but the slave had rights, but they did not have equal rights. Civic rights, too, were "not unfrequently unequal" in Virginia. This held true in other states too. In his *Lectures on Law*, delivered in 1790 and 1791, the Federalist politician, Supreme Court Justice, and College of Philadelphia law professor James Wilson systematically analyzed the different state constitutions to highlight how property and race determined the right to vote everywhere in America. Yet Wilson's conclusion from his catalogue of class and race exclusion was that far from falling short of revolutionary ideals, the state constitutions displayed a "close approximation" to "the true principles and correct theory of freedom." In Virginia the

American "theory of freedom" meant that the vast majority of the population were excluded from civic rights such as the right to vote. According to Tucker, "aliens, women, children under the age of discretion, ideots and lunatics, during their state of insanity, and negroes and mulattoes, though natives of the state and born free, have no civil rights in Virginia."[18]

Tucker's Virginia, and the other American republics, were societies characterized by relative rather than universal rights, and by hierarchy of status rather than equality. It is a type of rights regime better captured by ancient and early modern ideas of *republican* citizenship than by modern ideas of *liberal* citizenship. Republican thought conditions a citizen's public status on his private status as a master of a household, on his command over property and labor. Highlighting this link makes it possible to appreciate why it was no contradiction for the American founders to radically recast the relationship between the citizen and his government—the sphere of civic and political rights, in Tucker's terminology—while at the same time strengthening the rights of the household head over his dependents in the "*private* oeconomical relations" of the family, or what Blackstone, Tucker, and others thought of as the sphere of social rights.

"We have it in our power to begin the world over again," Thomas Paine declared in the appendix to *Common Sense*. Paine's stirring words is an important reminder that the American Revolution was a moment in time when social and economic relations were reimagined and therefore could also have been reinvented. There were many calls for economic, racial, and gender equality in this period, which demonstrate that people could, and did, imagine a radically different order of things. Yet this was not to be. The American Revolution altered social or relational rights within the household much less than the civic and political relations between the citizen and his government. Describing the postrevolutionary order, Noah Webster explained that the American citizen was "a subject" of the self-governing state of which he formed a part. This meant that he had the right to participate in the decision-making of the republic but also the duty to abide by the outcome of this decision-making process. But in the household a different order reigned. As "the head of a family," said Webster, the citizen was "sovereign in his domestic economy." The language of the law recognized as much. Despite the advent of ideals of companionate marriage and parental affection, the common law spoke of "the empire of the father" and defined the husband as the "baron" or "lord" of his wife. A servant who made an attempt on his master's life was guilty of "petty treason," a parallel but lesser crime to high treason against the sovereign of the realm. In the republic, citizens were equal. In the household, members were ordered hierarchically and rights were distributed unequally. In his position as husband, father, and master, the common law invested the household head with considerable authority, but also with responsibility, over his wife, children, and servants.[19]

The household was primarily a productive unit whose goal was the realization of autarky for the household and, ideally, leisure for the household head and his immediate family. That leisure was what made it possible for the *kyrios* to also be a *polites*, or citizen. The household was therefore intimately bound up with property because property in some form was necessary for the family to subsist and to generate the surplus that made leisure possible. Absence of property spelled need. And in early America, the common law's response to need was to dissolve the family and to bind its members to service, turning them into the servants of other family heads. Little wonder, then, that property—typically measured by state constitutions and state laws in land or in the ability to pay taxes—became the necessary qualification for the right to vote and other civic rights such as jury duty and militia service.

We may picture the central character of the early American bodies politic as a Janus-faced individual who combined the outward-looking role of the citizen with the inward-looking role of the household head. In the first capacity, this man (for it was almost always a man) participated in the running of the government at local, state, and federal level, at a minimum as an elector, possibly as an office holder. As a citizen he was also subject to the decisions made by these popular governments of which he formed a constituent part. In the second capacity, this man ruled a household made up by a retinue of legal dependents. The household was no republic of equals. The common law, which regulated the relationships within the household, was unhesitant about giving the master far-ranging authority over his dependents and severely constricting the right of dependents to oppose his authority.

Under common law, the head of the family had the right to "controul, restrain, and regulate" the conduct of his dependents and to keep them "under due subordination and subjection." The ultimate purpose was to give the household head control over the labor of the household. A husband also had the right to the "comfort and company" of his wife, which included access to her body, to her earnings within and without the household, to her personal property, and to the use of her real property. Fathers had the right to bind their children to servitude under another master. Masters were protected in different ways from the loss of servant labor. If the servant was enslaved, he or she lived under the most extreme form of servitude whereby "one man is subject to be directed by another in all his actions."[20]

Although legal writers habitually praised the common law for refusing to interfere in the "interiour government of a family," early American law and government in fact supported the authority of fathers and masters against rebellions in the household. In the South, slave patrols and slave codes kept the plantation labor force in subjection. In Connecticut, "stubborn children and servants" could be sent to houses of correction to be whipped, shackled, and deprived of food until "they are reduced to better order and obedience." In the Northwest Territory, disobedient children and servants who struck their parents or masters were whipped. Local government and local courts also interfered when household heads failed in their obligations to their dependents. This could happen in cases of excessive cruelty or when a woman's property had to be protected from an insolvent husband. More commonly it happened to prevent household dependents from becoming public charges. Overseers of the poor could take and bind children to servitude thereby depriving the father of his children's labor. They could also dissolve and bind to servitude entire families that had fallen on hard times.[21]

Throughout the founding period we find little appetite for restricting the rights of husbands, fathers, and masters. As Shammas remarks, "considering the amount of constitution writing that went on, what is most remarkable is the reluctance to rein in the powers of the household head." Her observation also holds true of the Constitutional Convention, which left the regulation of household government to the states. Nor did the convention delegates show any interest in extending rights beyond white, male, property owners. This is hardly surprising. In a system of unequal relative rights, the liberty of the citizen rested on the right of the *kyrios* to the labor, bodies, and property of his dependents. In a system of relative rights, any extension of the rights of dependents by definition amounted to the curtailment of the rights of husbands, fathers, and masters.[22]

Over time the relationship between household heads and household dependents would change. But it took a long and difficult struggle for oppressed and excluded groups to achieve an American social order of equal formal rights. Crucial to this development was their use of the national government to overrule state restrictions on civic rights to impose a national standard of citizenship. In a dramatic extension of federal government authority that fundamentally transformed the American union, Congress and the Supreme Court began to regulate the internal police of the states.

In their fight for justice and equality, American social movements have a long tradition of enlisting in their struggle the language of liberty and equality of the founding documents. The strategy is to shame the American public by pointing to the glaring incompatibility between the nation's founding ideals and contemporary reality. But it would be a mistake to interpret the gradual extension of rights in the nineteenth and twentieth century, which would eventually ensure the alignment between citizen and inhabitant, on the one hand, and the abolition of relative rights in the household, on the other, as the realization of founding ideals. To the contrary, generations of American emancipators inscribed the rhetoric of the founders with new meaning. In so doing they rewrote as charters of universal freedom instruments that were originally designed to privilege the few by the legal subjection and oppression of the many.

NOTES

Introduction

1. "From George Washington to the States, 8 June, 1783," Founders Online, National Archives, last modified April 12, 2018, https://founders.archives.gov/documents/Washington/99-01-02-11404.
2. John Fiske, *The Critical Period of American History, 1783–1789* (Boston: Houghton Mifflin, 1899 [1888]), 55; Gordon S. Wood, *The Creation of the American Republic, 1776–1787* (Chapel Hill: University of North Carolina Press, 1969), 393.
3. "Congressional Ratification of the Definitive Treaty of Peace," in *The Emerging Nation: A Documentary History of the Foreign Relations of the United States under the Articles of Confederation, 1780–1789*, ed. Mary A. Giunta, 3 vols. (Washington, DC: National Historical Publications and Records Commission, 1996), I, 963–67.
4. Fiske, *Critical Period*, 223.
5. Ibid., vi–vii.
6. Ibid., 308–309; Charles A. Beard and Mary R. Beard, *The Rise of American Civilization*, 2 vols. (New York: Macmillan, 1955 [1930 rev. ed.]), I, 332–33.
7. Charles A. Beard, *An Economic Interpretation of the Constitution of the United States* (New York: Macmillan, 1913), 48; Beard and Beard, *Rise of American Civilization* I, 303–304.
8. Merrill Jensen, *The Articles of Confederation: An Interpretation of the Social-Constitutional History of the American Revolution 1774–1781* (Madison: University of Wisconsin Press, 1976 [1940]), 245 ("engineered"); Jensen, *The New Nation: A History of the United States during the Confederation, 1781–1789* (New York: Knopf, 1950), 128 ("democratization"), 423 ("extraordinary").
9. Peter S. Onuf, "A Declaration of Independence for Diplomatic Historians," *Diplomatic History* 22, no. 1 (January 1998): 71–83; David Armitage, *The Declaration of Independence: A Global History* (Cambridge, MA: Harvard University Press, 2007); Leonard J. Sadosky, *Revolutionary Negotiations: Indians, Empires, and Diplomats in the Founding of America* (Charlottesville: University of Virginia Press, 2009); David M. Golove and Daniel J. Hulsebosch, "A Civilized Nation: The Early American Constitution, the Law of Nations, and the Pursuit of International Recognition," *New York University Law Review* 85, no. 4 (October 2010): 932–1066, quotation at 934; Eliga H. Gould, *Among the Powers of the Earth: The American Revolution and the Making of a New World Empire* (Cambridge, MA: Harvard University Press, 2012); Robbie J. Totten, "Security, Two Diplomacies, and the Formation of the U.S. Constitution: Review, Interpretation, and New Directions for the Study of the Early American Period," *Diplomatic History* 36, no. 1 (January 2012): 77–117; Gregory Ablavsky, "The Savage Constitution," *Duke Law Journal* 63, no. 5 (February 2014): 999–1090. Some recent works in the Beard-Jensen tradition are Terry Bouton, *Taming Democracy: "The People," the Founders, and the Troubled Ending of the American Revolution* (New York: Oxford

University Press, 2007); Woody Holton, *Unruly Americans and the Origins of the Constitution* (New York: Hill and Wang, 2007); Barbara Clark Smith, *The Freedoms We Lost: Consent and Resistance in Revolutionary America* (New York: The New Press, 2010); and Michael J. Klarman, *The Framers' Coup: The Making of the United States Constitution* (New York: Oxford University Press, 2016).

10. Carl Lotus Becker, *The History of Political Parties in the Province of New York, 1760–1776* (Madison: Bulletin of the University of Wisconsin, no. 286, History series 2, no. 1, 1909): 5. On the concept of a "dual revolution," see Robert Gough, "Charles H. Lincoln, Carl Becker, and the Origins of the Dual-Revolution Thesis," *William and Mary Quarterly* 38, no. 1 (January 1981): 97–109.

11. Mary Sarah Bilder, *Madison's Hand: Revising the Constitutional Convention* (Cambridge, MA: Harvard University Press, 2015), 76–77; Max Farrand, ed., *The Records of the Federal Convention of 1787*, 4 vols. (New Haven, CT: Yale University Press, 1966 [1937]), I, 169; *Supplement to Max Farrand's The Records of the Federal Convention of 1787*, ed. James H. Hutson (New Haven, CT: Yale University Press, 1987), 60–61. Alison L. La Croix, *The Ideological Origins of American Federalism* (Cambridge, MA: Harvard University Press, 2010), 30–131 analyses the American debates of the 1760s and 1770s and shows how Daniel Dulaney (50–1), the Massachusetts House of Representatives (90), and John Dickinson (102) all approached the question of the respective powers of Parliament and the colonial assemblies as a matter of "drawing a line" between the different levels of government.

12. "Final Version of an Opinion on the Constitutionality of an Act to Establish a Bank, [February 23, 1791]," *PAH* VIII, 97–134, quotation at 107.

13. "From James Madison to Thomas Jefferson, 24 October 1787," in *Papers of James Madison*, ed. William T. Hutchinson and William M. E. Rachal, 17 vols. (Chicago: University of Chicago Press, 1962–1991), X, 205–20.

14. Quotations from Ernst-Wolfgang Böckenförde, "The Historical Evolution and Changes in the Meaning of the Constitution," in his *Constitutional and Political Theory: Selected Writings*, ed. Mirjam Künkler and Tine Stein, 2 vols. (Oxford: Oxford University Press, 2017), I, 159, 169.

15. Gordon S. Wood, "Interests and Disinterestedness in the Making of the Constitution," in *Beyond Confederation: Origins of the Constitution and American National Identity*, ed. Richard Beeman, Stephen Botein, and Edward C. Carter II (Chapel Hill: University of North Carolina Press, 1987), 70; John L. Brooke, "Cultures of Nationalism, Movements of Reform, and the Composite-Federal Polity: From Revolutionary Settlement to Antebellum Crisis," *Journal of the Early Republic* 29, no. 2 (Spring 2009): 6.

16. Christopher Ryan Pearl, *Conceived in Crisis: The Revolutionary Creation of an American State* (Charlottesville: University of Virginia Press, 2020); John Joseph Wallis, "The Other Founding: Federalism and the Constitutional Structure of American Government," in *Founding Choices: American Economic Policy in the 1790s*, ed. Douglas A. Irwin and Richard Sylla (Chicago: University of Chicago Press, 2011), 177–213.

Chapter 1

1. David Thelen, introduction to "The Constitution and American Life: A Special Issue," *Journal of American History* 74, no. 3 (December 1987): 661; James H. Hutson, "The Creation of the Constitution: Scholarship at a Standstill," *Reviews in American History* 12, no. 4 (December 1984): 436–77.

2. The historiography is discussed in Robert E. Shalhope, "Toward a Republican Synthesis: The Emergence of an Understanding of Republicanism in American Historiography," *William and Mary Quarterly* 29, no. 1 (January 1972): 49–80 and Robert E. Shalhope, "Republicanism and Early American Historiography," *William and Mary Quarterly* 39, no. 2 (April 1982): 334–56.

3. Daniel T. Rodgers, "Republicanism: The Career of a Concept," *Journal of American History* 79, no. 1 (June 1992): 34–38; Isaac Kramnick, "The 'Great National Discussion': The Discourse of Politics in 1787," *William and Mary Quarterly* 45, no. 1 (January 1988): 4, 12 (quotations).

4. Peter S. Onuf, "Reflections on the Founding: Constitutional Historiography in Bicentennial Perspective," *William and Mary Quarterly* 46, no. 2 (April 1989): 341–75, quotations at 342 and 344. Other attempts to present the Unionist interpretation in systematic form are David

C. Hendrickson, "The Constitution in History: A Bibliographical Essay," in *Peace Pact: The Lost World of the American Founding* (Lawrence: University Press of Kansas, 2003), 281–97; Alan Gibson, *Interpreting the Founding: Guide to the Enduring Debates over the Origins and Foundations of the American Republic* (Lawrence: University of Kansas Press, 2010, 2nd ed.), ch. 8; Robbie J. Totten, "Security, Two Diplomacies, and the Formation of the US Constitution: Review, Interpretation, and New Directions for the Study of the Early American Period," *Diplomatic History* 36, no. 1 (January 2012): 77–117; Tom Cutterham, "The International Dimension of the Federal Constitution," *Journal of American Studies* 48, no. 2 (May 2014): 501–15.

5. Peter S. Onuf, *The Origins of the Federal Republic: Jurisdictional Controversies in the United States, 1775–1787* (Philadelphia: University of Pennsylvania Press, 1983); Peter S. Onuf, *Statehood and Union: A History of the Northwest Ordinance* (Bloomington and Indianapolis: Indiana University Press, 1987); Cathy D. Matson and Peter S. Onuf, *A Union of Interests: Political and Economic Thought in Revolutionary America* (Lawrence: University Press of Kansas, 1990).

6. Jack P. Greene, *Peripheries and Center: Constitutional Development in the Extended Polities of the British Empire and the United States, 1607–1788* (Athens: University of Georgia Press, 1986), 3, abridged and updated as Jack P. Greene, *The Constitutional Origins of the American Revolution* (New York: Cambridge University Press, 2011); Peter S. Onuf, "A Declaration of Independence for Diplomatic Historians," *Diplomatic History* 22, no. 1 (Winter 1998): 79. Jack N. Rakove, *The Beginnings of National Politics: An Interpretive History of the Continental Congress* (New York: Knopf, 1979). The antebellum period is explored in Peter Onuf and Nicholas Onuf, *Federal Union, Modern World: The Law of Nations in an Age of Revolutions, 1776–1814* (Madison, WI: Madison House, 1993) and Nicholas Onuf and Peter Onuf, *Nations, Markets, and War: Modern History and the American Civil War* (Charlottesville: University of Virginia Press, 2006). Unrelated to Greene's work was the simultaneous publication of the first volume of Donald Meinig's masterful *The Shaping of America*, the final chapters of which treat the disintegration of empires and the problems of federations. Neither volume I nor II, which covers the period to the aftermath of the Civil War, cite Greene or Onuf, apart from Onuf's book on the Northwest Ordinance. D. W. Meinig, *The Shaping of America: A Geographical Perspective on 500 Years of History*. Vol. I, *Atlantic America, 1492–1800* (New Haven, CT: Yale University Press, 1986).

7. Greene, *Peripheries and Center*, 2–12, 164 (quotation). A similar account is Christopher Tomlins, "The Legal Cartography of Colonization, the Legal Polyphony of Settlement: English Intrusions on the American Mainland in the Seventeenth Century," *Law and Social Inquiry* 26, no. 2 (Spring 2001): 315–72, reworked into ch. 3 and 4 of Christopher Tomlins, *Freedom Bound: Law, Labor, and Civic Identity in Colonizing English America, 1580–1865* (New York: Cambridge University Press, 2010), 93–190.

8. J. G. A. Pocock, "States, Republics, and Empires: The American Founding in Early Modern Perspective," *Social Science* Quarterly 68, no. 4 (December 1987): 703–23, quotation at 708. Pocock's discussion of the terms *commonwealth* and *state* should be read alongside Quentin Skinner, "A Genealogy of the Modern State," in *Proceedings of the British Academy*, vol. 162, *2008 Lectures* (Oxford: Oxford University Press, 2009), 325–70, Oxford: Published for the British Academy by Oxford University Press.

9. Montesquieu, *Spirit of the Laws*, ed. Anne M. Cohler Basia Carolyn Miller, and Harold Samuel Stone (Cambridge: Cambridge University Press, 1989), part II, book 9, ch. 1, 131–32; Pocock, "States, Republics, and Empires," 708, 713–20; Hendrickson, *Peace Pact*, ix ("body politic"; "readily recognizable"), 67–157; Onuf, "Declaration of Independence," 78 quoting *The Constitutions of the Several Independent States of America; The Declaration of Independence; The Articles of Confederation* (London, 1782). On the intellectual history of federalism in American political thought before the Constitution, see Alison L. LaCroix, *The Ideological Origins of American Federalism* (Cambridge, MA: Harvard University Press, 2010), 30–131.

10. Onuf, "Declaration of Independence," 73; "Confederation Congress Calls the Constitutional Convention, 21 February 1787," in *The Documentary History of the Ratification of the Constitution*, ed. Merrill Jensen, John P. Kaminski, and Gaspare J. Saladino, 34 vols. to date (Madison: Wisconsin Historical Society Press, 1976–), I, 187. On independence and union, see also Pocock, "States, Republics, and Empires," 57–61; David Armitage, "The Declaration of Independence and International Law," *William and Mary Quarterly* 59, no. 1 (January

2002): 34–64. On the postwar period, see Matson and Onuf, *Union of Interests*, 50–100; John J. McCusker, "Estimating Early American Gross Domestic Product," *Historical Methods* 33, no. 3 (2000): 155–62; Peter H. Lindert and Jeffrey G. Williamson, "American Incomes Before and After the Revolution," *Journal of Economic History* 73, no. 3 (September 2013): 725–65; Allan Kulikoff, "'Such Things Ought Not to Be': The American Revolution and the First National Great Depression," in *The World of the Revolutionary American Republic: Land, Labor, and the Conflict for a Continent*, ed. Andrew Shankman (New York: Routledge, 2014), 134–64; George Van Cleve, *We Have Not a Government: The Articles of Confederation and the Road to the Constitution* (Chicago: University of Chicago Press, 2017).

11. Michael P. Zuckert, "Federalism and the Founding," *Review of Politics*, vol. 48, no. 2 (Spring 1986): 174; "Preface to the Debates in the Convention," in James Madison, *Notes on Debates in the Federal Convention of 1787 Reported by James Madison*, ed. Adrienne Koch (Athens: Ohio University Press, 1966), 3.

12. Onuf, *Origins of the Federal Republic*, 205; Onuf and Onuf, *Federal Union*, 141.

13. Daniel H. Deudney, "The Philadelphian System: Sovereignty, Arms Control, and Balance of Power in the American States-Union, Circa 1787–1861," *International Organization* 49, no. 2 (Spring 1995): 191–228; David M. Golove and Daniel J. Hulsebosch, "A Civilized Nation: The Early American Constitution, the Law of Nations, and the Pursuit of International Recognition," *New York University Law Review* 85, no. 4 (October 2010): 932–1066; Eliga H. Gould, *Among the Powers of the Earth: The American Revolution and the Making of a New World Empire* (Cambridge, MA: Harvard University Press, 2012); Leonard J. Sadosky, *Revolutionary Negotiations: Indians, Empires, and Diplomats in the Founding of America* (Charlottesville: University of Virginia Press, 2009).

14. Samuel Johnson, *A Dictionary of the English Language*, 2 vols. (London: W. Strahan, 1755), quoted in Jonathan Gienapp, *The Second Creation: Fixing the American Constitution in the Founding Era* (Cambridge, MA: Harvard University Press, 2018), 25. For standard definitions of the meaning of the term *constitution*, see for example *The Oxford Companion to Politics of the World*, ed. Joel Krieger (Oxford: Oxford University Press, 2001, 2nd ed.), s.v. "Constitution"; *A Dictionary of Law*, ed. Jonathan Law (Oxford: Oxford University Press, 2018, 9th ed.), s.v. "Constitution."

15. Thomas Paine, *The Rights of Man, Pt I*, in Paine, *Political Writings*, ed. Bruce Kuklick (Cambridge: Cambridge University Press, 1989), 81; Gerard N. Magliocca, *The Heart of the Constitution: How the Bill of Rights Became the Bill of Rights* (New York: Oxford University Press, 2018), 9–21; Richard Rush, *Observations upon the Present State of the Government of Pennsylvania* (Philadelphia: Steiner and Cist, 1777), quoted in Gienapp, *Second Creation*, 51, emphasis in the original. It is not clear that the American revolutionaries distinguished between constitutions and systems of government. The recommendation by Congress to the states to write new constitutions as part of the independence process, which was adopted on May 10, 1776, does not use the term *constitution* at all. It recommends that the "respective assemblies and conventions of the United Colonies . . . adopt such *government* as shall . . . best conduce to the happiness and safety of their constituents in particular, and America in general," *The Journals of the Continental Congress, 1774–1789*, ed. C. Ford Worthington Gaillard Hunt, John Clement Fitzpatrick, Roscoe R. Hill, Kenneth E. Harris, and Steven D. Tilley, 34 vols. (Washington, DC: US Government Printing Office, 1904–1937), IV, 342. Mary Sarah Bilder argues that this uncertainty persisted well beyond the adoption of the Constitution in "The *Ordeal* and the Constitution," *New England Quarterly* 91, no. 1 (January 2018): 129–46. On the variable meaning of the term *constitution*, see Gerald Stourzh, "Constitution: Changing Meaning of the Term from the Early Seventeenth to the Late Eighteenth Century," in *Conceptual Change and the Constitution*, ed. Ball and Pocock, 35–54. The fluid meaning of the term in the American founding is the thesis of Gienapp, *Second Creation*.

16. Ernst-Wolfgang Böckenförde, "The Historical Evolution and Changes in the Meaning of the Constitution," in *Constitutional and Political Theory: Selected Writings*, 2 vols., ed. Mirjam Künkler and Tine Stein (Oxford: Oxford University Press, 2017), I, 152–68, quotation at 159. On the European state-system, see Hendrickson, *Peace Pact*, x–xi, 40–54. On the Imperial constitution, see Barbara A. Black, "The Constitution of Empire: The Case for the Colonists," *University of Pennsylvania Law Review* 124, no. 5 (1976): 1157–2011; Greene,

Peripheries and Center; John P. Reid, *The Constitutional History of the American Revolution* (Madison: University of Wisconsin Press, 1995); Daniel J. Hulsebosch, *Constituting Empire: New York and the Transformation of Constitutionalism in the Atlantic World, 1664–1830* (Chapel Hill: University of North Carolina Press, 2005), 71–144; Greene, *Ideological Origins*. Discussions about federal republics by natural law thinkers can be found in Montesquieu, *Spirit of the Laws*, part II, book 9, ch. 1, 131–32; Emer de Vattel, *The Law of Nations, Or, Principles of the Law of Nature, Applied to the Conduct and Affairs of Nations and Sovereigns*, ed. Béla Kapossy and Richard Whatmore (Indianapolis: Liberty Fund, 2008), book 1, ch. 1, §10, 84–85; and Jean-Jacques Burlamaqui, *The Principles of Natural and Politic Law*, ed. Petter Korkman (Indianapolis: Liberty Fund, 2006), vol. II, pt II, ch. 2, §§xl–xlv, 336–37.

17. Mary Sarah Bilder, *Madison's Hand: Revising the Constitutional Convention* (Cambridge, MA: Harvard University Press, 2015), 15; Bilder, "The *Ordeal* and the Constitution," 138–39.

18. Michael P. Zuckert, "A System Without Precedent: Federalism in the American Constitution," in *The Framing and Ratification of the Constitution*, ed. Leonard W. Levy and Dennis J. Mahoney (New York: Macmillan, 1987), 141; Zuckert, "Federalisms and the Founding," 166–210; Onuf, *Origins of the Federal Republic*, 173–85; Pocock, "States, Republics, and Empires," 66–70; Hendrickson, *Peace Pact*, x–xi; David C. Hendrickson, "Bringing the State System Back In: The Significance of the Union in Early American History, 1763–1865," in *State and Citizen: British America and the Early United States*, ed. Peter Thompson and Peter S. Onuf (Charlottesville: University of Virginia Press, 2013), 114.

19. Deudney, "Philadelphian System," 193, 195; Hendrickson, "Bringing the State System Back In," 114; Hendrickson, *Peace Pact*, quotation at 10; Max M. Edling, *A Hercules in the Cradle: War, Money, and the American State, 1783–1867* (Chicago: University of Chicago Press, 2014), 224–27. Hendrickson is quoting Jefferson's words from *Notes on the State of Virginia*.

20. Vattel, *Law of Nations*, book 1, ch. 1, §10, 84.

21. Onuf, *Origins of the Federal Republic*, 186–209; Zuckert, "System Without Precedent," 132–50; Hendrickson, *Peace Pact*. See also chapter 2.

22. Matson and Onuf, *Union of Interests*, 101–23.

23. David Waldstreicher, *Slavery's Constitution: From Revolution to Ratification* (New York: Hill and Wang, 2009), 57–105; George Van Cleve, *A Slaveholders' Union: Slavery, Politics, and the Constitution in the Early American Republic* (Chicago: University of Chicago Press, 2011), 103–83. Among legal historians Paul Finkelman has consistently argued for the importance of slavery in the Constitution, for example in "Slavery and the Constitutional Convention: Making a Covenant with Death," in *Beyond Confederation: Origins of the Constitution and American National Identity*, ed. Richard Beeman, Stephen Botein, and Edward C. Carter (Chapel Hill: University of North Carolina Press, 1987), 188–225. In the Progressive tradition, Staughton Lynd was unusual in stressing the role of slavery in the making of the Constitution. His essays on the topic are collected in *Class Conflict, Slavery, and the United States Constitution* (Indianapolis: Bobbs-Merrill, 1967), 135–213.

24. Lynd, "The Compromise of 1787," in *Class Conflict*, 185–213; Matson and Onuf, *Union of Interests*, 113–19; Waldstreicher, *Slavery's Constitution*, 87–88; Van Cleve, *Slaveholders' Union*, 153–67; Max M. Edling, *A Revolution in Favor of Government: Origins of the US Constitution and the Making of the American State* (New York: Oxford University Press, 2003).

25. Hendrickson, *Peace Pact*, xii.

26. Edling, *Hercules in the Cradle*, 50–107; Golove and Hulsebosch, "Civilized Nation," 993–44.

27. St. George Tucker, "View of the Constitution of the United States," in *View of the Constitution of the United States With Selected Writings*, ed. Clyde N. Wilson (Indianapolis: Liberty Fund, 1999), 248; Vattel, *Law of Nations*, preliminaries, §18, 75 (quotation) and book 1, ch. 1, §§1–11, 81–84.

28. Totten, "Security," 101–109; Max M. Edling, "'A Vigorous National Government': Hamilton on Security, War, and Revenue," in *The Cambridge Companion to The Federalist*, ed. Jack N. Rakove and Colleen Sheehan (New York: Cambridge University Press, 2020), 82–113.

29. John E. Crowley, *Privileges of Independence: Neo-Mercantilism and the American Revolution* (Baltimore: Johns Hopkins University Press, 1993) argues that American statesmen failed to appreciate that Britain maintained a difference between the exchange of goods, where

British postindependence policy was liberal, and shipping, where it was mercantilist. After independence, American political leaders wished for a return to the colonial order that allowed American ships to carry goods within the British Empire with few restrictions. On the Atlantic commercial regime, see also Matson and Onuf, *Union and Interest*, 67–81; Onuf and Onuf, *Federal Union, Modern World*; Van Cleve, *We Have Not a Government*.

30. Golove and Hulsebosch, "Civilized Nation," 935; Gould, *Among the Powers of the Earth*, 130.

31. Gould, *Among the Powers of the Earth*, 3; Daniel J. Hulsebosch, "The Revolutionary Portfolio: Constitution-Making and the Wider World in the American Revolution," *Suffolk University Law Review* 47, no. 4 (December 2014): 759–822. On the law of nations and American political development, see also Onuf and Onuf, *Federal Union, Modern World* and Onuf and Onuf, *Nations, Markets, and War*. The geographic expansion and limits to the law of nations is a major theme of Gould's *Among the Powers of the Earth*.

32. Golove and Hulsebosch, "Civilized Nation," 945–46 (quotation); Gould, *Among the Powers of the Earth*, 119, 127.

33. Gould, *Among the Powers of the Earth*, 132; Golove and Hulsebosch, "Civilized Nation," 989–90.

34. Golove and Hulsebosch, "Civilized Nation," 993–94; Daniel J. Hulsebosch, "Being Seen Like a State: How Americans (and Britons) Built the Constitutional Infrastructure of a Developing Nation," *William and Mary Law Review* 59, no. 4 (2018): 1239–1319.

35. On the actions of the federal courts and the reception of the Constitution in Britain see Daniel J. Hulsebosch, "Magna Carta for the World? The Merchant's Chapter and Foreign Capital in the Early American Republic," *North Carolina Law Review* 94, no. 5 (2016): 1599–1634, and Hulsebosch, "Being Seen Like a State." Trade and diplomacy in the period 1789–1795 are expertly treated in Stanley Elkins and Eric McKitrick, *The Age of Federalism: The Early American Republic, 1788–1800* (New York: Oxford University Press, 1993), 375–449.

36. Gould, *Among the Powers of the Earth*, 11 (quotation); Sadosky, *Revolutionary Negotiations*, 1–9 and passim. Lisa Ford, *Settler Sovereignty: Jurisdiction and Indigenous People in American and Australia, 1788–1836* (Cambridge, MA: Harvard University Press, 2010) analyzes the transition from legal pluralism in the Georgia borderlands to "perfect settler sovereignty." See also Richard White, *The Middle Ground: Indians, Empires, and Republics in the Great Lakes Region, 1650–1815* (New York: Cambridge University Press, 1993); Eric Hinderaker, *Elusive Empires: Constructing Colonialism in the Ohio Valley, 1673–1800* (New York: Cambridge University Press, 1997); Stuart Banner, *How the Indians Lost Their Land* (Cambridge, MA: Harvard University Press, 2005), 112–227; Gregory Ablavsky, "Species of Sovereignty: Native Nationhood, the United States, and International Law, 1783–1795," *Journal of American History* 106, no 3 (December 2019): 591–613. The consequences of ratification are also treated in Sadosky, *Revolutionary Negotiations*, 176–215; Gould, *Among the Powers of the Earth*, 178–218; and Alan Taylor, "The War of 1812 and the Struggle for a Continent," in *World of the Revolutionary American Republic*, ed. Shankman, 246–67.

37. Peter S. Onuf, "Liberty, Development and Union: Visions of the West in the 1780s," *William and Mary Quarterly* 43, no. 2 (April 1986): 179–213; Gregory Ablavsky, "The Savage Constitution," *Duke Law Journal*, 63, no. 5 (February 2014): 999–1090, quotation at 1011; Bethel Saler, *The Settlers' Empire: Colonialism and State Formation in America's Old Northwest* (Philadelphia: University of Pennsylvania Press, 2014), 16–17.

38. Sadosky, *Revolutionary Negotiations*, 127–40; Ablavsky, "Savage Constitution," 1042–43; Saler, *Settlers' Empire*, 29–32.

39. Ordinance for the Government of the Territory of the United States Northwest of the River Ohio, 13 July 1787, in *Documentary History of the Ratification of the Constitution* I, 168–74; Onuf, *Statehood and Union*; Saler, *Settlers' Empire*, 17–26.

40. Saler, *Settlers' Empire*, 3–5, 26–29, 83–120, quotation at 27. Kathleen DuVal, *Independence Lost: Lives on the Edge of the American Revolution* (New York: Random House, 2015), 219–351 describes this process from the American Indian side in the Old Southwest, William H. Bergmann, *The American National State and the Early West* (New York: Cambridge University Press, 2012) treats the Northwest Territory. On US policy toward American Indian nations, see Bernard W. Sheehan, *Seeds of Extinction: Jeffersonian Philanthropy and the American Indian* (New York: Norton, 1974); Bernard W. Sheehan, "The Indian Problem in

the Northwest: From Conquest to Philanthropy," in *Launching the "Extended Republic": The Federalist Era*, ed. Ronald Hoffman and Peter J. Albert (Charlottesville: University of Virginia Press, 1996), 190–222; Peter S. Onuf, *Jefferson's Empire: The Language of American Nationhood* (Charlottesville: University Press of Virginia, 2000).

41. Bilder, *Madison's Hand*, 74–80, 89–101.

Chapter 2

1. Montesquieu, *Spirit of the Laws*, ed. Anne M. Cohler, Basia Carolyn Miller, and Harold Samuel Stone (Cambridge: Cambridge University Press, 1989), Part. II, book. 9, ch. 1, 131–32; Emer de Vattel, *The Law of Nations, Or, Principles of the Law of Nature, Applied to the Conduct and Affairs of Nations and Sovereigns*, ed. Richard Whatmore and Béla Kapossy (Indianapolis: Liberty Fund, 2008), book 1, ch. 1, §10, 84; Jean-Jacques Burlamaqui, *The Principles of Natural and Politic Law*, ed. Petter Korkman (Indianapolis: Liberty Fund, 2006), vol. II, pt II, ch. 2, §§xl-xlv, 336–37; Samuel von Pufendorf, *Of the Law of Nature and of Nations* (London: J. Walthoe, R. Wilkin, J. J. Bonwicke, S. Birt, T. Ward, and T. Osborne, 1729), bk VII, ch V, §§16–18, 681–84.

2. John Locke, *Two Treatises of Government*, ed. Peter Laslett (Cambridge: Cambridge University Press, 1988), 365, emphasis in the original; Montesquieu, *Spirit of the Laws*, Part. II, book. 11, ch. 6, 156–57.

3. James Wilson, "Lectures on Law, Delivered in the College of Philadelphia," in *Collected Works of James Wilson*, ed. Kermit L. Hall and Mark David Hall, 2 vols. (Indianapolis: Liberty Fund, 2007), I, 664; St. George Tucker, *View of the Constitution of the United States, with Selected Writings*, ed. Clyde N. Wilson (Indianapolis: Liberty Fund, 1999), 79–80; "Committee Report on Carrying the Confederation into Effect and on Additional Powers Needed by Congress," in *Documentary History of the Ratification of the Constitution*, ed. Merrill Jensen, John P. Kaminski, and Gaspare J. Saladino, 34 vols. to date (Madison: Wisconsin Historical Society Press, 1976–), I, 145.

4. For the axiom, see David C. Hendrickson, *Peace Pact: The Lost World of the American Founding* (Lawrence: University Press of Kansas, 2003), xii.

5. Richard Bland, *An Inquiry into the Rights of the British Colonies* (1766), quoted in Alison L. LaCroix, *The Ideological Origins of American Federalism* (Cambridge, MA: Harvard University Press, 2010), 60; Alexander Hamilton, *The Farmer Refuted, &c.*, in *Papers of Alexander Hamilton*, ed. Harold C. Syrett, 27 vols. (New York: Columbia University Press, 1961–1987), I, 81–165, quotation at 98; Thomas Jefferson, "Draft of Instructions to the Virginia Delegates in the Continental Congress (MS Text of *A Summary View*, &c.), [July 1774]," in *The Papers of Thomas Jefferson*, ed. Julian P. Boyd, 44 vols. to date (Princeton, NJ: Princeton University Press, 1950–), I, 121–37, quotation at 123; James Wilson, "Considerations of the Nature and Extent of the Legislative Authority of the British Parliament, 1774," in *Collected Works of James Wilson* I, 30 note r; John Adams, "Novanglus VII: To the Inhabitants of the Colony of Massachusetts-Bay, 6 March 1775," *Papers of John Adams*, ed. Robert J. Taylor, Mary-Jo Kline, Gregg L. Lint, 18 vols. to date (Cambridge, MA: Harvard University Press, 1977–), II, 307–27, quotation at 324. On the American debate about the imperial federal union in the 1760s and 1770s, and the belief that sovereignty could be divided "along substantive lines, defined by subject matter," see LaCroix, *Ideological Origins of American Federalism*, 30–105, 113–20.

6. John Adams, "Novanglus VII," *Papers of John Adams* II, 307–27, quotations at 321, 322, and 323. See also the discussion in Wilson, "Considerations of the Nature and Extent of the Legislative Authority of the British Parliament," in *Collected Works of James Wilson* I, 30–31 note r.

7. Heather Schwartz, "Re-Writing the Empire: Plans for Institutional Reform in British America, 1675–1791" (PhD diss., SUNY Binghamton, 2011), Appendix A, 245–55; Jack N. Rakove, *The Beginnings of National Politics: An Interpretative History of the Continental Congress* (New York: Knopf, 1979), 136–38.

8. For the text of these plans, see Joseph Galloway's "Plan of Union," September 28, 1774, in *Journals of the Continental Congress*, ed. C. Ford Worthington, Gaillard Hunt, John Clement Fitzpatrick, Roscoe R. Hill, Kenneth E. Harris, and Steven D. Tilley, 34 vols. (Washington, DC: Library of Congress, 1904–1937), 1:49–51; Franklin's "Articles of Confederation," on or before July 21, 1775, in *Journals of the Continental Congress*, 2:195–99; Silas Deane's

proposal to Congress, November 1775 [?], in *Letters of the Delegates to Congress, 1774–1789*, ed. Paul H. Smith et al., 25 vols. (Washington, DC: Library of Congress, 1776–2000), 418–20; Connecticut plan, *Pennsylvania Evening Post*, March 5, 1776. The plans are discussed in Rakove, *Beginnings of National Politics*, 139–50; LaCroix, *Ideological Origins of American Federalism*, 111–13, 126–31.

9. *Journals of the Continental Congress* V, 425, 428–29, 431, 433. The historical record of the drafting of the Articles of Confederation is very limited and stands in sharp contrast to the wealth of sources available for the Constitutional Convention. The principal treatments are Merrill Jensen, *The Articles of Confederation: An Interpretation of the Social-Constitutional History of the American Revolution, 1774–1781* (Madison: University of Wisconsin Press, 1940), 107–84 and Rakove, *Beginnings of National Politics*, 135–91. I have also benefitted from the analysis in Hendrickson, *Peace Pact*, 115–49.

10. Articles of Confederation and Perpetual Union, *Documentary History of the Ratification of the Constitution* I, 86–91. Jensen, *Articles of Confederation*, 161–76; Rakove, *Beginnings of National Politics*, 164–75. Hendrickson argues that Burke's view reflected that of the majority in Congress and was therefore uncontroversial, see Hendrickson, *Peace Pact*, 134.

11. Pufendorf, *Of the Law of Nature and of Nations*, bk VII, ch V, §18, 682–84. Burlamaqui, another writer with whom Americans were familiar and whose treatise relied heavily on Pufendorf, also used the term "perpetual confederacy of several states," Burlamaqui, *Principles of Natural and Politic Law*, vol. II, pt II, ch. 2, §xliii, 337.

12. The drafts of the Dickinson committee are in *Journals of the Continental Congress* V, 674–89.

13. For the tension between the states and Congress over Indian diplomacy in the 1780s, see Leonard J. Sadosky, *Revolutionary Negotiations: Indians, Empires, and Diplomats in the Founding of America* (Charlottesville: University of Virginia Press, 2009).

14. Rakove, *Beginnings of National Politics*, 157–58, 162, 172, 276; John M. Murrin, "1787: The Invention of American Federalism," in *Essays on Liberty and Federalism: The Shaping of the U.S. Constitution*, ed. David E. Narrett and Joyce S. Goldberg (College Station: Texas A&M University Press, 1988), 20–47; Hendrickson, *Peace Pact*, 136. There was a Court of Appeals that heard admiralty appeals from state trial courts during the Confederation, see Henry J. Bourguignon, *The First Federal Court: The Federal Appellate Prize Court of the American Revolution, 1775–1787* (Philadelphia: American Philosophical Society, 1977). Executive departments also developed toward the close of the War of Independence. A post office was set up already in 1775, and departments for foreign affairs, war, and finance were created in 1781. The Continental army can of course be seen as a field service of Congress, and there were diplomatic agents and collectors of revenue. See Jennings B. Sanders, *Evolution of Executive Departments of the Continental Congress, 1774–1789* (Chapel Hill: University of North Carolina Press, 1935).

15. Richard S. Patterson and Richardson Dougall, *The Eagle and the Shield: A History of the Great Seal of the United States* (Washington, DC: Office of the Historian, Bureau of Public Affairs, Department of State, 1976), 6–88, du Simitière and Thompson quoted on 20 and 84–85.

16. An Act to provide for the safe-keeping of the Acts, Records and Seal of the United States, and for other purposes, September 15, 1789, ch. XIV, *US Statutes at Large* I: 68–70.

17. John J. McCusker, "Estimating Early American Gross Domestic Product," *Historical Methods* 33, no. 3 (Summer 2000): 155–62. On the economic consequences of independence and the War of Independence, see also Peter H. Lindert and Jeffrey G. Williamson, "American Incomes Before and After the Revolution," *Journal of Economic History* 73, no. 3 (September 2013): 725–65, and Allan Kulikoff, "'Such Things Ought Not to Be': The American Revolution and the First National Great Depression," in *The World of the Revolutionary American Republic: Land, Labor, and the Conflict for a Continent*, ed. Andrew Shankman (New York: Routledge, 2014), 134–64.

18. A recent discussion of the term *mercantilism* can be found in Steve Pincus, "Rethinking Mercantilism: Political Economy, the British Empire, and the Atlantic World in the Seventeenth and Eighteenth Centuries," *William and Mary Quarterly* 69, no. 1 (January 2012): 3–34 and Jonathan Barth, "Reconstructing Mercantilism: Consensus and Conflict in British Imperial Economy in the Seventeenth and Eighteenth Centuries, *William and Mary Quarterly* 73, no. 2 (April 2012): 257–90.

19. John Holroyd, Earl of Sheffield, *Observations on the Commerce of the American States with Europe and the West Indies* (London: J. Debrett, 1783), 68. On commercial restrictions, see Frederick W. Marks III, *Independence on Trial: Foreign Affairs and the Making of the Constitution* (Baton Rouge: Louisiana State University Press, 1973), 52–95; Cathy D. Matson and Peter S. Onuf, *A Union of Interests: Political and Economic Thought in Revolutionary America* (Lawrence: University Press of Kansas, 1990), 67–81; Peter Onuf and Nicholas Onuf, *Federal Union, Modern World: The Law of Nations in an Age of Revolutions, 1776–1814* (Madison, WI: Madison House, 1993); John E. Crowley, *Privileges of Independence: Neo-Mercantilism and the American Revolution* (Baltimore: Johns Hopkins University Press, 1993); George W. Van Cleve, *We Have Not a Government: The Articles of Confederation and the Road to the Constitution* (Chicago: University of Chicago Press, 2017).

20. Benjamin Franklin to Robert R. Livingston, July 22[-26], 1783, in *Papers of Benjamin Franklin*, ed. Ellen R. Cohn, 43 vols. to date (New Haven, CT: Yale University Press, 1959–), XL, 369. Early US relations to the North African principalities are treated in Robert Allison, *The Crescent Obscured: The United States and the Muslim World, 1776–1815* (Chicago: University of Chicago Press, 2000); William Earl Weeks, *The New Cambridge History of American Foreign Relations*. Vol. I, *Dimensions of the Early American Empire, 1754–1865* (New York: Cambridge University Press, 2015), 75–77.

21. Jedediah Morse, *Geography Made Easy: Being an Abridgement of the American Geography* (Boston: Isaiah Thomas & Ebenezer T. Andrews, 1790), 231. This and the following four paragraphs build on Marks, *Independence on Trial*, 3–51; Peter S. Onuf, *Statehood and Union: A History of the Northwest Ordinance* (Bloomington: Indiana University Press, 1987); Patrick Griffin, *American Leviathan: Empire, Nation, and Revolutionary Frontier* (New York: Hill and Wang, 2007); Sadosky, *Revolutionary Negotiations*; Weeks, *New Cambridge History of American Foreign Relations*, I, 36–39; Gregory Ablavsky, "The Savage Constitution," *Duke Law Journal* 63, no. 5 (February 2015): 999–1088; Bethel Saler, *The Settler's Empire: Colonialism and State Formation in America's Old Northwest* (Philadelphia: University of Pennsylvania Press, 2015), 1–82; Collin G. Calloway, *The Victory With No Name: The Native American Defeat of the First American Army* (New York: Oxford University Press, 2015), 11–60.

22. This and the following two paragraphs are based on E. James Ferguson, *The Power of the Purse: A History of American Public Finance, 1776–1790* (Chapel Hill: University of North Carolina Press, 1961); Rakove, *Beginning of National Politics*, 297–329; Roger H. Brown, *Redeeming the Republic: Federalists, Taxation, and the Origins of the Constitution* (Baltimore: Johns Hopkins University Press, 1993); and Max M. Edling, *A Hercules in the Cradle: War, Money, and the American State, 1783–1867* (Chicago: University of Chicago Press, 2014), 50–107.

23. Alexander Hamilton, "Federalist 30," in *The Federalist*, ed. Jacob E. Cooke (Middletown, CT: Wesleyan University Press, 1961), 192; Hamilton, "Defence of the Funding System," *Papers of Alexander Hamilton* XIX, 60.

24. Peter S. Onuf, *The Origins of the Federal Republic: Jurisdictional Controversies in the United States 1775–1787* (Philadelphia: University of Pennsylvania Press, 1983), 149–72; Van Cleve, *We Have Not a Government*; Daniel J. Hulsebosch, "Being Seen Like a State: How Americans (and Britons) Built the Constitutional Infrastructure of a Developing Nation," *William and Mary Law Review* 59, no. 4 (2018): 1239–319.

25. Alexander Hamilton, "Federalist 15," *Federalist*, ed. Cooke, 91.

26. "Grant of temporary power to regulate commerce," April 30, 1784, *Documentary History of the Ratification of the Constitution* I, 154; "Amendment to grant commercial powers to Congress," March 28, 1785, *Documentary History of the Ratification of the Constitution* I, 155; "Amendments to the Articles of Confederation proposed by a Grand Committee of Congress," August 7, 1786, *Documentary History of the Ratification of the Constitution* I, 164.

27. Noah Webster, *Sketches of American Policy* (Hartford, CT: Hudson and Goodwin, 1785), 44, emphasis in the original.

28. Pelatiah Webster, *A Dissertation on the Political Union and Constitution of the Thirteen United States, of North-America* (Philadelphia: T. Bradford, 1783), 6–7, 42.

29. "Amendment to give Congress coercive power over the states and their citizens," *Documentary History of the Ratification of the Constitution* I, 142–43.

30. "Grant of power to collect import duties," *Documentary History of the Ratification of the Constitution* I, 140–41; "Grant of temporary power to collect import duties and request for supplementary funds," April 18, 1783, *Documentary History of the Ratification of the Constitution* I, 146–48.

31. "Proceedings and Report of the Commissioners at Annapolis, Maryland," September 11–14, 1786, *Documentary History of the Ratification of the Constitution* I, 184.

32. Van Cleve, *We Have Not a Government*; Rakove, *Beginning of National Politics*, 333–99, analyses Congress in the period leading up to the Constitutional Convention.

33. "Confederation Congress Calls the Constitutional Convention," February 21, 1787, *Documentary History of the Ratification of the Constitution* I, 187.

34. "Notes and Ancient and Modern Confederacies" and "Vices of the Political System of the United States," in *Papers of James Madison*, ed. William T. Hutchinson and William M. E. Rachal, 17 vols. (Chicago: University of Chicago Press, VA, 1962–1991), IX, 3–24, 345–58. On Madison's changes of the "Vices" memorandum, see Mary Sarah Bilder, *Madison's Hand: Revising the Constitutional Convention* (Cambridge, MA: Harvard University Press, 2015), 44–46, 94–95, 243–44.

35. Madison to Thomas Jefferson, October 24, 1787, *Papers of James Madison* X, 207–208; Madison to George Washington, April 16, 1787, *Papers of James Madison* IX, 383; James Madison, "The Federalist No. 45," in *Federalist*, ed. Cooke, 314. In recent years the idea that Madison, the alleged "Father of the Constitution," shaped the Constitution to his liking has been questioned. On the one hand, it has long been evident that the finished document fell well short of his expectations. On the other, it has been questioned to what extent Madison was really representative of the broader movement to reform the union. In very different ways, this interpretative shift is evident in both Lance Banning, *The Sacred Fire of Liberty: James Madison and the Founding of the Federal Republic* (Ithaca, NY: Cornell University Press, 1995), 111–91, and in Gordon S. Wood, "Is There a 'James Madison Problem'?" in *Liberty and American Experience in the Eighteenth Century*, ed. David Womersley (Indianapolis: Liberty Fund, 2006), 425–47, and most recently in Bilder, *Madison's Hand*.

36. There is a large literature on the convention. Standard scholarly accounts are Max Farrand, *The Framing of the Constitution of the United States* (New Haven, CT: Yale University Press, 1913); Charles Warren, *The Making of the Constitution* (Boston: Little, Brown, 1928); and Clinton Rossiter, *1787: The Grand Convention* (New York: Macmillan, 1966). Recent narrative histories are Carol Berkin, *A Brilliant Solution: Inventing the American Constitution* (New York: Harcourt, 2002); Richard Beeman, *Plain, Honest Men: The Making of the American Constitution* (New York: Random House, 2009); and Michael Klarman, *The Framers' Coup: The Making of the United States Constitution* (New York: Oxford University Press, 2016), 126–304. The best analytical works, to which the interpretation offered in the following pages is deeply indebted, are Banning, *Sacred Fire of Liberty*, 1–191; Matson and Onuf, *A Union of Interests*, 101–23; Jack N. Rakove, *Original Meanings: Politics and Ideas in the Making of the Constitution* (New York: Knopf, 1996); Michael P. Zuckert, "A System without Precedent: Federalism in the American Constitution," in *The Framing and Ratification of the Constitution*, ed. Leonard W. Levy and Denis J. Mahoney (New York: Macmillan, 1987), 132–50; and Bilder, *Madison's Hand*.

37. Bilder, *Madison's Hand*, 179–222, 244–46, 257–62 and passim. Bilder's important study of Madison's Notes demonstrate the many additional reasons why they cannot be regarded as a full, impartial and contemporary record of the convention. Madison's original rough notes have been lost or destroyed. The content of the replaced pages of the Notes can therefore only be conjectured from the reports of other note takers at the convention and from Madison's correspondence around the time of the Convention. The other note takers at the Constitutional Convention were Gunning Bedford, Pierce Butler, Alexander Hamilton, Rufus King, John Lansing, George Mason, James McHenry, William Paterson, William Pierce, James Wilson, and Robert Yates. Although the list looks impressive, many times these notes are bare outlines of convention debates and most reporters covered only a handful of the days of the convention.

38. Max Farrand, ed., *The Records of the Federal Convention of 1787*, 4 vols. (New Haven, CT: Yale University Press, 1966), I, 18–19, 20–22. In Madison's Notes, Randolph' speech is

in Randolph's own hand. He sent his original notes for the speech to Madison in 1789, see Bilder, *Madison's Hand*, 180–81.

39. Farrand, *Records* I, 34, 133 (Sherman), 243. The quotation is from the version of Sherman's speech in Madison's Notes. King reported Sherman saying that "the State Governments must continue—Few objects then will be before the Genl. Government—foreign War, Treaties of commerce &c—in short let the Genl. Government be a sort of collateral Government which shall secure the States in particular difficulties such as foreign war, or a war between two or more States" (Farrand, *Records* I, 142–43).

40. Farrand, *Records* II, 158–59.

41. Farrand, *Records* I, 20.

42. Farrand, *Records* I, 242–45 (New Jersey Plan), 313, and Farrand, *Records* II, 13–15. On the Connecticut compromise and the convention's debate about representation, see Rakove, *Original Meanings*, 57–70 and Beeman, *Plain, Honest Men*, 200–25.

43. Bilder, *Madison's Hand*, 96–101, quotation at 98; Farrand, *Records* I, 323 ("corporations," "subordinate," "abolished"), 328–29, 331–32, 449 ("counties"), 477 ("not sovereign," "Bye Laws"), 479. Madison's account of Hamilton and King is similar to Yates's and King's notes. King reported Madison's speech of June 19 as did Paterson whose notes say: "Mr. Madison Will have the States considered as so many great Corporations, and not otherwise."

44. James Wilson, "Lectures on Law," in *Collected Works of James Wilson* I, 632; II, 1035–37; Farrand, *Records* I, 332. King's remarks in the Convention point to two different meanings of *sovereignty* circulating in the 1780s. Natural law thinkers like Pufendorf, Vattel and others were clear that states in a federal republic could delegate their power over war and peace to a common council without thereby giving up their status as sovereign powers. As long as a state governed itself "without dependence on any foreign power" it was "a *sovereign state*." As such, it could engage in voluntary agreements to curtail the exercise of sovereign power without ceasing to be sovereign, just like "a person does not cease to be free and independent, when he is obliged to fulfil engagements which he has voluntarily contracted," Vattel, *Law of Nations*, book I, ch. I, §4 and §10, 83, 84. But in the eighteenth century it was also customary to speak of the powers of war and peace as expressions of sovereign power, "the Gt. & distinguishing acts of Sovereignty." This seem to be what King had in mind. He argued that the American states were not sovereign "under the confed.," i.e. the Articles of Confederation, because they "could not make war, nor peace, nor alliances, nor treaties. Considering them as political Beings, they were dumb, for they could not speak to any forign [sic] Sovereign whatever. They were deaf, for they could not hear any propositions from such Sovereign. They had not even the organs or faculties of defence or offence, for they could not of themselves raise troops, or equip vessels, for war." King's own notes also say that the states "can do no act but such as are of a subordinate nature or such as terminate in themselves—and even then in some instances they are restrained—Coinage, P. Office &c.," Farrand, *Records* I, 323, 331. Such as it is, the record of the debate in the convention does not support the conclusion that delegates who spoke of the states as corporations envisaged terminating the power of the states to regulate their internal affairs. However, those who supported Madison's veto proposal were certainly in favor of national supervision of such affairs, see Bilder, *Madison's Hand*, 98–100.

45. Farrand, *Records* I, 124. No other note taker reported Madison's metaphor and the quote is from a sheet of Madison's notes that Madison later replaced. It appears in the context of his argument about the federal judiciary in response to the argument that federal courts should only be appellate courts. King reported that "Madison proposes to vest the Genl. Govt. with authority to erect an Independent Judicial, coextensive wt. ye. Nation." King, Yates and Pierce all noted that Madison was in favor of the Senate appointing judges, which he may have later regarded as controversial. Alternatively, any compromising statements on the replaced sheet may have been made the following day, June 6 (Farrand, *Records* I, 126–29).

46. Farrand, *Records* I, 21, 164–68, and II, 27–28, 390–92 (Mason quoted at 390); Madison to George Washington, April 16, 1787, *Papers of James Madison* IX, 383–84 (Madison quotations). Madison's veto is analyzed in Charles F. Hobson, "The Negative on State Laws: James Madison, the Constitution, and the Crisis of Republican Government," *William and Mary Quarterly* 36, no. 2 (April 1979): 215–35.

47. Farrand, *Records*, II, 27–28. No note taker other than Madison left a record of the debates of this day.

48. Farrand, *Records* I, 21, 34, 54. No other note taker apart from Madison recorded either Mason's or Madison's remark. In a letter to Thomas Jefferson, Madison remarked that an administration of the laws relying on coercion of delinquent states resembled "much more a civil war, than the administration of a regular Government," Madison to Thomas Jefferson, October 24, 1787, *Papers of James Madison X*, 207.

49. Farrand, *Records* I, 243, 256, 339–40. Paterson's notes from the debate reports that Randolph said "Coercion two Ways—1. As to Trade—2. as to an Army—Legislation affecting Individuals the only Remedy" (Farrand, *Records* I, 273). Yates heard Mason say "What, would you use military force to compel the observance of a social compact? It is destructive to the rights of the people. Do you expect the militia will do it, or do you mean a standing army? The first will never on such an occasion, exert any power; and the latter may turn its arms against the government which employs them" (Farrand, *Records* I, 346).

50. Farrand, *Records* I, 21.

51. Farrand, *Records* I, 179 (Paterson), 447–48 ("Staple of Mast."), 466 (Hamilton), 486 ("principally from"), and 492 (Bedford). Neither Yates nor King reported Paterson's threat that New Jersey would rather submit to, presumably, the British monarch. However, Yates noted Paterson's strong objection that "Myself or my state will never submit to tyranny or despotism" and King his declaration that "New Jersey will never agree to the Scheme" (I, 183, 185). Their notes certainly convey that Madison captured the spirit of the speech correctly. Yates reported Bedford's words as "Sooner than be ruined, there are *foreign powers who will take us by the hand*. I say not this to threaten or intimidate, but that we should reflect seriously before we act" (I, 501). Madison had access to Yates's notes (which are not without their own problems as a reliable source to the convention), however, and made changes in, and additions to, his notes to ensure a match between the two records, see Bilder, *Madison's Hand*, 226–29. In the Constitutional Convention and the ratification debates that followed participants often argued that the states in the American union had their own distinct interests that were sometimes incompatible or even conflicting. The most commonly identified conflict of interest was between the staple-producing planters, who dominated the southern states, and the merchant and shipowners, who were powerful in the northern states. This could be presented as a conflict between noncarrying and carrying states, in Hamilton's terms, or between slave and non–slave states, in Madison's terms. It appears that mention of this distinction was first made on June 29 and 30 to change the terms of debates from size to section. Madison's remark about the staples of the three large states made on June 28 is repeated by Yates, Farrand, *Records* I, 456. King's notes say: "of the small states being swallowed up by large ones. of combinations between Mass. Penn. & Virgin. no circumstance of Religion, Habits, manners, mode of thinking, course of Business, manufactures, commerce, or natural productions establishes a common interest between them exclusive of all the other States" (I, 458). In Madison's notes, the record of debates on June 29 appears on sheets of paper that Madison substituted for his original notes after the convention and Madison is alone among note takers to report Hamilton's remark. Yates, however, reported Madison saying on June 29 that "If there was real danger, I would give the smaller states the defensive weapons—But there is none from that quarter. The great danger to our general government *is the great southern and northern interests of the continent, being opposed to each other. Look to the votes in congress, and most of them stand divided by the geography of the country, not according to the size of the states*" (I, 476). This statement resembles the content of Madison's words from his June 30 speech as reported in Madison's notes. No other note taker referred to Madison's mention of a conflict of interest between slave and non–slave states on June 30. According to Bilder, the June 30 speech was part of the original notes and not a later substitution, see Bilder, *Madison's Hand*, 101. When Yates's notes were published in 1821 his account of Madison's June 29 speech, caused a stir. At this period of the convention, Madison and his allies attacked the proposal for equal state representation in the new congress by challenging the sovereignty of the states, describing them as "corporations" and "districts." Madison later replaced his original notes of his June 29 speech with a new version and there is reason to believe that he manipulated the record. In correspondence from the 1820s and 1830s about Yates's notes he claimed he had been

misrepresented by Yates, see James Madison to Joseph Gales, 26 Aug. 1821, Farrand, *Records* III, 446–47; Madison to J. C. Cabell, 2 Feb. 1829 (III, 477–78); Madison to Nicholas P. Trist, Dec. 1831 (III, 516–18); Madison to W.C. Rives, 21 Oct. 1833 (III, 521–24).

52. Farrand, *Records* I, 604 and 605. No note takers other than Madison recorded the debates of this day.

53. Farrand, *Records* II, 182–83.

54. Farrand, *Records* II, 307–308, 449, 450. On July 26 the Convention adjourned until August 6 when it reconvened to consider the report of the Committee of Detail. Bilder notes that from this point on, Madison took much less extensive notes compared to earlier in the convention. She argues that on August 21 Madison abandoned his practice of writing up his rough notes on the evening of the proceedings, or soon after, to which he had adhered up to this point. He may have continued to take rough notes, but he completed the account of the last few weeks of the convention only two or more *years* after the Convention rose, see Bilder, *Madison's Hand*, 121–37, 141–50, 179–89, 246–49, 261–62. The only other contemporary source from the later stages of the Convention is the sparse notes taken by James McHenry. This means that the record of the Convention from August 6 is particularly problematic and even more so the period from August 22.

55. Farrand, *Records* II, 307, 360, 363–64.

56. Farrand, *Records* II, 305–308, 359–65, 369–75, quotations at 364, 374.

57. Farrand, *Records* II, 396, 408, 414–17, 446, 449–53, quotations at 449–50, 453.

58. Farrand, *Records* I, 20; "Amendment to Share Expenses According to Population," April 18, 1783, *Documentary History of the Ratification of the Constitution* I, 148–50. On the South, slavery, and the Constitution, see Howard A. Ohline, "Republicanism and Slavery: Origins of the Three-Fifths Clause in the United States Constitution," *William and Mary Quarterly* 28, no. 4 (October 1971): 563–84; Staughton Lynd, *Class Conflict, Slavery, and the United States Constitution* (Indianapolis: Bobbs-Merrill, 1967), 135–213; Paul Finkelman, "Slavery, and the Constitutional Convention: Making a Covenant with Death," in *Beyond Confederation: Origins of the Constitution and American National Identity*, ed. Richard Beeman, Stephen Botein, and Edward C. Carter, II (Chapel Hill: University of North Carolina Press, 1987), 188–225; David Waldstreicher, *Slavery's Constitution: From Revolution to Ratification* (New York: Hill and Wang, 2009); and George W. Van Cleve, *A Slaveholders' Union: Slavery, Politics, and the Constitution in the Early American Republic* (Chicago: University Press of Chicago, 2010).

59. Farrand, *Records* I, 177, 178, 462. These are Madison's reports of speeches by Brearley, Paterson, and Gorham. Yates and King both report that David Brearley spoke of redrawing a map of the United States. Yates has Paterson saying "if a consolidated government must take place, then state distinctions must cease, or the states be equalized" (Farrand, *Records* I, 182, 183, 184). Yates notes records Gorham's remark about Massachusetts (Farrand, *Records*470). Bilder notes that Madison's advocacy for proportional representation "raised the threat of governance by Virginians." But she also notes that in the convention Madison wished to diminish the power of the Virginia *state government*, see Bilder *Madison's Hand*, 77–79.

60. Farrand, *Records* I, 343 and 467. No other note taker apart from Madison reported Sherman's and Gerry's words.

61. "Virginia Resolutions," in *Documentary History of the Ratification of the Constitution*, 1:245; "Resolutions of the Convention Recommending the Procedures for Ratification and for the Establishment of Government under the Constitution of the Confederation Congress, 17 September 1787" (318); "Proceedings of Congress on the Constitution" (322–42).

62. For the history of the ratification struggle, see *The Constitution and the States: The Role of the Original Thirteen in the Framing and Adoption of the Federal Constitution*, ed. Patrick T. Conley and John P. Kaminski (Madison: University of Wisconsin Press, 1988); *Ratifying the Constitution*, ed. Michael Allen Gillespie and Michael Lienesch (Lawrence: University Press of Kansas, 1989); Pauline Maier, *Ratification: The People Debate the Constitution 1787–1788* (New York: Simon & Schuster, 2010); Jürgen Heideking, *The Constitution before the Judgment Seat: The Prehistory and Ratification of the American Constitution, 1787–1791*, ed. John P. Kaminski and Richard Leffler (Charlottesville: University of Virginia Press, 2012).

63. The literature on the debate over ratification is vast. Some important works are Herbert J. Storing, *What the Antifederalists Were For: The Political Thought of the Opponents of*

the *Constitution* (Chicago: University of Chicago Press, 1981); Saul Cornell, *The Other Founders: Anti-Federalism and the Dissenting Tradition in America, 1788–1828* (Chapel Hill: University of North Carolina Press, 1999); Max M. Edling, *A Revolution in Favor of Government: Origins of the U.S. Constitution and the Making of the American State* (New York: Oxford University Press, 2003). A recent study of *The Federalist* is Max M. Edling, "'A Vigorous National Government': Alexander Hamilton on Security, War, and Revenue," in *The Cambridge Companion to The Federalist*, ed. Jack N. Rakove and Colleen Sheehan (New York: Cambridge University Press, 2020), 82–113.

64. James Madison, "Political Observations," April 20, 1795, *Papers of James Madison* XV, 558.
65. Kenneth R. Bowling, "'A Tub to the Whale': The Founding Fathers and Adoption of the Federal Bill of Rights." *Journal of the Early Republic* 8, no. 3 (November 1988): 223–51; Gerard N. Magliocca, *The Heart of the Constitution: How the Bill of Rights Became the Bill of Rights* (New York: Oxford University Press, 2018).
66. Madison to Edmund Randolph, June 15, 1789, *Papers of James Madison* XII, 219; Grayson to Patrick Henry 12 June 1789, quoted in Kenneth R. Bowling, *Politics in the First Congress, 1789–1791* (New York: Garland, 1990), 136.
67. Gerstle, *Liberty and Coercion: The Paradox of American Government from the Founding to the Present* (Princeton, NJ: Princeton University Press, 2015), 89–123, quotation at 93.

Chapter 3

1. "The Dissent of the Minority of the Convention," *Pennsylvania Packet*, December 18, 1787, in *Documentary History of the Ratification of the Constitution*, ed. Merrill Jensen, John P. Kaminski, and Gaspare J. Saladino, 34 vols. to date (Madison: Wisconsin Historical Society Press, 1976–), II: 629; "Federal Farmer, Letters to the Republican," [*Observations Leading to a Fair Examination of the System of Government Proposed by the Late Convention; and to Several Essential and Necessary Alterations in It. In a Number of Letters from the Federal Farmer to the Republican* (New York, 1787)], *Documentary History of the Ratification of the Constitution* XIV: 24; "The Address of the Seceding Assemblymen," [*An Address of the Subscribers Members of the late House of Representatives of the Commonwealth of Pennsylvania to their Constituents* (Philadelphia, 1787)] *Documentary History of the Ratification of the Constitution* II: 116; "Mason's Objections to the Constitution of Government formed by the Convention," *Documentary History of the Ratification of the Constitution* XIII, 348–51; "Elbridge Gerry to the Massachusetts General Court," *Massachusetts Centinel*, November 3, 1787, *Documentary History of the Ratification of the Constitution* XIII, 548–50; "Edmund Randolph and the Constitution," [*A Letter of His Excellency Edmund Randolph, Esquire, On the Federal Constitution* (Richmond?, 1787)], *Documentary History of the Ratification of the Constitution* XV, 122–34.
2. "Brutus I," *New York Journal*, October 18, 1787, *Documentary History of the Ratification of the Constitution* XIII, 413; "Dissent of the Minority," *Documentary History of the Ratification of the Constitution* II, 626, emphasis in the original.
3. "Address of the Seceding Assemblymen," *Documentary History of the Ratification of the Constitution* II, 116. There is a large literature on the Antifederalists, for some of the main interpretations see Jackson Turner Main, *The Anti-Federalists: Critics of the Constitution, 1781–1788* (Chapel Hill: University of North Carolina Press, 1961); Herbert J. Storing, *What the Antifederalists Were For: The Political Thought of the Opponents of the Constitution* (Chicago: University of Chicago Press, 1981); Gordon S. Wood, "Interest and Disinterestedness in the Making of the Constitution," in *Beyond Confederation: Origins of the Constitution and American National Identity*, ed. Richard Beeman, Stephen Botein, and Edward C. Carter II. (Chapel Hill: University of North Carolina Press, 1987), 69–109; Saul Cornell, *The Other Founders: Anti-Federalism and the Dissenting Tradition in America, 1788–1828* (Chapel Hill: University of North Carolina Press, 1999); Max M. Edling, *A Revolution in Favor of Government: The U.S. Constitution and the Making of the American State* (New York: Oxford University Press, 2003).
4. "Centinel I," *Independent Gazetteer*, October 5, 1787, *Documentary History of the Ratification of the Constitution* II, 164; "Brutus I," *Documentary History of the Ratification of the Constitution* XIII, 414; "Dissent of the Minority," *Documentary History of the Ratification of the Constitution*

II, 624. As can be seen, the dissenting minority was citing Article II of the Articles of Confederation.

5. "Federal Farmer, Letters to the Republican," *Documentary History of the Ratification of the Constitution* XIV, 24–25.

6. On the first ten amendments, see Kenneth R. Bowling, "'A Tub to the Whale': The Founding Fathers and Adoption of the Federal Bill of Rights." *Journal of the Early Republic* 8, no. 3 (1988): 223–51; Gerard N. Magliocca, *The Heart of the Constitution: How the Bill of Rights Became the Bill of Rights* (New York: Oxford University Press, 2018).

7. "James Wilson: Speech at a Public Meeting in Philadelphia 6 October," *Pennsylvania Herald,* October 9, 1787, *Documentary History of the Ratification of the Constitution* II, 167–68. The idea that the national government was a government of enumerated powers was of course not new but had been the accepted understanding of the national government also under the Articles of Confederation. What was new in Wilson's analysis was the claim that the national government under the Constitution was formed by a grant of power made directly by the people of the respective states and not through a compact between sovereign states.

8. "A Citizen of Philadelphia: Remarks on the Address of the Sixteen Members," [*Remarks on the Address of Sixteen Members of the Assembly of Pennsylvania, To Their Constituents, Dated September 29, 1787. With some Strictures on the Objections to the Constitution, Recommended by the Late Federal Convention, Humbly Offered to the Public* (Philadelphia, 1787)], *Documentary History of the Ratification of the Constitution* XIII, 301, emphasis in the original.

9. "A Citizen of Philadelphia: The Weakness of Brutus Exposed, 8 November," [*The Weakness of Brutus Exposed: or, some Remarks in Vindication of the Constitution Proposed by the Late Federal Convention, against the Objections and Gloomy Fears of that Writer* (Philadelphia, 1787)], *Documentary History of the Ratification of the Constitution* XIV, 66 (quotation), 71, emphasis in the original; "America," *New York Daily Advertiser, Documentary History of the Ratification of the Constitution* XV, 200, emphasis in the original.

10. Noah Webster, "Sketches of the Rise, Progress and Consequences of the Late Revolution," in *A Collection of Essays and Fugitiv* [*sic*] *Writings on Moral, Historical, Political and Literary Subjects* (Boston: I. Thomas and E.T. Andrews, 1790), 164; David Ramsay, *The History of the American Revolution,* 2 vols. (Philadelphia: R. Aitken & Son., 1789), I, 42. Webster's essay was originally serialized and published in newspapers in 1787–1789. Without attribution, Jedediah Morse lifted the quoted passage from Webster for his *American Geography, or, A View of the Present Situation of the United States of America* (London: John Stockdale, 1794), 244.

11. Declaration of Rights and Grievances, October 14, 1774, *Journals of the Continental Congress, 1774–1789,* ed. C. Ford Worthington , Gaillard Hunt, John Clement Fitzpatrick, Roscoe R. Hill, Kenneth E. Harris, and Steven D. Tilley, 34 vols. (Washington, DC: Library of Congress, 1904–1937), I, 68; Rules and Regulations, June, 30, 1775, *Journals of the Continental Congress* II, 111; The Twelve United Colonies, by Their Delegates in Congress, to the Inhabitants of Great Britain, July 8, 1775, *Journals of the Continental Congress* II, 168. The draft version of the Declaration of Rights and Grievances was even more clear about reserving internal police or "polity" to the respective colonies. The first draft resolution stated "That the power of making laws for ordering or regulating the internal polity of these Colonies, is, within the limits of each Colony, respectively and exclusively vested in the Provincial Legislature of such Colony; and that all statutes for ordering or regulating the internal polity of the said Colonies, or any of them, in any manner or in any case whatsoever, are illegal and void" (I, 67).

12. "The Virginia Petition to the King and Parliament, December 18, 1764: The Petition to the King," in *Prologue to Revolution: Sources and Documents on the Stamp Act Crisis, 1764–1766,* ed. Edmund S. Morgan (New York: Norton, 1973), 14; "Twelve United Colonies . . . to the Inhabitants of Great Britain," *Journals of the Continental Congress* II, 168. The colonists' view of the distribution of duties or powers between the imperial and colonial governments was echoed in British pamphlets. An anonymous member of London's Inner Temple conceded that when considered individually, every colony had "in what relates to their *internal Police,* a Right to make Laws, by their Representatives, on the same Principles, as the British Parliament, provided they are not repugnant to the Laws of their Mother Country." But "when considered as a *collective* Body of colonies" there were issues "respecting the *general good* of the *whole,* which

can only be regulated by the *Legislative Authority* of the Mother-Country," even if such regulation had local consequences. Among such "issues" were the regulation of commerce; the
militia; currency and payments; Indian affairs; naturalization; and defense. As students of the
Constitution will readily recognize, this list of legislative authority corresponds closely to the
powers that the states would invest in the federal government by the reform of the American
union in 1787, see J. M., of the Inner Temple, *The Legislative Authority of the British Parliament*
(London: W. Nicoll, 1766), 6, 8, and 9–10, emphasis in the original. The distinction made
between internal and external government in the writings and declarations of the colonial
opposition to the Stamp Act is discussed in Jack P. Greene, *The Constitutional Origins of the
American Revolution* (New York: Cambridge University Press, 2011), 79–88 and in Alison L.
LaCroix, *The Ideological Origins of American Federalism* (Cambridge, MA: Harvard University
Press, 2010), 30–67.

13. [Joseph Galloway] "A Plan of Proposed Union between Great Britain and the Colonies,"
Journals of the Continental Congress I, 49–51, quotation at 49; Jacob Green, *Observations: On
the Reconciliation of Great-Britain, and the Colonies; in which are Exhibited, Arguments For, and
Against, that Measure. By a Friend of American Liberty* (Philadelphia: Robert Bell, 1776), 35.

14. The right to regulate the internal police of the state was the third article in the Pennsylvania
and New Ireland declarations and the fourth article in the Delaware and Vermont declarations.
The wording of the second article of the Maryland and North Carolina declarations was "That,
the People of this state ought to have the sole and exclusive right of regulating the internal
police thereof." See *The Federal and State Constitutions, Colonial Charters, and Other Organic
Laws*, ed. Francis Newton Thorpe, 7 vols. (Washington, DC: Government Printing Office,
1909), III, 1686 (DE); V, 2787 (NC) and 3082 (PA); and VI, 3740 (VT); Max Farrand,
"The Delaware Declaration of Rights of 1776," American Historical Review 3, no. 4 (July
1898): 643; Alexander McNutt, *The Constitution and Frame of Government of... New Ireland*
(Philadelphia: R. Aitken, 1780), 8.

15. First and second printed forms of draft Articles of Confederation, July 12 and August 20,
1776, *Journals of the Continental Congress* V, 675; Thomas Burke to Richard Caswell, April
29, 1777, in *Letters of Delegates to Congress, 1774–1789*, ed. Paul H. Smith Gerard W. Gawalt,
Rosemary Fry Plakas, and Eugene R. Sheridan, 25 vols. (Washington, DC: Library of
Congress, 1976–2000), VI, 673; Act of Confederation of the United States of America,
November 15, 1777, in *Documentary History of the Ratification of the Constitution* I, 86–94. For
the proposals, see "Franklin's Articles of Confederation," *Journals of the Continental Congress*
II, 195–99; "Silas Deane's Proposal to Congress," *Letters of Delegates to Congress* II, 419–20;
Pennsylvania Evening Post, March 5, 1776. The drafting of the Articles of Confederation is
analyzed in Jack N. Rakove, *The Beginnings of National Politics: An Interpretive History of the
Continental Congress* (New York: Knopf, 1979), 135–91; and Merrill Jensen, *The Articles of
Confederation: An Interpretation of the Social-Constitutional History of the American Revolution,
1774–1781* (Madison: University of Wisconsin Press, 1940), 161–76. Hendrickson argues
that Burke's view reflected that of the majority in Congress and was therefore uncontroversial, see David C. Hendrickson, *Peace Pact: The Lost World of the American Founding*
(Lawrence: University Press of Kansas, 2003), 134.

16. "A Letter from Phocion to the Considerate Citizens of New York, [1–27 January 1784]," in
The Papers of Alexander Hamilton, ed. Harold C. Syrett (New York: Columbia University
Press, 1962), III, 483–97.

17. William Blackstone, *Commentaries on the laws of England.... By William Blackstone, Esq.
Vinerian Professor of Law, and solicitor general to her Majesty*, 4 vols. (Oxford: Clarendon
Press, 1765–1769), IV, 161–75, quotation at 162, emphasis in the original. Blackstone
discussed *police* in a chapter titled "Of Offences against the Public Health, and the Public
Police or Oeconomy." It formed part of his fourth book, on public wrongs. Elsewhere
in Europe, an early nineteenth-century Bavarian police criminal code proscribed
actions or inactions in a manner reminiscent of Blackstone, including the failure to
sweep the sidewalk on Sundays, blocking streets with carts, public drinking after 11 pm,
blaspheming, and endangering the life of a pregnant woman or her fetus, see Markus
Dirk Dubber, *The Police Power: Patriarchy and the Foundations of American Government*
(New York: Columbia University Press, 2005), 75–76. For the American context, see

William J. Novak, *The People's Welfare: Law and Regulation in Nineteenth-Century America* (Chapel Hill: University of North Carolina Press, 1996), 3–6; William J. Novak, "The American Law of Association: The Legal-Political Construction of Civil Society," *Studies in American Political Development* 15, no. 2 (Fall 2001): 179; William J. Novak, "A State of Legislatures," *Polity* 40, no. 3 (July 2008): 345–46. Mariana Valverde has identified three characteristics of police power-lists: "(1) the heterogeneity of governance objects; (2) the simultaneous institution of very broad categories ('public nuisance,' for example) that create swamps of discretion; and (3) the dearth of theoretical justification for selecting these particular objects," quoted in Dubber, *Police Power*, n27, 240. Christopher Tomlins notes that the "vocabulary of *police* [was] vital to the politics of the eighteenth century" but has since then been "largely lost" creating a problematic gap in the literature, see Christopher L. Tomlins, *Law, Labor, and Ideology in the Early American Republic* (New York: Cambridge University Press, 1993), 35–59, quotation at 36. For the literature on the American discourse on *police*, see in addition to the works by Tomlins, Novak, and Dubber already cited, Santiago Legarre, "The Historical Background of the Police Power," *Journal of Constitutional Law* 9, no. 3 (2007): 745–96; Christopher L. Tomlins, "The Supreme Sovereignty of the State: A Genealogy of Police in American Constitutional Law, from the Founding Era to *Lochner*," in *Police and the Liberal State*, ed. Markus D. Dubber and Mariana Valverde (Stanford, CA: Stanford University Press, 2008), 33–53; William J. Novak, "Police Power and the Hidden Transformation of the American State," in *Police and the Liberal State*, 54–73; Gary Gerstle, "The Resilient Power of the States across the Long Nineteenth Century: An Inquiry into a Pattern of American Governance," in *The Unsustainable American State*, ed. Lawrence Jacobs and Desmond King (New York, 2009), 61–87; John L. Brooke, "Patriarchal Magistrates, Associated Improvers, and Monitoring Militias: Visions of Self-Government in the Early American Republic, 1760–1840," in *State and Citizen: British America and the Early United States*, ed. Peter Thompson and Peter S. Onuf (Charlottesville: University of Virginia Press, 2013), 178–217.

18. Thomas Pownall, *Administration of the Colonies* (London: J. Dodsley and J. Walter, 1766, 3d ed.), 154 (currency); Jonas Hanway, *Letters on the Importance of the Rising Generation of the Laboring Part of Our Fellow-Subjects* (London: A. Millar and T. Cadell, 1767), 173 (poor relief); *First Annual Report of the Corporation Instituted for the Relief of the Poor* (Kilkenny: Edmund Finn, 1776), n. pag. (poor relief); *To the Inhabitants of Old England* (Exeter, 1779), 1; Henry Sacheverell Homer, *An Enquiry into the Means of Preserving and Improving the Publick Roads in This Kingdom* (Oxford: S. Parker, 1767) (roads); Thomas Mortimer, *The Elements of Commerce, Politics, and Finance* (London: S. Hooper et al., 1774), 71 (wages and contracts); Speech by Charles Mellish in House of Commons on October 27, 1775, and reported in *Parliamentary Register; or, History of the Proceedings and Debates of the House of Commons; ... and a List of the Acts*, 17 vols. (London, 1775–1780), III, 57 (hospitals, pine trees, hats, debts, and naturalization); Caroline Mathilde, *Memoirs of an Unfortunate Queen* (London: J. Bew, 1776), 58 (censorship). *A Copy of a Remonstrance, of the Council of the State of Vermont, against the Resolution of Congress of the 5th of December Last* (Hartford, CT: Hudson and Goodwin, 1783).

19. *Pennsylvania Mercury, and Universal Advertiser*, January 7, 1785 (China); *Thomas's Massachusetts Spy: Or, The Worcester Gazette*, March 3, 1785 (Aztecs), an extract from William Robertson's multivolume *History of America* (1777); *The Columbian Herald or the Patriotic Courier of North-America*, September 28, 1785 (North America); *Newport Herald*, April 26, 1787 (Ha-Tien), a translated extract from Pierre Poivre, *Voyages d'un philosophe, ou observations sur les moeurs & les arts des peuples de l'Afrique, de l'Asie et de l'Amérique* (1769); *The New-Jersey Journal, and Political Intelligencer*, October 10, 1787 (Louis XIII); *Pennsylvania Journal*, September 28, 1785 (Rotterdam); *The Pennsylvania Packet, and Daily Advertiser*, November 17, 1785 ("property and the person"); *Pennsylvania Evening Herald and the American Monitor*, May 27, 1786 (Dublin); *The Pennsylvania Packet, and Daily Advertiser*, June 1, 1786 (Dublin); *The Daily Advertiser; Political, Historical, and Commercial*, July 18, 1786 (Philadelphia); *The Charleston Morning Post and Daily Advertiser*, April 11, 1787 (Charleston); *The Columbian Herald or the Independent Courier of North-America*, August 28, 1788 (Paris police force); *Independent Journal*, November 29, 1788 (Paris police force); *The Independent Ledger and the American Advertiser*, December 13, 1784 (Boston); *Massachusetts Centinel*, December

18, 1784 (Boston); *The Pennsylvania Packet, and Daily Advertiser*, November 17, 1785 (Philadelphia); *The Independent Gazeteer*, June 6, 1787 (Philadelphia).

20. *The Massachusetts Gazette*, April 27, 1787 ("boys"); *Federal Gazette and Philadelphia Daily Advertiser*, August 10, 1791 (watermelon rinds).

21. *The Pennsylvania Packet, and Daily Advertiser*, November, 17, 1785; *Pennsylvania Packet, and Daily Advertiser*, 8 September 1786; *The Pennsylvania Packet, and Daily Advertiser*, June, 7, 1787; *The Columbian Herald or the Patriotic Courier of North America*, July 26, 1787; *The Daily Advertiser*, January 22, 1788 (repackaging of meat); *Pennsylvania Gazette*, September 23, 1789 ("vagrants, beggars" and "nuisances, obstructions"). A spirited account of the mingling of people in the contracted space of the City of Philadelphia is provided by Billy G. Smith and Michelle Maskiell, "A *Flâneur* in Philly: Class, Gender, Race, and All That Jazz," *Early American Studies* 13, no. 3 (Summer 2015): 512–43.

22. *The Continental Journal, and Weekly Advertiser*, March 20, 1783 (provisions); *The Freeman's Journal; or, The North-American Intelligencer*, June 2, 1790 ("the first object"; promote manufactures); *Thomas's Massachusetts Spy: Or, The Worcester Gazette*, June 9, 1785 ("system of internal policy"), an extract from Robertson's *History of America*; *Pennsylvania Journal*, September 28, 1785 ("rasp houses"); *The Independent Gazetteer*, August 14, 1787 ("take away"); *The Independent Ledger and the American Advertiser*, March 27, 1786 ("disturb their internal police"); *Thomas's Massachusetts Spy: Or, The Worcester Gazette*, March 3, 1785 ("refinement of policy"), and extract from Robertson's *History of America*.

23. *OED* s.v. "Police" definitions 3a, 3c, and 5a. British eighteenth-century use of the term *police* appear in both narrowly focused discussions about public order, especially in cities, and in broader debates about political economy. Magistrates and social reformers such as Henry and John Fielding, Jonas Hanway, Edward Sayer, Henry Zouch, and Patrick Colquhoun wrote extensively on the related issues of poverty, idleness, and crime. Operating with a concept of *police* very similar to the French idea of city regulation they wrote about London although other writers contributed occasional pamphlets and books on other rapidly growing cities in the British Isles. With the exception of the Fieldings and Hanway's first pamphlet, these works date from the two final decades of the century when debate on the police of London had achieved an urgency in the aftermath of the Gordon Riots in 1780. Henry Fielding and Colquhoun created the precursors of the Metropolitan Police (1829) and they were instrumental in popularizing the understanding of police as "[t]he civil force of a state responsible for maintaining public order and enforcing the law, including preventing and detecting crime," which is by far the most common use of the term today. Fielding created the so-called Bow Street Runners, operating in Westminster and beyond, and Colquhoun the Marine Police Force, which patrolled the River Thames. John Fielding, *An Account of the Origin and Effects of a Police Set on Foot by His Grace the Duke of Newcastle in the Year 1753* (London: A. Millar, 1758); Jonas Hanway, *Observations on the Causes of the Dissoluteness which Reigns among the Lower Classes of the People . . . With a Proposal for New Regulating of Bridewell, in Order to Render it of Important Service to the Police of London . . .* (London: J and F Rivington, 1772); Jonas Hanway, *The Defects of Police the Cause of Immorality, and the Continual Robberies Committed, Particularly in and about the Metropolis: With Various Proposals for Preventing Hanging and Transportation: Llikewise [sic] for the Establishment of Several Plans of Police on a Permanent Basis . . .* (London: J. Dodsley et al., 1775); Jonas Hanway, *The Citizen's Monitor: Shewing the Necessity of a Salutary Police, Executed by Resolute and Judicious Magistrates . . .* (London: Dodsley et al., 1780); Jonas Hanway, *Reflections on Mr. Hanway's Report to the General Court of the Marine Society . . . Proving the Necessity of a Peace Establishment for Instructing the Poor and Distressed Boys Who are the Objects of It . . . The Design Being Equally Practicable and Correspondent with the General Wishes of the People for a Reform of our Police, the Promotion of True Piety, and the Most Useful Industry; With the Addition of Learning the Duty of an Able Mariner, and a Worthy Man* (London: s.n., 1785); Thomas Gilbert, *Plan for the Better Relief and Employment of the Poor; for Enforcing and Amending the Laws Respecting Houses of Correction, and Vagrants; and for Improving the Police of This Country . . .* (London: G. Wilkie, 1781); Thomas Gilbert, *A Plan of Police: Exhibiting the Causes of the Present Increase of the Poor, and Proposing a Mode for Their Future More Effectual Relief and Support* (London: s.n., 1781); Thomas Gilbert., *A Bill Intended to Be Offered to Parliament, for the Better Relief and Employment of the Poor, and for the*

Improvement of the Police of This Country (Manchester, UK: Harrop, 1786); Edward Sayer, *Observations on the Police or Civil Government of Westminster, with a Proposal for a Reform* (London: J. Debrett, 1784); William Bizard, *Desultory Reflections on Police: With an Essay on the Means of Preventing Crimes and Amending Criminals* (London: Baker and Galabin, 1785); George Barrett, *An Essay towards Establishing a System of Police . . . Consisting of Propositions for the Effectual and Immediate Suppression of Vagrancy, Thefts, Burglaries, Swindling, and other Enormities; Also, for the Future better Discipline, Instruction, Provision, and Employment of our Numerous Poor . . .* (London: H. Reynell, 1786); Henry Zouch, *A Few Words in Behalf of the Poor, being Remarks upon a Plan proposed by Mr. Gilbert, for Improving the Police of this Country* (London: G. Robinson, 1782); Henry Zouch, *Hints Respecting the Public Police* (London: John Stockdale, 1786); Anon., *Some Hints towards a Revisal of the Penal Laws, the Better Regulating the Police, and the Necessity of Enforcing the Execution of Justice . . . By a magistrate* (London: J. Debrett, 1787); William Godschall, *A General Plan of Parochial and Provincial Police* (London: T. Payne and Son, 1787); Patrick Colquhuon, *A Treatise on the Police of the Metropolis . . .* (London: H. Fry, 1796); Patrick Colquhuon, *A General View of the National Police System, Recommended by the Select Committee of Finance to the House of Commons . . .* (London: H. Baldwin and Son, 1799); Patrick Colquhuon, *The State of Indigence, and the Situation of the Casual Poor in the Metropolis, Explained; With Reasons Assigned Why the Prevailing System, with Respect to this Unfortunate Class of the Community, Contributes . . . to the Increase and Multiplication of Crimes: with Suggestions, Shewing the Necessity and Utility of an Establishment of Pauper Police . . .* (London: H. Baldwin and Son, 1799); Patrick Colquhuon, *A Treatise on the Commerce and Police of the River Thames* (London: Joseph Mawman, 1800); Anon., *Cursory Remarks on the Police. By a Magistrate* (London: P. Elmsly, 1797); William Bleamire, *Remarks on the Poor Laws, and the Maintenance of the Poor* (London: J. Richardson, 1800). Occasional other works addressed the police of provincial cities, John Ferriar, *To the Committee for the Regulation of the Police, in the Towns of Manchester and Salford* (Manchester, UK: s.n., 1792); James Wallace, *A General and Descriptive History of the Ancient and Present State, of the Town of Liverpool, Comprising, A Review Of Its Government, Police, Antiquities, And Modern Improvements . . .* (Liverpool: R. Phillips, 1795); Alexander Park, *Abstract of an Act for Establishing and Regulating the Police of the City of Glasgow, and Other Purposes* (Glasgow: James Mundell, 1800). See generally F. M. Dodsworth, "The Idea of Police in Eighteenth-Century England: Discipline, Reformation, Superintendence, c. 1780–1800," *Journal of the History of Ideas* 69, no. 4 (October 2008): 583–604.

24. Adam Smith, "Lectures on Jurisprudence: Report of 1762–3," in Smith, *Lectures on Jurisprudence*, ed. R. L. Meek, D. D. Raphael, and P. G. Stein (Oxford: Oxford University Press, 1978), 5. Tomlins also identifies German *Polizeiwissenschaft* and French city regulation as two important strands of police thinking, see Tomlins, *Law, Labor, and Ideology*, 39–43. The only social theorist of note to have written about police is Michel Foucault. In lectures he delivered at the Collège de France in 1977–1978, Foucault attempted to fit police into early modern ideas of governance. Although a mere sketch, this is the most insightful treatment of the concept of *police* to date. Foucault notes that from "the seventeenth century 'police' begins to refer to the set of means by which the state's forces can be increased while preserving the state in good order. In other words, police will be the calculation and technique that will make it possible to establish a mobile, yet stable and controllable relationship between the state's internal order and the development of its forces." Generalizing from an early seventeenth-century treatise by Louis Turquet de Mayerne, Foucault notes that police represented a novel fourth field of government activity alongside justice, the military, and finance. In Turquet de Mayerne, police legislation and regulation were responsible for education; the poor, public health, and disaster relief; markets and manufactures; landed property, including conveyance, price, and inheritance; and roads, rivers, public buildings, and forests. In his own summary, Foucault lists the five objects of police as population numbers, necessities of life, health, work, and the circulation of goods and people. Michel Foucault, *Security, Territory, Population: Lectures at the Collège de France 1977–1978*, ed. Michel Senellart (New York: Palgrave Macmillan, 2007), 311–61, quotation at 313.

25. Cesare Birignani, "The Police and the City: Paris, 1660–1750" (PhD diss., Columbia University, 2013), 195–328; Foucault, *Security, Territory, Population*, 334–36; *Encyclopédie*

ou Dictionnaire raisonné des sciences, des arts et des métiers (Paris, 1751–1772), s.v. "sauvages." Foucault argues that a key aim of police was to ensure not only that the people of a state lived, but that they *lived well*, thus drawing attention to its role in creating and maintaining civilized, as distinct from primitive, societies, see Foucault, *Security, Population, Territory*, 326–28, 338–39.

26. Samuel Johnson, *A Dictionary of the English Language*, 2 vols. (London: W. Strahan, 1755), II, s.v. "Police"; Noah Webster, *American Dictionary of the English Language*, 2 vols. (New Haven, CT: Hezekiah Howe, 1828), II, s.v. "Police"; Keith Tribe, "Cameralism and the Sciences of the State," in *The Cambridge History of Eighteenth-Century Political Thought*, ed. Mark Goldie and Robert Wokler (Cambridge: Cambridge University Press, 2006), 525–46. Justi's *Grundsätze der Policey-Wissenschaft* (1756), quoted at 541. See also Marc Raeff, "The Well-Ordered Police State and the Development of Modernity in Seventeenth- and Eighteenth-Century Europe: An Attempt at a Comparative Approach," *American Historical Review* 80, no. 5 (December 1975): 1221–43.

27. Jean-Jacques Burlamaqui, *The Principles of Natural and Politic Law*, ed. Petter Korkman (Indianapolis: Liberty Fund, 2006), vol. II, pt. I, ch. I, §xv, 275; Emer de Vattel, *The Law of Nations, Or, Principles of the Law of Nature, Applied to the Conduct and Affairs of Nations and Sovereigns*, ed. Richard Whatmore and Béla Kapossy (Indianapolis: Liberty Fund, 2008), bk I, ch. VI–XIII, 126–97, quotation at 193–94.

28. Malachy Postlethwayt, *Britain's Commercial Interest Explained and Improved; in a Series of Dissertations on Several Important Branches of Her Trade and Police*, 2 vols. (London: D. Browne, 1757); Sir James Steuart, *An Inquiry into the Principles of Political Oeconomy: Being an Essay on the Science of Domestic Policy in Free Nations* (London: A. Millar and T. Cadell, 1767), quotation at xiv–xv; Blackstone, *Commentaries on the Laws of England* I, 264. Postlethwayt based his *Universal Dictionary of Trade and Commerce* (1751–1755) on Richard Cantillion's *Essai sur la nature du commerce en géneral* (1755), which circulated widely in manuscript before its publication, see Terence Hutchinson, *Before Adam Smith: The Emergence of Political Economy, 1662–1776* (Oxford: Blackwell, 1988), 241–44. Other British eighteenth-century titles dealing with police in this sense were Patrick Lindsay, *The Interest of Scotland Considered, with Regard to its Police in Imploying of the Poor, its Agriculture, its Trade, its Manufactures, and Fisheries* (Edinburgh: R. Fleming, 1733); William Mildmay, *The Laws and Policy of England, Relating to Trade, Examined by the Maxims and Principles of Trade in General; and by the Laws and Policy of other Trading Nations* (London: T. Harrison, 1765); Société oeconomique de Berne, *Essays on the Spirit of Legislation, in the Encouragement of Agriculture, Population, Manufactures, and Commerce. Containing Observations on the Political Systems at Present Pursued in Various Countries of Europe, for the Advancement of Those Essential Interests. Interspersed with Various Remarks on the Practice of Agriculture. Societies of Agriculture. Rewards. Bounties. The Police. Luxury. Industry. Machines. Exportation. Taxes. Inoculation. Marriage. Naturalization, &c.* (London: W. Nicoll, 1772); Matthew Peters, *Agricultura: Or the Good Husbandman, being a Tract of Antient and Modern Experimental Observations on the Green Vegetable System. Interspersed with Exemplary Remarks on the Police of other Nations: To Promote Industry, Self-Love, and Public Good, by Reducing Forests, Chaces, and Heaths into Farms. Together with some Observations on the large Exports that Must Unavoidably Arise from Thence, as Well as the Increase of Population. Depopulation Considered. Tables Calculated for the Use and Ease of the Good Husbandman, for Enclosing Land, Degrees in Strength of Various Food for Cattle, and Strength of Dungs, &c. With Many Interesting Instructions, in Order to Stimulate Industry, and Accumulate Wealth* (London: W. Flexney, 1776); David Loch, *Essays on the Trade, Commerce, Manufactures, and Fisheries of Scotland; Containing, Remarks on the Situation of most of the Sea-Ports; the Number of Shipping Employed; their Tonnage: Strictures on the Principal Inland Towns; the Different Branches of Trade and Commerce Carried On; and the Various Improvements Made in Each: Hints and Observations on the Constitutional Police* (Edinburgh: Walter and Thomas Ruddiman, 1778). Interestingly, the use of the term appears to trail off at the point in time when "police" came to be more used in discourses about law and order.

29. Smith, "Lectures on Jurisprudence: Report of 1762-3, in *Lectures on Jurisprudence*, contents page (n.p.), 5–7; Millar quoted in R. L. Meek, D. D. Raphael, and P. G. Stein, "Introduction," in *Lectures on Jurisprudence*, 3. Compare Foucault's discussion of Turquot de Mayerne's

division of government activity into justice, finance, the military, and police, see Foucault, *Security, Territory, Population*, 319–21, 339–41.

30. Smith, "Lectures of Jurisprudence: Report of 1762-3," in *Lectures on Jurisprudence*, 5-6 ("system," "internal"), 331 ("cleanlyness"); "Lectures on Jurisprudence: Report dated 1766," in *Lectures on Jurisprudence*, 398, 486–87 ("too mean")); Jakob Friedrich von Bielfeld, *Institutions politiques* (The Hague: P. Gosse, 1760), 34, emphasis in the original.

31. "Report of 1762-3" in *Lectures on Jurisprudence*, 331–94; "Report dated 1766," in *Lectures on Jurisprudence*, 486–541. In vol. II, book V, ch. I, pt. III of the *Wealth of Nations*, Smith discusses expenditures on public works and public institutions that facilitate commerce and provide for the education of youth and the general population. Here he lists items such as roads, bridges, canals, harbors, coinage, and street lightning. He takes a critical view of trading companies and monopolies and a favorable view of widespread education, Adam Smith, *An Inquiry into the Nature and Causes of the Wealth of Nations*, ed. R. H. Campbell and A. S. Skinner, 2 vols. (Oxford: Oxford University Press, 1976), II, 723–814.

32. Ian K. Steele, *The English Atlantic, 1675–1740: An Exploration of Communication and Community* (New York: Oxford University Press, 1986); The Atlantic exchange of information arose on the back of an integrated Atlantic economy, for which see D. W. Meinig, *The Shaping of America: A Geographic Perspective on 500 Years of History*. Vol. I: *Atlantic America, 1492–1800* (New Haven, CT: Yale University Press, 1986), 3–254; Bernard Bailyn, *Atlantic History: Concepts and Contours* (Cambridge, MA: Harvard University Press, 2005), 81–111. Dubber, *Police Power*, 81–82, makes a similar argument about the transfer of knowledge about the concept of *police* to America.

33. For the literature on the Constitutional Convention, see the references cited in chapter 2, n34.

34. James Madison to George Washington, 16 April 1787, in *Papers of James Madison* ed. William T. Hutchinson and William M. E. Rachal 17 vols. (Chicago: University of Chicago Press, VA, 1962–1991), IX, 382–87. See also Madison to Thomas Jefferson, 19 March 1787, *Papers of James Madison* IX, 317–22; Madison to Edmund Randolph, 8 April 1787, *Papers of James Madison* IX, 368–71.

35. Madison to Jefferson, 24 October 1787, *Papers of James Madison* X, 205–20, quotation at 212; Max Farrand, ed., *The Records of the Federal Convention of 1787*, 4 vols. (New Haven, CT: Yale University Press, 1966), I, 30 ("merely federal"), 377, 449 ("counties"). Looking back at the Convention almost fifty years later, Madison presented unjust state legislation as a problem of both federalism and individual rights, noticing that "In the internal administration of the States a violation of Contract had become familiar in the form of depreciated paper made a legal tender, of property substituted for money, of Instalment laws, and of the occlusions of the Courts of Justice; although evident that all such interferences affected the rights of other States, Relatively creditor, as well as Citizens Creditors within the State," James Madison, *Notes of Debates in the Federal Convention of 1787 Reported by James Madison*, ed. Adrienne Koch (Athens, OH: Ohio University Press, 1966), 88–89. The problematic nature of Madison's notes from the Constitutional Convention is discussed in Mary Sarah Bilder, *Madison's Hand: Revising the Constitutional Convention* (Cambridge, MA: Harvard University Press, 2015).

36. Farrand, *Records* II, 56–57; Cathy D. Matson and Peter S. Onuf, *A Union of Interests: Political and Economic Thought in Revolutionary America* (Lawrence: University Press of Kansas, 1990), 101–23. No note taker apart from Madison recorded this debate.

37. Farrand, *Records* I, 21. On Madison's veto, see Charles F. Hobson, "The Negative on State Laws: James Madison, the Constitution, and the Crisis of Republican Government," *William and Mary Quarterly* 36, no. 2 (April 1979): 215–35.

38. Farrand, *Records* I, 162, 165 (Williamson and Gerry), 169, 171; *Supplement to Max Farrand's The Records of the Federal Convention of 1787*, ed. James H. Hutson (New Haven, CT: Yale University Press, 1987), 60 ("State Governments"), 61 ("precise Line"); Bilder, *Madison's Hand*, 76–77. The accounts of the speeches by other note takers are similar to Madison's in content. King's notes report that Williamson said "internal *policy*," rather than *police*, see Farrand, *Records* I, 171.

39. Farrand, *Records* II, 21, 26, emphasis added. No note taker apart from Madison reported this debate.

40. Farrand, *Records* II, 21, 26–27.

41. Farrand, *Records* II, 21–22, 27–28.

42. Farrand, *Records* II, 22, 28–29, 382, 390–91, quotation at 391. No note taker apart from Madison reported the August 23 debate. For Martin's later explanation for his motion, see Farrand, *Records* III, 286–87. See also the discussion in Jonathan Gienapp, *The Second Creation: Fixing the American Constitution in the Founding Era* (Cambridge, MA: Belknap Press, 2018), 70.

43. Farrand, *Records* II, 181–82, 321–22, 324–26, 334–37, 340–42; Bilder, *Madison's Hand*, 130–37. On the problematic nature of the records from the Convention in August and September, see chapter 2, n50.

44. For a discussion of the Constitution relative to foreign and fiscal affairs, see David M. Golove and Daniel J. Hulsebosch, "A Civilized Nation: The Early American Constitution, the Law of Nations, and the Pursuit of International Recognition," *New York University Law Review* 85, no. 4 (2010): 932–1066; Leonard J. Sadosky, *Revolutionary Negotiations: Indians, Empires, and Diplomats in the Founding of America* (Charlottesville: University of Virginia Press, 2009); Max M. Edling, *A Hercules in the Cradle: War, Money, and the American State, 1783–1867* (Chicago: University of Chicago Press, 2014), 17–49.

45. Farrand, *Records* II, 335–36, 342–44.

46. *Documentary History of the First Federal Congress of the United States of America, March 4, 1789–March 3, 1791*, ed. Linda Grant DePauw, 20 vols. (Baltimore: Johns Hopkins University Press, 1972–2012), X, 725 ("territorial possessions"), 743 ("by enumerating"), 759. On the creation of the Department of the Interior, see Henry Barrett Learned, "The Establishment of the Secretaryship of the Interior," *American Historical Review* 16, no. 4 (July 1911): 751–73.

47. "Federalist 45," in *The Federalist*, ed. Jacob E. Cooke (Middletown, CT: Wesleyan University Press, 1961), 314. Article IX of the Articles of Confederation contains the following passage: "The united states in congress assembled shall also have the sole and exclusive right and power of regulating the alloy and value of coin struck by their own authority or by that of the respective states—fixing the standard of weights and measures throughout the united states—regulating the trade and managing all affairs with the Indians, not members of any of the states, provided that the legislative right of any state within its own limits be not infringed or violated—establishing and regulating post-offices from one state to another, throughout all the united states, and exacting such postage on the papers passing thro' the same as may be requisite to defray the expenses of the said office," *Documentary History of the Ratification of the Constitution* I, 91. Article IX also says that Congress has "sole and exclusive right and power" of "entering into treaties and alliances, provided that no treaty of commerce shall be made whereby the legislative power of the respective states shall be restrained from imposing such imposts and duties on foreigners, as their own people are subjected to, or from prohibiting the exportation or importation of any species of goods or commodities whatsoever" (89).

48. James Madison, "Vices of the Political System of the United States," *Papers of James Madison* IX, 348–57, "Federalist 44," in *Federalist*, ed. Cooke, 301; Sherman and Ellsworth to Huntington 26 September 1787, Farrand, *Records* III, 100. For this interpretation of the restrictions of the police powers of the states I am indebted to Daniel J. Hulseboch, "Being Seen Like a State: How Americans (and Britons) Built the Constitutional Infrastructure of a Developing Nation," *William and Mary Law Review* 59, no. 4 (2018): 1239–1319. In the ratification debate, Antifederalist critique of the paper money ban was muted, see George Van Cleve, "The Antifederalists' Toughest Challenge: Paper Money, Debt Relief, and the Ratification of the Constitution," *Journal of the Early Republic* 34, no. 4 (Winter 2014): 529–60.

49. Farrand, *Records* II, 322, 565–79, 615.

50. Farrand, *Records* II, 615–16; Farrand, *Records* III, 362 (Sherman). Bilder has shown that Madison completed the section of his notes that cover proceedings from August 22 several years after the convention rose. In doing so, Madison used the official journal of the convention and, probably, his rough notes that are now lost. She notes the particular problems facing Madison when trying to write up the proceedings from September 6 and onward when the journal becomes spotty and confused, Bilder, *Madison's Hand* 184–89, 261–62. On the convention journal, see Mary Sarah Bilder, "How Bad Were the Official Records of the Federal Convention?," *George Washington Law Review* 80, no. 6 (2012): 1620–82. McHenry's brief

notes from 14 September records the three motions on canals, incorporation, and the university, and the opposition to them, see Farrand, *Records* II, 620. The question of Congress's power of incorporation became controversial when Congress debated the constitutionality of chartering the Bank of the United States in 1791. Jefferson's report on the constitutionality of the bank evidently drew on Madison's notes and in the exchanges in Congress, several congressmen turned to their recollection of the debate in the Constitutional Convention. For later recollections, see James Madison in the House of Representatives, February 2, 1791, Farrand, *Records* III, 362; Oliver Ellsworth in the House of Representatives, February 7, 1791, Farrand, *Records* III, 362–63; Thomas Jefferson on the constitutionality of the national bank, Farrand, *Records* III, 363; Alexander Hamilton on the constitutionality of a national bank, Farrand, *Records* III, 363; Thomas Jefferson's *Anas*, 11 March 1798, Farrand, *Records* III, 375; James Madison to Reynolds Chapman, January 6, 1831, Farrand, *Records* III, 495. Bilder and Gienapp discuss the use of the debates in the Constitutional convention in the later interpretation of the Constitution and the constitutionality of the Bank, see Bilder, *Madison's Hand*, 205–208; Gienapp, *Second Creation*, 232–38.

51. "Brutus I," *Documentary History of the Ratification of the Constitution* XIII, 415–16; Antoine de Laforêt to Comte de Montmorin, 28 September 1787, *Documentary History of the Ratification of the Constitution* XIII, 259 Louis Guillaume Otto to Comte de Montmorin, 20 October 1787, *Documentary History of the Ratification of the Constitution* XIII, 424–25.

52. Roger Sherman to ——, December 8, 1787, in *Supplement to Max Farrand*, ed. Hutson, 288; "Federalist 17," in *Federalist*, ed. Cooke, 105–106.

53. "A Native of Virginia, Observations on the Proposed Plan of Federal Government" [*Observations on the Proposed Plan of Federal Government. With an Attempt to Answer Some of the Principal Objections that Have Been Made to It* (1788)], *Documentary History of the Ratification of the Constitution* IX, 692.

54. "Federal Farmer, Letters to the Republican," *Documentary History of the Ratification of the Constitution* XIV, 35.

55. A Freeman I, *Pennsylvania Gazette*, 23 January 1788, *Documentary History of the Ratification of the Constitution* XV, 453n; A Freeman II, *Pennsylvania Gazette* 30 January 1788, *Documentary History of the Ratification of the Constitution* XV, 508–10, quotation at 510.

56. Novak, *People's Welfare*, quotations at 1 and 238; Dubber, *Police Power*, 81–153; Gerstle, "Resilient Power of the States," 61–87; Gerstle, *Liberty and Coercion*, 55–86; Brian Phillips Murphy, *Building the Empire State: Political Economy in the Early Republic* (Philadelphia: University of Pennsylvania Press, 2015).

Chapter 4

1. Charlene Bangs Bickford and Kenneth Bowling, *Birth of the Nation: The First Federal Congress 1789–1791* (Lanham, MD: Madison House, 1989), 9–13.

2. George Washington, First Inaugural Address to Congress, in *A Compilation of the Messages and Papers of the Presidents, 1789–1797*, ed. James D. Richardson, 10 vols. (New York: Bureau of National Literature, 1897), I, 44–45.

3. Bickford and Bowling, *Birth of the Nation*, 5, 107–10, Iredell and Osgood cited at 5; Kenneth Bowling, *Politics in the First Congress, 1789–1791* (New York: Garland, 1990), 16–17; Gordon S. Wood, *Empire of Liberty: A History of the Early Republic, 1789–1815* (New York: Oxford University Press, 2009), 57–58.

4. "Confederation Congress Calls the Constitutional Convention," in *The Documentary History of the Ratification of the Constitution*, ed. Merrill Jensen, John P. Kaminiski, and Gaspare J. Saladino, eds., 34 vols. to date (Madison: State Historical Society of Wisconsin, 1976–), I, 187; "The President of the Convention to the President of Congress" *Documentary History of the Ratification of the Constitution* I, 305. On attempts to reform the Articles of Confederation, see Merrill Jensen, *The New Nation: A History of the United States during the Confederation, 1781–1789* (New York: Knopf, 1950); Jack N. Rakove, *The Beginnings of National Politics: An Interpretive History of the Continental Congress* (New York: Knopf, 1979); and George W. Van Cleve, *We Have Not a Government: The Articles of Confederation and the Road to the Constitution* (Chicago: University of Chicago Press, 2017).

5. "From George Washington to Lafayette, January 29, 1789," *The Papers of George Washington: Presidential Series*, ed. Dorothy Twohig, 19 vols. to date (Charlottesville: University Press of Virginia, 1987–), I, 262–64; "From James Madison to Edmund Pendleton, April 8, 1789," *The Papers of James Madison*, ed. Charles F. Hobson and Robert A. Rutland, 17 vols. (Charlottesville: University Press of Virginia, 1979), XII, 51–52; "Import and Tonnage Duties, [8 April] 1789," *Papers of James Madison* XII, 64–66; Debates in the House of Representatives, April 8 and 25, 1789, in *Documentary History of the First Federal Congress of the United States of America, March 4, 1789–March 3, 1791*, ed. Linda Grant DePauw, 20 vols. (Baltimore: Johns Hopkins University Press, 1972–2012), X, 4–5, 313–14.

6. Bowling, *Politics in the First Congress* and Bickford and Bowling, *Birth of the Nation* are the major treatments of the first Congress. See also *The House and Senate in the 1790s: Petitioning, Lobbying, and Institutional Development*, ed. Kenneth R. Bowling and Donald R. Kennon (Athens: Ohio University Press, 2002). David P. Currie and Jonathan Gienapp have written about the interpretation and development of constitutional law in the first congresses, see Currie, *The Constitution in Congress: The Federalist Period, 1789–1801* (Chicago: University of Chicago Press, 1997) and Gienapp, *The Second Creation: Fixing the American Constitution in the Founding Era* (Cambridge, MA: Belknap Press, 2018). Overviews of the Federalist era include Stanley Elkins and Eric McKitrick, *The Age of Federalism: The Early American Republic, 1788–1800* (New York: Oxford University Press, 1993); James Roger Sharp, *American Politics in the Early Republic: The New Nation in Crisis* (New Haven, CT: Yale University Press, 1993); and Wood, *Empire of Liberty*, 53–208. On the Bill of Rights, see Kenneth R. Bowling, "'A Tub to the Whale': The Founding Fathers and Adoption of the Federal Bill of Rights," *Journal of the Early Republic* 8, no. 3 (Fall 1988): 223–51; on the reform of the debt, Max M. Edling, *A Hercules in the Cradle: War, Money, and the American State, 1783–1867* (Chicago: University of Chicago Press, 2014), 81–107; on the location of the capital, Jacob E. Cooke, "The Compromise of 1790," *William and Mary Quarterly* 27, no. 4 (October 1970): 523–45; Kenneth R. Bowling with a rebuttal by Jacob E. Cooke, "Dinner at Jefferson's: A Note on Jacob E. Cooke's 'The Compromise of 1790,'" *William and Mary Quarterly* 28, no. 4 (October 1971): 629–48. The literature on party formation in the early Congress is substantial, e.g., Noble E. Cunningham, *The Jeffersonian Republicans: The Formation of Party Organization, 1789–1801* (Chapel Hill: University of North Carolina Press, 1957); Norman K. Risjord, *The Early American Party System* (New York: Harper & Row, 1969); Rudolph M. Bell, *Party and Faction in American Politics: The House of Representatives, 1789–1801* (Westport, CT: Greenwood Press, 1973); John F. Hoadley, *Origins of American Political Parties, 1789–1803* (Lexington: University Press of Kentucky, 1986); John H. Aldrich and Ruth W. Grant, "The Antifederalists, the First Congress, and the First Parties," *Journal of Politics* 55, no. 2 (May 1993): 295–326; John H. Aldrich, *Why Parties? A Second Look* (Chicago: University of Chicago Press, 2011, 2nd ed.).

7. North Carolina and Rhode Island initially rejected the Constitution and joined the Union only in 1789 and 1790, respectively. Vermont joined the Union in 1791, Kentucky in 1792, and Tennessee in 1796.

8. William J. Novak, "A State of Legislatures," *Polity* 40, no. 3 (July 2008): 342; Julian Hoppit, "Patterns of Parliamentary Legislation, 1660–1800," *The Historical Journal* 31, no. 1 (March 1996): 116, 118. Julian Hoppit and Joanna Innes, "Introduction" to *Failed Legislation, 1660–1800: Extracted from the Commons and Lords Journal*, ed. Hoppit (London: Hambledon Press, 1997), 30–32 presents the subject classifications used by the project. American political scientists have studied US legislative output in the twentieth century, see for example David Mayhew, *Divided We Govern: Party Control, Lawmaking, and Investigations, 1946–2002* (New Haven, CT: Yale University Press, 2005, 2nd ed.) and John S. Lapinski, *The Substance of Representation: Congress, American Political Development, and Lawmaking* (Princeton, NJ: Princeton University Press, 2013). Innes has employed the parliamentary legislation database to analyze Parliament and legislation in numerous publications discussing the relationship of economic and social developments to the politics of the British union, see Innes, "Parliament and the Shaping of Eighteenth-Century English Social Policy," *Transactions of the Royal Historical Society* 40 (1990): 63–92; Innes, "The Domestic Face of the Military-Fiscal State: Government and Society in Eighteenth-Century Britain," in *An Imperial State at War: Britain from 1689 to 1815*, ed. Lawrence Stone (London: Routledge, 1994), 96–127;

Innes, "The Local Acts of a National Parliament: Parliament's Role in Sanctioning Local Action in Eighteenth-Century Britain," *Parliamentary History* 17, no. 1 (1998): 23–47; Innes, "Legislating for Three Kingdoms: How the Westminster Parliament Legislated for England, Scotland and Ireland, 1707–1830," in *Parliaments, Nations and Identities in Britain and Ireland, 1660–1860*, ed. Julian Hoppit (Manchester, UK: Manchester University Press, 2003), 15–47. Hoppit reports his findings in *Britain's Political Economies: Parliament and Economic Life, 1660–1800* (Cambridge; Cambridge University Press, 2017).

9. Novak makes the point that the study of the American state has suffered from the use of abstract theories and concepts of the state drawn from a theoretical model developed from European historical experiences, William J. Novak, "The Myth of the 'Weak' American State," *American Historical Review* 113, no. 3 (June 2008): 761–65.

10. John Brewer, *The Sinews of Power: War, Money, and the British State, 1688–1783* (Boston: Unwin Hyman, 1989); Patrick K. O'Brien, "The Political Economy of British Taxation, 1660– 1815," *Economic History Review* 41, no. 1 (February 1988): 1–32; Hoppit, "Patterns of Parliamentary Legislation," 125–27; Bob Harris, "Parliamentary Legislation, Lobbying and the Press in Eighteenth-Century Scotland," *Parliamentary History* 26, no. 1 (2007): 76, citing *Stilling the Grumbling Hive. The Response to Social and Economic Problems in England, 1689–1750*, ed. Lee Davison, T. Hitchcock, T. Keirn, and R.B. Shoemaker (Stroud: Allan Sutton, 1992); Innes, "The Local Acts of a National Parliament"; Julian Hoppit, "Compulsion, Compensation and Property Rights in Britain, 1688–1833," *Past and Present* 210, no 1 (February 2011): 93–128.

11. Hoppit, "Patterns of Parliamentary Legislation," 109 and Table 1, 117; Julian Hoppit, "The Nation, the State, and the First Industrial Revolution," *Journal of British Studies* 50, no. 2 (April 2011): 316.

12. Hoppit, "Patterns of Parliamentary Legislation," 126–27, quotation at 127; Innes, "The Local Acts of a National Parliament"; Hoppit, "Compulsion, Compensation and Property Rights," 99–103.

13. Hoppit, "Patterns of Parliamentary Legislation," table 3, 119.

14. Dan Bogart and Gary Richardson, "Making Property Productive: Reorganizing Rights to Real and Equitable Estates in Britain, 1660–1830," *European Review of Economic History* 13, no. 1 (April 2009): 3–30.

15. Hoppit, "Patterns of Parliamentary Legislation," 121–22; Julian Hoppit, Joanna Innes, and John Styles, "Parliamentary Acts, 1660–1800," Excel file in author's possession; Robert C. Allen, "Agriculture during the Industrial Revolution, 1700–1850," in *The Cambridge Economic History of Modern Britain. Vol. 1: Industrialisation 1700–1860*, ed. Roderick Floud and Paul Johnson (Cambridge: Cambridge University Press, 2004), 96–116. On the enclosure movement, see Michael Turner, *Enclosures in Britain, 1750–1830* (London and Basingstoke, 1984).

16. Hoppit, "Patterns of Parliamentary Legislation," 121; Hoppit et al., "Parliamentary Acts, 1660–1800," Excel file in author's possession; Dan Bogart, "Turnpike Trusts and Property Income: New Evidence on the Effects of Transport Improvements and Legislation in Eighteenth-Century England," *Economic History Review* 62, no. 1 (2009): 128–52. On turnpikes, canals, and bridges, see William Albert, *The Turnpike Road System in England, 1663–1840* (Cambridge: Cambridge University Press, 1972); J. Ginarlis, and S. Pollard, "Roads and Waterways, 1750–1850," in *Studies in Capital Formation in the United Kingdom, 1750–1920*, ed. C. H. Feinstein and S. Pollard (Oxford: Oxford University Press, 1988), 182–224; D. F. Harrison, "Bridges and Economic Development, 1300–1800," *Economic History Review* 45, no 2 (May 1992): 755–93; Simon Ville, "Transport," in *Cambridge Economic History of Modern Britain* I, 295–331.

17. Jack P. Greene, *Peripheries and Center: Constitutional Development in the Extended Polities of the British Empire and the United States, 1607–1788* (Athens: University of Georgia Press, 1986); Alison G. Olson "Eighteenth-Century Colonial Legislatures and Their Constituents," *Journal of American History* 79, no. 2 (September 1992): 543–67, quotation at 566. Peverill Squire, "The Evolution of American Colonial Assemblies as Legislative Organizations," *Congress & the Presidency* 32, no. 2 (Autumn 2005): 109–31, reviews the literature on the colonial assembly.

18. Novak, "A State of Legislatures"; Douglas Bradburn, *The Citizenship Revolution: Politics and the Creation of the American Union, 1774–1804* (Charlottesville: University of Virginia

Press, 2009), 47. For more on the rise of the state legislatures in the revolutionary pe-
riod, see Christopher Tomlins, *Law, Labor, and Ideology in the Early American Republic*
(New York: Cambridge University Press, 1993), 35–59; James Henretta, "Magistrates,
Common Law Lawyers, Legislators: The Three Legal Systems of British America," in *The
Cambridge History of Law in America*, ed. Christopher Tomlins and Michael Grossberg, 3
vols. (Cambridge: Cambridge University Press, 2008), I, 586–89; Bradburn, "The Rise of the
States: Governance, Institutional Failure, and the Causes of American Independence," paper
presented at the conference on Political Economy and Empire in the Early Modern World,
Yale University, May 2013, 14–36; Christopher R. Pearl, *Conceived in Crisis: The Revolutionary
Creation of an American State* (Charlottesville: University of Virginia Press, 2020).

19. William J. Novak, *The People's Welfare: Law and Regulation in Nineteenth-Century America*
(Chapel Hill: University of North Carolina Press, 1996).

20. On the Confederation Congress, see Rakove, *Beginnings of National Politics*, 175; David C.
Hendrickson, *Peace Pact: The Lost World of the American Founding* (Lawrence: University
Press of Kansas, 2003), 135–36, quotation at 136; Benjamin H. Irvin, *Clothed in the Robes
of Sovereignty: The Continental Congress and the People Out of Doors* (New York: Oxford
University Press, 2011).

21. Donald L. Eilenstine, David L. Farnsworth, and James S. Fleming, "Trends and Cycles in the
Legislative Productivity of the United States Congress, 1789–1976," *Quality and Quantity* 12,
no. 1 (1978): Table 1, 22–23.

22. Note that Table 4.1 presents my coding of US and Pennsylvania legislation together with the
Hoppit team's coding of British legislation. In methodological terms Table 4.1 does not present a comparative analysis because such analysis would require that the same researcher or
team of researcher coded all data.

23. James H. Kettner, *The Development of American Citizenship, 1608–1870* (Chapel
Hill: University of North Carolina Press, 1978), 235–44; Aristides Zolberg, *A Nation by
Design: Immigration Policy in the Fashioning of America* (Cambridge, MA: Harvard University
Press, 2006), 24–98; Edwin Maxey, "Federal Quarantine Laws," *Political Science Quarterly* 23,
no. 4 (December 1908): 617–19; Richard R. John, *Spreading the News: The American Postal
System from Franklin to Morse* (Cambridge, MA: Harvard University Press, 1995); Allen S.
Miller, "'The Lighthouse Top I See': Lighthouses as Instruments and Manifestations of State
Building in the Early Republic," *Buildings & Landscapes: Journal of the Vernacular Architecture
Forum* 17, no. 1 (Spring 2010): 13–34. On the Federalists largely unrealized visions of communications improvements, see John Lauritz Larson, *Internal Improvement: National Works
and the Promise of Popular Government in the Early United States* (Chapel Hill: University of
North Carolina Press, 2001), 9–38. The federal government's importance for the development of arms technology has long been noted, see Merrit Roe Smith, *Harpers Ferry Armory
and the New Technology: The Challenge of Change* (Ithaca, NY: Cornell University Press, 1977)
and Andrew J. B. Fagal, "'The Next Great Work to be Accomplished': American Armament
Policy," in *The Washington Administration and the Creation of the Federal Government*, ed. Max
M. Edling and Peter J. Kastor (Charlottesville: University of Virginia Press, 2021), ch. 6. It
should be noted that the quantitative analysis undertaken here concerns Congress only. The
federal government promoted the economy in other ways than legislation. The patent and
copyright administration and the rulings of the federal courts are two important examples of
nonlegislative federal government action.

24. The full list of legislation categories is in Hoppit and Innes, "Introduction" to Hoppit, ed.,
Failed Legislation, 30–32. The pattern of legislative activity in Congress in the 1790s supports
the argument about the early American state made in *Shaped by War and Trade: International
Influences on American Political Development*, ed. Ira Katznelson and Martin Schefer
(Princeton, NJ: Princeton University Press, 2002).

25. Ira Katznelson and John S. Lapinski, "The Substance of Representation: Studying Policy
Content and Legislative Behavior," in *The Macropolitics of Congress*, ed. John S. Lapinski and
E. Scott Adler (Princeton, NJ: Princeton University Press, 2011), 100–26; Lapinski, *The
Substance of Representation*.

26. On the Army, see Richard H. Kohn, *Eagle and Sword: The Federalists and the Creation of the
Military Establishment in America, 1783–1802* (New York: Free Press, 1975); on Indian Affairs,

see Leonard J. Sadosky, *Revolutionary Negotiations: Indians, Empires, and Diplomats in the Founding of America* (Charlottesville: University of Virginia Press, 2009), 119–75 and Bernard W. Sheehan "The Indian Problem in the Northwest: From Conquest to Philanthropy," in *Launching the "Extended Republic": The Federalist Era*, ed. Ronald Hoffman and Peter J. Albert (Charlottesville: University of Virginia Press, 1996), 190–222; on the western lands see Malcolm J. Rohrbough, *The Land Office Business: The Settlement and Administration of American Public Lands, 1789–1837* (New York: Oxford University Press, 1968); on territorial government, see Bethel Saler, *The Settlers' Empire: Colonialism and State Formation in America's Old Northwest* (Philadelphia: University of Pennsylvania Press, 2014), 40–82; on the customs and revenue legislation, see Gautham Rao, *National Duties: Custom Houses and the Making of the American State* (Chicago: University of Chicago Press, 2016); on diplomacy, see David M. Golove and Daniel J. Hulsebosh, "A Civilized Nation: The Early American Constitution, the Law of Nations, and the Pursuit of International Recognition," *New York University Law Review* 85, no. 4 (2010): 932–1066 and Eliga H. Gould, *Among the Powers of the Earth: The American Revolution and the Making of a New World Empire* (Cambridge, MA: Harvard University Press, 2012).

27. Morgan Sherwood, "The Origins and Development of the American Patent System," *American Scientist* 71, no. 5 (September–October 1983): 500–506. The first congressional bankruptcy act was passed in 1800, but was only a temporary measure. The first stable act was passed in 1898, see Peter J. Coleman, *Debtors and Creditors in America: Insolvency, Imprisonment for Debt, and Bankruptcy* (Washington, DC: Beard Books, 1999 [1974]), 16–30. There is a very substantial literature on early American federalism, but it focuses on political principles and ideology rather than on administration and legislation. For key work see Cathy D. Matson and Peter S. Onuf, *A Union of Interests: Political and Economic Thought in Revolutionary America* (Lawrence: University Press of Kansas, 1990); Andrew C. Lenner, *The Federal Principle in American Politics, 1790–1833* (Lanham, MD: Madison House, 2001); and Hendrickson, *Peace Pact*.

28. There were roads built in the federal territories and the National Road would later become a contentious exception, see *The National Road*, ed, Karl B. Raitz (Baltimore: Johns Hopkins University Press, 1996); Pamela L. Baker, "The Washington National Road Bill and the Struggle to Adopt a Federal System of Internal Improvements," *Journal of the Early Republic* 22, no. 3 (Autumn, 2002): 437–64.

29. Louis Hartz, *Economic Policy and Democratic Thought: Pennsylvania, 1776–1860* (Cambridge, MA: Harvard University Press, 1948), 3; Thomas Jefferson, "First Annual Message," *The Papers of Thomas Jefferson*, ed. Julian P. Boyd. 44 vols. to date (Princeton, NJ: Princeton University Press, 1950–), XXXVI, 60. More than any other scholar of the early republic, Richard John has stressed the importance of government to social, economic and political development. In addition to John *Spreading the News*, see Richard R. John, "Governmental Institutions as Agents of Change: Rethinking American Political Development in the Early Republic, 1787–1835," *Studies in American Political Development* 11, no. 2 (Fall 1997): 347–80 and John, "The State Is Back In: What Now?" *Journal of the Early Republic* 38, no. 1 (Spring, 2018): 105–18.

30. There is a large literature on Pennsylvania politics in the period of the American Revolution and on the Pennsylvania Constitutions of 1776 and 1790. For some key works, see Steven Rosswurm, *Arms, Country, and Class: The Philadelphia Militia and the Lower Sort in the American Revolution* (New Brunswick, NJ: Rutgers University Press, 1987); Owen S. Ireland, *Religion, Ethnicity, and Politics: Ratifying the Constitution in Pennsylvania* (University Park: Penn State University Press, 1995); *Pennsylvania's Revolution*, ed. By William Pencak (University Park: Penn State University Press, 2010); Pearl, *Conceived in Crisis*.

31. See Pearl, *Conceived in Crisis* for a discussion of such claims.

32. Hartz, *Economic Policy and Democratic Thought*, 38–39. On the early American corporation and early American incorporation, see James Willard Hurst, *The Legitimacy of the Business Corporation in the Law of the United States, 1780–1970* (Charlottesville: University Press of Virginia, 1969); Pauline Maier, "The Revolutionary Origins of the American Corporation," *William and Mary Quarterly* 50, no.1 (January 1993): 51–84; Novak, *People's Welfare*, 105–106; Andrew Schocket, *Founding Corporate Power in Early National Philadelphia* (DeKalb: Northern Illinois University Press, 2007); John Joseph Wallis, "The Other

Foundings: Federalism and the Constitutional Structure of American Government," in
Founding Choices: American Economic Policy in the 1790s, ed. Douglas A. Irwin and Richard
Sylla (Chicago: University of Chicago Press, 2011), 177–213; Robert E. Wright, "Rise of the
Corporate Nation," in Irwin and Sylla, *Founding Choices,* Table 7.1, 220–21; Robert E. Wright,
Corporation Nation (Philadelphia: University of Pennsylvania Press, 2013).

33. An Act to provide for the opening and improving sundry navigable waters and roads within
this Commonwealth, 13 April 1791, in *Acts of the General Assembly of the Commonwealth
of Pennsylvania, Passed at a Session which was Begun and Held at the City of Philadelphia on
Tuesday, the Seventh Day of December, in the Year One Thousand Seven Hundred and Ninety, and
of the Independence of the United States of America, the Fifteenth* (Philadelphia: Hall and Sellers,
1791), 77–81.

34. Robert E. Wright, "The Pivotal Role of Private Enterprise in America's Transportation Age,
1790–1860," *Journal of Private Enterprise* 29, no. 2 (Spring 2014): 3–4. Klein and Majewski report that turnpike corporations made up 27 percent of all business incorporations between
1800 and 1830 in the northeast, Daniel B. Klein and John Majewski, "Economy, Community,
and Law: The Turnpike Movement in New York, 1797–1845," *Law and Society Review* 26, no. 3
(1992): Table 1, 470. On the development of transportation in the antebellum period, see George
Rogers Taylor, *The Transportation Revolution, 1815–1860* (New York: Harper & Row, 1951) and
John Majewski, *A House Dividing: Economic Development in Pennsylvania and Virginia before the
Civil War* (New York: Cambridge University Press, 2000). On roads, see Joseph Durrenberger,
Turnpikes: A Study of the Toll Road Movement in the Middle Atlantic States and Maryland (Cos Cob,
CT: John E. Edwards, 1968 [1931]); Daniel B. Klein, "The Voluntary Provision of Public Goods?
The Turnpike Companies of Early America," *Economic Inquiry* 28, no. 4 (October 1990): 788–
812; and Klein and Majewski "Economy, Community, and Law," 469–512.

35. For the background of the Pennsylvania initiatives, see Jessie L. Hartman, "Pennsylvania's
Grand Plan of Post Revolutionary Internal Improvement," *Pennsylvania Magazine Of
History and Biography* 65, no. 4 (October 1941): 437–57. On canal building generally, see
Carter Goodrich, *Government Promotion of American Canals and Railroads, 1800–1890*
(New York: Columbia University Press, 1960); *Canals and American Economic Development,*
ed. Carter Goodrich (New York: Columbia University Press, 1961); and Ronald Shaw, *Canals
for a Nation: The Canal Era in the United States, 1790–1860* (Lexington: The University Press
of Kentucky, 1990).

36. For the unprofitability of turnpike companies, see Klein and Majewski, "Turnpike Movement
in New York," 469–512.

37. Novak, *People's Welfare,* 1–50 and passim; Emma Hart, "City Government and the State
in Eighteenth-Century South Carolina," *Eighteenth-Century Studies* 50, no. 2 (Winter
2017): 195–211. The University of Pennsylvania was created by merging the University of the
State of Pennsylvania with the College, Academy and Charitable School of Philadelphia. On
the nonbusiness corporation in the early United States, see Ronald Seavoy, *The Origins of the
American Business Corporation, 1784–1855: Broadening the Concept of Public Service During
Industrialization* (Westport, CT: Greenwood Press, 1982), 9–38; Johann Neem, *Creating a
Nation of Joiners: Democracy and Civil Society in Early Massachusetts* (Cambridge, MA: Harvard
University Press, 2008); Sarah Barringer Gordon, "The African Supplement: Religion, Race,
and Corporate Law in Early National America," *William and Mary Quarterly* 72, no. 3 (July
2015): 385–422. On health regulations in Philadelphia, see Simon Finger, *The Contagious
City: The Politics of Public Health in Early Philadelphia* (Ithaca, NY: Cornell University Press,
2012). For the literature on internal police see references cited in n17, chapter 3.

38. Novak, *People's Welfare,* 237. I am indebted to Christopher Pearl for information about the
workings of borough government in Pennsylvania in the revolutionary period.

39. "A further Supplement to the Act, entitled 'An Act for erecting the town of Carlisle, in the
county of Cumberland, into a borough, for regulating the buildings, preventing nuisances and
encroachments on the commons, squares, streets, lanes and alleys of the same, and for other
purposes therein mentioned,' passed the thirteenth day of April, one thousand seven-hundred
and eighty-two," April 19, 1794, *Acts of the Commonwealth of Pennsylvania [3 December 1793],*
ch. CCXXXVI, 543; "An Act to erect the town of Pittsburg, in the county of Allegheny, into

a borough, and for other purposes therein mentioned," April 22, 1794, ch. CCLI (590–91); "An Act for Erecting the Borough of Reading in the County of Berks Into a Borough; For Regulating the Buildings, Preventing Nuisances and Encroachments on the Squares, Streets, Lanes and Alleys of the Same, And for Other Purposes Therein Mentioned, September 12, 1783," *The Statutes at Large of Pennsylvania from 1682–1801*, vol. XI, ch. MXXXI, 123–46. On the incorporation of towns and the delegation of power in the system of early American government, see William J. Novak, "The American Law of Association. The Legal-Political Construction of Civil Society," *Studies in American Political Development* 15 (Fall 2001): 163–88; Novak, "A State of Legislatures," 340–47. Novak, *People's Welfare*, 51–233, deals with fire regulations, markets, public ways, prostitution and drunkenness, and health.

40. Pearl, *Conceived in Crisis*, 175, 179 (quotation).
41. There is a need for systematic investigations of state activity in the founding period. Although he takes a different approach to the analysis of Pennsylvania presented here, Gregory Scott King-Owen's investigation of petitions to the North Carolina assembly confirms the Pennsylvania pattern of a legislative output dominated by the requests from communities and private individuals for local regulations and the protection of property, see Gregory Scott King-Owen, "The People's Law: Popular Sovereignty and State Formation in North Carolina, 1776–1805," PhD diss., Ohio State University, 2011.
42. James Wilson, *Lectures on Law, Delivered in the College of Philadelphia, In the Years One Thousand Seven Hundred and Ninety, and One Thousand Seven Hundred and Ninety One*, in *Collected Works of James Wilson*, ed. Kermit L. Hall and Mark David Hall (Indianapolis: Liberty Fund, 2007), 870–72, quotation at 870; St. George Tucker, "Of the Several Forms of Government," in *View of the Constitution of the United States. With Select Writings*, ed. Clyde N. Wilson (Indianapolis: Liberty Fund, 1999), 45.

Conclusion

1. Pew Research Center, "Technology Triumphs, Morality Falters," July 3, 1999, https://www. pewresearch.org/politics/1999/07/03/technology-triumphs-morality-falters/; Annenberg Public Policy Center, "Americans' Civics Knowledge Increases But Still Has a Long Way to Go," September 12, 2019, https://www.annenbergpublicpolicycenter.org/americans-civics-knowledge-increases-2019-survey/. The number who could correctly name the three branches of the federal government rose to 39 percent in 2019 probably as a result of highly publicized tensions between the president and Congress.
2. *ABA Journal*, September 1, 1987, 44; *We the People: The Commission on the Bicentennial of the United States Constitution, 1985–1992, Final Report* (1992), 85; Doonesbury, *Washington Post*, February 22, 1987.
3. "Founding Documents in the Rotunda for the Charters of Freedom," https://museum. archives.gov/founding-documents, accessed October 24, 2019; Leader, *The Guardian*, 17 September 2007.
4. George Washington, "Seventh Annual Address," in *A Compilation of the Messages and Papers of the Presidents, 1789–1908*, ed. James D. Richardson (Washington, DC: Bureau of Art and Literature, 1908), 182–86.
5. *Indian Affairs: Laws and Treaties*, ed. Charles J. Kappler, 7 vols. (Washington, DC: Government Printing Office, 1904), II (Treaties); *Eighteenth Annual Report of the Bureau of American Ethnology to the Secretary of the Smithsonian Institution 1896–97, pt. 2: Indian Land Cesssions in the United States 1784–1894*, 56th Cong., 1st Sess., H.R. Doc. No. 736/3, 56th Cong., 1st Sess. (1899), U.S. Serial Set Number 4015; *Indians Removed to West Mississippi from 1789*, H.R. Doc. 147, 25th Cong., 3d Sess. (1838), Statement B, 9.. U.S. Bureau of the Census, *Historical Statistics of the United States, Colonial Times to 1970*. Bicentennial Edition, 2 vols. (Washington, DC: Government Printing Office 1975), I, 24–37.
6. John Holroyd, Earl of Sheffield, *Observations on the Commerce of the American States with Europe and the West Indies* (London: J. Debrett, 1783), 69–70; *Treaties and Other International Acts of the United States of America*, ed. David Hunter Miller, 8 vols. (Washington, DC: Government Printing Office, 1931–1948), I, 55–62.

7. Washington, "Sixth Annual Address," *Messages and Papers*, ed. Richardson, I, 167; Report of the Secretary of the Treasury on the State of the Finances for the Year 1866, 39th Cong., 2nd Sess., H.R. Ex. Doc. 4, 306–307.

8. Max M. Edling, *A Hercules in the Cradle: War, Money, and the American State, 1783–1867* (Chicago: University of Chicago Press, 2014).

9. Jack P. Greene, "Colonial History and National History: Reflections on a Continuing Problem," *William and Mary Quarterly* vol. 64, no. 2 (April 2007): 235–50.

10. William J. Novak, *The People's Welfare: Law and Regulation in Nineteenth-Century America* (Chapel Hill: University of North Carolina Press, 1996); Oscar Handlin and Mary Flug Handlin, *Commonwealth: A Study of the Role of Government in the American Economy: Massachusetts, 1774–1861* (New York: New York University Press, 1947); Louis Hartz, *Economic Policy and Democratic Thought: Pennsylvania, 1776–1860* (Cambridge, MA: Harvard University Press, 1948). Much less known than the works by Hartz and the Handlins are the two other books on state development sponsored by the Commission on Research in Economic History of the Social Science Research Council during the Second World War: Milton S. Heath, *Constructive Liberalism: The Role of the State in Economic Development in Georgia to 1860* (Cambridge, MA: Harvard University Press, 1954) and J. N. Primm, *Economic Policy in the Development of a Western State: Missouri, 1820–1860* (Cambridge, MA: Harvard University Press, 1954). John Brooke has outlined a political history over clashing visions of state regulation in the early republic, which is centered on the states yet national in aspiration, see John L. Brooke, "Patriarchal Magistrates, Associated Improvers, and Monitoring Militias: Visions of Self-Government in the Early American Republic, 1760–1840," in *State and Citizen: British America and the Early United States*, ed. Peter Thompson and Peter S. Onuf (Charlottesville: University of Virginia Press, 2013), 178–217.

11. J. G. A. Pocock, "Virtue and Commerce in the Eighteenth Century," *Journal of Interdisciplinary History* 3, no. 1 (Summer 1972): 119–34, quotation at 120.

12. An Act directing the trial of Slaves, committing capital crimes; and for the more effectual punishing conspiracies and insurrections of them; and for the better government of Negros, Mulattos, and Indians, bond or free, Virginia Statutes at Large, May 1723, ch. IV, sect. 23, in *The Statutes at Large; Being a Collection of All the Laws of Virginia, From the First Session of the Legislature in the Year 1619*, ed. William Waller Hening, 13 vols. (New York: R. & W. & G. Bartow, 1819–1823), IV, 133–34. This restriction on voting rights was repeated in An Act concerning election of members of general assembly, Virginia Statutes at Large, October 1785, ch. LV, sect. 2, Hening's *Statutes at Large* XII, 120.

13. Mary Sarah Bilder points out that the Constitution "contained a strikingly robust list of rights, albeit not in the form of a 'bill'," but also that "the embrace of a Constitution without a list of individual protections from government emphasizes the distance from our modern concept [of the Constitution]," see Mary Sarah Bilder, "The *Ordeal* and the Constitution," *The New England Quarterly* 91, no. 1 (January 2018): 141.

14. My understanding of the early modern republic and of the place of the household in the early American political order is indebted to William James Booth, *Households: On the Moral Architecture of the Economy* (Ithaca, NY: Cornell University Press, 1993), 15–93; Stephanie McCurry, *Masters of Small Worlds: Yeoman Households, Gender Relations, and the Political Culture of the Antebellum South Carolina Low Country* (New York: Oxford University Press, 1995), quotation at 89; Quentin Skinner, *Liberty Before Liberalism* (Cambridge: Cambridge University Press, 1998), 1–57; Carole Shammas, *A History of Household Government in America* (Charlottesville: University of Virginia Press, 2002); Laura F. Edwards, *The People and Their Peace: Legal Culture and the Transformation of Inequality in the Post-Revolutionary South* (Chapel Hill: University of North Carolina Press, 2009); Christopher Tomlins, *Freedom Bound: Law, Labor, and Civic Identity in Colonizing English America, 1580–1865* (New York: Cambridge University Press, 2010); and Barbara Young Welke, *Law and the Borders of Belonging in the Long Nineteenth Century United States* (New York: Cambridge University Press, 2010).

15. Shammas, *History of Household Government*, xiii.

16. William Blackstone, *Commentaries on the laws of England. . . . By William Blackstone, Esq. Vinerian Professor of Law, and solicitor general to her Majesty*, 4 vols. (Oxford: Clarendon Press, 1765–1769), I, 410.

17. St George Tucker, *Blackstone's Commentaries with Notes of Reference to the Constitution and Laws of the Federal Government of the United States, and of the Commonwealth of Virginia with an Appendix to Each Volume, Containing Short Tracts upon Such Subjects as Appeared Necessary to Form a Connected View of the Laws of Virginia, as a Member of the Federal Union*, 5 vols. (Philadelphia: W. Y. Birch and A. Small, 1803), I, 145. Tucker wrote an eight-page essay on political and civil liberty as a comment on Blackstone's reference to Montesquieu's assertion "that the English is the only nation in the world, where political or civil liberty is the direct end of it's constitution." The essay is placed after Blackstone's first chapter, "Of the Absolute Rights of Individuals."

18. Ibid. I, 145; James Wilson, *Lectures on Law, Delivered in the College of Philadelphia, In the Years One Thousand Seven Hundred and Ninety, and One Thousand Seven Hundred and Ninety One*, in *Collected Works of James Wilson*, ed. Kermit L. Hall and Mark David Hall (Indianapolis: Liberty Fund, 2007), 839–43.

19. Thomas Paine, *Common Sense* (Philadelphia: R. Bell, 1776), 70; Noah Webster, *Sketches of American Policy* (Hartford, CT: Hudson and Goodwin, 1785), 34–35; Tucker, *Blackstone's Commentaries* I, 433, 441, 445, 453; Wilson, *Lectures on Law*, in *Collected Works of James Wilson* II, 1079. When Webster argued for a stronger national government he wrote that "Congress must have the same power in matters that concern the whole, as a man has in his own family, as a city has within the limits of its corporation, and as the legislature of a state has in the limits of that state, respecting matters that fall within their several jurisdictions."

20. Zephaniah Swift, *A System of the Laws of Connecticut*, 2 vols. (Windham, CT: John Byrne, 1795–1796), I, 199, 201, 205–206, 221; Tucker, *Blackstone's Commentaries* I, 422–58; St. George Tucker, "Of the State of Slavery in Virginia," in *View of the Constitution of the United States. With Select Writings*, ed. Clyde N. Wilson (Indianapolis: Liberty Fund, 1999), 409–10.

21. Wilson, *Lectures on Law*, 1079–80; Swift, *A System of the Laws of Connecticut*, 113, 119, 121–24; Ch. VI, A Law Respecting Crimes and Punishment," in *Laws Passed in the Territory North-West of the River Ohio . . . to the 31st of December, 1791* (Philadelphia: Francis Childs and John Swaine, 1792), 20; Tucker, *Blackstone's Commentaries* I, 426, 458; Marylynn Salmon, *Women and the Law of Property in Early America* (Chapel Hill: University of North Carolina Press, 1986), 81–140; Sally E. Hadden, *Slave Patrols: Law and Violence in Virginia and the Carolinas* (Cambridge, MA: Harvard University Press, 2003); Thomas D. Morris, *Southern Slavery and the Law, 1619–1860* (Chapel Hill: University of North Carolina Press, 1996); Kelly A. Ryan, "'The Spirit of Contradiction:' Wife Abuse in New England, 1780–1820," *Early American Studies* 13, no. 3 (Summer 2015): 586–625.

22. Shammas, *History of Household Government*, 65.

INDEX

Tables are indicated by *t* following the page number
For the benefit of digital users, indexed terms that span two pages (e.g., 52–53) may, on occasion, appear on only one of those pages.

Ablavsky, Gregory, 7–8, 31
absolute *vs.* relative rights, 145–46, 147
Adams, John, 38–39, 56, 107, 141
Adams, John Quincy, 4
administrative law, 30–31, 55, 122, 135
African Americans
    free blacks, 146–47
    voting rights, 143–44, 146–47
    See also slavery
Age of Federalism, 107, 140–41
Age of Revolutions, 21–22, 30–31
agriculture and agricultural interests, 25, 26, 83, 85, 87, 97–98
    commercial interests *vs.* agricultural interests, 6, 19–20
    cotton plantations, 67–68
    early legislation, 117–21
    enclosure acts, 113, 116–17
    exports, river navigation, 47
    freehold farms, 31–32
    standard of living, access to new agricultural land, 43–44
    western economic prospects (*see* trans-Appalachian West)
alcohol, taxation, 140, 141
d'Alembert, Jean-Baptiste le Rond, 84
The Algerine Captive (Tyler), 45
ambassadors. *See* diplomatic relations
American Dictionary of the English Language (Webster), 84–85
American exceptionalism, 29
American Indians. *See* Indian nations
American Revolution. *See* American War of Independence

American union
    framers' concept of union, 11–12
    structure *vs.* purpose, 10–11
American War of Independence, 1–3
    economic effect of, 44
    Peace of Paris, 3–4, 44–45, 46–47, 50
    war debts, 2–3, 47–48, 122, 124, 140–41
Annapolis convention, 53
Antifederalists and anti-federalism, 6, 69–71, 72–73, 101, 105, 114–15
    Bill of Rights, 72
    terminology, 75, 135–36
    See also residual power of states
Appalachian expansion. *See* trans-Appalachian west
armed forces. *See* military defense
Armitage, David, 7–8
Articles of Confederation, 2–3, 5, 36–43
    amending *vs.* replacing, 9, 23, 36, 53–54, 57, 105–6
    analysis of Constitution in light of, 35–36
    commerce, regulation of, 35–36, 42–50
    executors of decisions, state governments as, 35–36
    goal, 20, 43–44
    "perpetual union", 41–43
    police powers granted under, 98–99
    requisitions system, 2, 48, 49–53, 55, 57, 62
    sovereign American people under, 43
    states under, 1–3, 36–43, 48, 49–53, 55, 57, 60–61, 62, 67–68
    as treaty organization, 19–20
    unanimous agreement of states, 41
    veto powers, 41
    voluntary compliance of states, 2, 48, 49–53, 55, 57, 62

Atlantic marketplace
    access to, 11, 14, 17–18, 20, 26, 28, 31, 44, 47–
        48, 136, 139–40
    early legislation, 121t, 130–31
    See also international commerce
Aztec Empire, 81–82

Bailyn, Bernard, 16–17, 33
bankruptcy, legislation of early Congresses,
        117–21, 122
banks
    Bank of the United States, 9–10, 106,
        107, 122–23
    early legislation, 112t, 115–17, 125–26
    incorporation of, 125–26, 136
Barbary States, 5, 45, 53, 140
bars and taverns, within police powers to be
        exercised by state governments, 102–3
Battle of Fallen Timber, 138
Beard, Charles, 6–8, 14–15, 16–17, 33
Beard, Mary, 6–7
Becker, Carl, 8
Bedford, Gunning, 63, 91
bicentennial response to U.S.
        Constitution, 133–34
von Bielfeld, Jakob Friedrich, 84, 87
Bilder, Mary Sarah, 9, 23, 34, 56, 58–59
bills of credit, 99
bills of rights, 21–22, 69, 72–73, 76, 107, 144–45
Black people
    free blacks, 146–47
    voting rights, 143–44, 146–47
    See also slavery
Blackstone, William, 80–81, 83, 86, 87–88,
        117, 145–46
Blackstone's *Commentaries on the Laws of England*,
        80–81, 117, 146
Bland, Richard, 38
bonds and notes, within police powers to be
        exercised by state governments, 102
borderlands. *See* trans-Appalachian west
boroughs, creation, 102–3, 129, 136
Boston police, 81–82, 84–85
boundary disputes, 27, 102
bridges, 112t, 115–17, 126–28, 136
Britain, 108–9, 110–14
    colonists as transplanted Britons, 79
    commercial discrimination against U.S., 106
    common market/"commonwealth" concept of
        British empire, 20, 37–38, 39, 41, 44
    constitution of, 21
    "contracts" between colonial sponsors and
        settlers, 18–19
    diplomatic relations with Indian nations, 20, 53
    in European wars, 137
    federal union, British Empire as, 37–39
    as fiscal-military state, 109, 131

Glorious Revolution, 108, 110
Home Department and Foreign Office, 98
internal police, British model, 78–81, 86,
        87–88, 113
military posts in U.S., 5, 20, 46–47, 53
mode of colonization, 18–19
Parliament, 9, 108–17
royal veto, 88–89
treaties with, 30
western states, interest in, 25
See also American War of Independence;
        colonies
*Britain's Commercial Interest Explained and
        Improved; In a Series of Dissertations on Several
        Important Branches of Her Trade and Police*
        (Postlethwayt), 86
Brooke, John, 142–43
"Brutus", 74–76, 77, 100–1, 102
Burke, Edmund, 21–22
Burke, Thomas, 41
Burlamaqui, Jean-Jacques, 36, 85, 87–88
Butler, Pierce, 64

"cameralism" (Kameralistik or
        Kameralwissenschaft), 84–85, 86, 87
canals and canal companies, 93–97, 99–100, 102–
        3, 112t, 113–14, 115–17, 126–28, 136
Caribbean/Gulf Coast trade, 44–45, 47, 49, 50,
        65, 138–39
categories of legislation, 108–9, 111, 112t,
        117–21, 118t
"Centinel", 74, 75–76
"central" government, 4, 5
charitable corporations, 93–97
Charleston police, 81–82
charters of incorporation, 99–100
Cherokee Nation v. Georgia (1831), 30–31
Chesapeake Bay, 53
children, social rights, 146–47, 148–49
China, 81–82
Chippewa people, 46
cities, police powers, 81–83, 84, 102–3
citizenship
    national standard, 134, 149
    naturalization, 55–56, 130–31
civic rights, 146, 149
    equal *vs.* unequal social rights, 146–47
    regulation of, 9–10, 11–12, 13–14, 15
"civilized nations", 28, 30–31, 32
"A Civilized Nation: The Early American
        Constitution, the Law of Nations, and
        the Pursuit of International Recognition"
        (Golove and Hulsebosch), 28
class issues, 6–7, 9, 17, 33–34
    changing class structures, 110–11
    redistribution of wealth, 99
    See also democratization

classification schema, 108–9, 111, 112t,
   117–21, 118t
coinage. *See* currency and legal tender
colleges and universities, 99–100, 102–3, 128
colonies
   assemblies mirroring British Parliament, 114
   Britain, relationship to, 79, 98, 109
   claims to land north of Ohio River, 46
   sociopolitical order, 10–11, 143
   as sovereign polities, 40
   See also Britain
Colquhoun, Patrik, 81
Commentaries on the Laws of England (Blackstone),
   80–81, 117, 146
commerce and trade, 5, 6, 12, 14, 29, 30,
   116–17, 130–31
   agricultural interests *vs.* commercial interests,
     6, 19–20
   under Articles of Confederation, 35–36, 42–50,
     53, 55–56, 57–58, 62–66
   fur trade, 47, 138–39
   Indian nations, trade with, 31, 32, 93–97, 98–99
   and internal police, 83, 85, 87, 99–100
   marketplace regulation, 12, 42–43, 82–83, 86,
     87, 93–97
   monopolization of commercial policy by federal
     government, 27
   slavery, 63, 64–66
   transition to liberal democracy and market
     economy, 142
   weights and measures, 42–43, 82–83, 86, 87,
     93–97, 98–99, 113
   See also international commerce; maritime
     issues; navigation of waterways
Commission on Bicentennial of United States
   Constitution, 133–34
Committee of Detail, 62–63, 64, 65–66, 92, 97–98
Committee of Style, 35, 92, 99–100
Common Sense (Paine), 147
"commonwealth" concept of British empire, 20,
   37–38, 39, 41, 44
Commonwealth school of economic
   history, 143–44
communications regulation, 9–10, 11–12, 13–14,
   35, 87, 97–98, 100
   Britain, 111–14
   early legislation, 116–17
   within internal police definition, 39
   See also navigation of waterways
"compleat consolidating plan", 76
confederation of states
   regional confederations, 9
   See also Articles of Confederation
Congress
   as central to fiscal-military state, 131
   comparisons of legislative activities, 107–32
   day-to-day operations, 107

expansion of legislative power, 74, 77
house (*see* House of Representatives)
party behavior, polarization, and leadership, 117
patterns in legislative output, 108
regulation of internal police of states, 149
as representation of American people or of
   sovereign states, 40, 59–60
senate (*see* Senate of U.S.)
See also first sessions of Congress; legislation
Connecticut, 58, 91
Connecticut Compromise, 58–60, 89
consent to become citizens, 19–20
"conservatives" as aristocrats and nationalists, 7
constabularies. *See* police
constitution
   of Britain, 21
   importance of written constitutions, 21–22
   meaning of term, 11, 21, 22, 23, 35–36
   See also U.S. Constitution
constitutional convention. *See* Philadelphia
   Convention
consumption/consumerism, 93–97, 113
contracts
   between colonial sponsors and
     settlers, 18–19
   impairment of obligation of contracts, 30, 70, 99
   interference, 27
copyrights, early legislation, 117–21, 122, 131–32
corporations
   laws regarding incorporation, 59, 102–3, 125–
     26, 129, 136, 142–43
   states as, 34, 58–59, 74, 100–1
cotton plantations, 67–68
Council of State, 97–98
counties, creation of, 102–3
county courts, 114
courts. *See* judiciary/judicial branch of
   government
Coxe, Tench, 102
Creation of the American Republic (Wood), 7–8
credit, state bills of, 99
credit of U.S., 48. *See also* indebtedness
Creek Nation, 48–49
crimes
   on high seas, 42
   against persons and property, 82–83
   state governments, list of police powers to be
     exercised by, 102–3
critical period, 1–15
critical period, explained, 4
currency and legal tender, 27, 30, 35–36, 42–43,
   70, 83, 86, 87, 90, 98–99
   early legislation, 117–21, 122, 130–31
   enumeration of powers, 93–97
   and internal police, 85
   paper money, 6, 16–17, 27, 30, 35–36, 48–49,
     61, 70, 83, 90, 91, 99, 144–45

customs and customs duties, 5, 27, 30, 52–53,
    55–56, 57–58, 62–63, 64, 65–66, 122–23,
    135, 137, 140

d'Alembert, Jean-Baptiste le Rond, 84
dam construction, 130
de Gardoqui, Diego, 49
de Laforêt, Antoine, 100–1
de Vattel, Emer, 21, 24, 27, 28, 36, 85, 87–88
Deane, Silas, 39–40
debts. See indebtedness
Declaration of Independence, 5, 7–8, 19, 29, 33,
    34, 40
Declarations and Resolves of First Continental
    Congress, 78–79
defense of nation. See military defense
Delamare, Nicolas, 84, 87
Delaware people, 46
Delaware (state), 40, 53–54, 58, 65, 66–67, 79
delegation of state supervisory authority, 103
"demand-led" legislation, 114
democratization, 7, 8, 13–14
    creation of modern democratic republic, 134
    See also class issues
demographics, 74–75
Deudney, David, 21
Dickinson, John, 40–42
Dickinson plan, 40–42
Dictionary of the English Language (Johnson),
    21, 84–85
Diderot, Denis, 84
diplomatic relations, 20, 24–25, 28, 29–30, 33–34,
    36–37, 39–40, 43
    foreign recognition as one nation vs. thirteen
        republics, 4–5
    with Indian nations (see Indian nations)
    between Indian nations and Britain, 20, 53
    states, 4–5, 30, 139–40
    See also international commerce
distilled spirits, 140, 141
Documentary History of the Ratification of the
    Constitution (Grant DePauw), 70
Domestic Affairs Department, 97–99
dual revolution, explained, 8

An Economic Interpretation of the Constitution of the
    United States (Beard), 6–7, 16
economy, 9–10, 11–12, 13–14, 136, 142
    Britain, legislation related to economy,
        111, 113
    and development of the West, 31
    distribution of wealth, 6, 8
    early legislation, 116–21, 122, 130
    economic depression, 20, 49
    economic interpretations of Constitution, 6–8,
        16, 33–34
    economic strata (see class issues)

incorporation acts, 142–43
    within internal police definition, 39
    old meaning of term, 146
    small states vs. large states, 63
socioeconomics (see class issues)
standard of living, 43–44
state-driven economic development,
    142–43
world power status of U.S., 142
See also fiscal matters
education, 9–10, 11–12, 13–14, 100, 128
    colleges and universities, 99–100, 102–3, 128
    within internal police definition, 39
elections and voting
    by "the people" or by the states, 143–44
    electoral districts, 59
    electoral votes for president, 104
    local government officers, 129
    within police powers to be exercised by state
        governments, 102
    ratio of legislators to electors, 74–75
    suffrage requirements, 143–44,
        146–47, 148
    three-fifths rule, 66–67
elite vs. ordinary. See class issues
Ellsworth, Oliver, 99
embassies and ambassadors. See diplomatic
    relations
employment, within police powers to be exercised
    by state governments, 102–3
enclosure acts, 113, 116–17
Encyclopédie (Diderot and d'Alembert), 84
England. See Britain
enumeration of powers, 9–10, 11, 24–25, 58, 71,
    77, 80, 92, 131–32
    list of police powers to be exercised by state
        governments, 102–3
    "surrogacy," as strategy to stretch enumerated
        powers, 73
    tables of state and federal powers, 94–97t
    See also residual power of states
equal vs. unequal social rights, 146–47
Essays and Treatises on Several Subjects
    (Hume), 87–88
estate and inheritance legislation, 102–3, 111–13,
    116, 129–30
European wars, 136–37, 140, 141
evolutionary theory of history, 6
ex post facto laws, 99
exceptionalism, American, 29
executive branch of government, 59–60
    administrative law, 30–31, 55, 122, 135
    executive and federative powers, 37
    See also president of U.S.
export markets. See international commerce
external vs. internal powers, 39, 131–32
extravagance, sumptuary laws, 93–97

Fallen Timber, Battle of, 138
families, rights and obligations within households, 145, 146, 147, 148–49
"family of civilized nations", 28, 29
Farmer Refuted (Hamilton), 38
federal constitution
    use of term, 23
    See also U.S. Constitution
Federal Convention. *See* Philadelphia Convention
federal courts, 27, 33–34, 55, 61, 71, 73, 74, 77, 105, 107, 122–23, 149
federal employees, number, 141
"Federal Farmer", 38, 74, 76, 102
federal government and states, line of demarcation, 9, 10–11, 12, 13–14. *See also* states
Federal Hall, 104–5
federal legislation. *See* legislation
federal mint, 117–21
"federal systems", 22
federal union
    British Empire as, 37–39
    explained, 36
    framers' concept of union, 11–12
    structure *vs.* purpose, 10–11
federalism, 17–18, 33
The Federalist, 55–56, 71–72, 98–99, 101
"the federal plan", 76
federations/"federal republics", 19–20, 22, 76
    explained, 36
    regional state confederations, 9
ferries, 102–3, 112t, 115–17, 126–28
finances. *See* fiscal matters
first sessions of Congress, 104–32
    amendments to Constitution, 104–5
    growth, number of states in union, 107–8
fiscal matters, 71, 76
    Articles of Confederation, structural flaw, 50–51
    Bank of the United States, 9–10, 106, 107, 122–23
    early legislation, 106, 117–21, 122, 124, 130–31
    fiscal-military states, ix, 109, 131
    requisitions system, 2, 48, 49–53, 55, 57, 62
    See also banks; currency and legal tender; indebtedness; taxation
Fiske, John, 4, 5–6, 7–8
flag of U.S., 122
foedus, 89. *See also* treaties
foreign relations. *See* diplomatic relations
foreign trade. *See* international commerce
founding fathers, critical period, 1–15
France, 44–45, 47–48, 137–38, 139–40, 141
    French Revolution, 136–37, 141
    internal police, 81–82, 84, 85, 87, 99, 100–1
Franklin, Benjamin, 39–40, 45, 93–97, 99–100
free blacks, 146–47
freeholders, 31–32, 143–44
"Freeman" essays (Coxe), 102

French Revolution, 136–37, 141
fugitive slave clause, 66
fur trade, 138–39

Galloway, Joseph, 39–40, 79
de Gardoqui, Diego, 49
"general" government, 2
general welfare clauses, 39–40, 42, 57, 71, 75, 76, 114–15
geographic size of states, 74–75
geographic size of U.S., 109–10
Geography Made Easy (Morse), 46
George I, 110
Georgia, 48–49, 53–54, 65, 91, 100
Germany, police, 84–85, 86, 87
Gerry, Elbridge, 68, 74, 90
Glorious Revolution (England), 108, 110
Golove, David, 7–8, 28, 30–31
Gorham, Nathaniel, 65–67
Gould, Eliga, 7–8, 21, 28, 31
Grand Convention at Philadelphia. *See* Philadelphia Convention
Grayson, William, 72–73
Great Lakes military posts, 138–39
Greece
    πολιτεία (politeia), 39
    kyrios (head of household), 145, 148, 149
    oikos (household), 145
    perpetual preparation for warfare, 6
Green, Jacob, 79
Greene, Jack, 18, 142
Greenville, Treaty of, 138–39
growth of U.S. between first Congress and fourth Congress, 107–8
Guardian newspaper, 134
guardians and wards, rights and duties of, 146
Gulf Coast and Mississippi River trade, 47, 49, 138–39

Hamilton, Alexander, 9–10, 38, 48, 49, 52–53, 58–59, 63, 64, 71–72, 80–81, 101, 106–7, 141
Hamilton-Madison alliance, 106–7
Handlin, Mary, 142–43
Handlin, Oscar, 142–43
Hartz, Louis, 123–24, 142–43
head of household, 145–46, 147, 148, 149
health regulations, 39, 128
heartland
    defined, 121
    early legislation regarding, 121t, 122
Hendrickson, David, 23–24, 26
Henry, Patrick, 56
high seas. *See* maritime issues
highways and streets, 82–83, 85, 87, 97–98, 136
    Britain, 113–14
    early legislation, 112t, 115–17, 126
    list of police powers to be exercised by state governments, 102–3

History of the Americas (Robertson), 83
Holroyd, John (Earl of Sheffield), 44–45
"home department", 98
Hoppit, Julian, 108, 110–11, 113, 129–30
hospitals, police powers to be exercised by state
        governments, 102–3
House of Representatives, 55, 58–59, 62–63,
        66–67, 70
    analysis of legislation by first sessions of
        Congress, 104–32
    average number of statutes enacted by early
        Congresses, 115
    "popular" House of Representatives *vs.*
        "aristocratic" Senate, 143–44
    proportional representation, 55, 58–59, 66–67
    See also first sessions of Congress; legislation
Hulsebosch, Daniel, 7–8, 21, 28, 30–31
Hume, David, 87–88
husband and wife, rights and duties, 143–44, 146,
        147, 148–49
Hutson, James, 16

Ideological historians, 143
immigration, 73
impairment of obligation of contracts, 30, 70, 99
import of goods. *See* international commerce
inauguration of president of U.S., 104–5
incorporation. *See* corporations
indebtedness, 2–3, 5, 6, 20, 27, 46–51, 53, 70,
        71–72, 137–38, 140–41
    first Congress, public finance reform, 106, 107
    national debt obligations of states, 47–51
    private debts, within police powers to be
        exercised by state governments, 102
    of states, 99
Indian nations, 8, 39–40, 46, 48–49, 53,
        135, 138–39
    under Articles of Confederation, 20, 25, 26, 28,
        31, 32
    "civilizing" of, 32
    Indian removal, 30–31, 67–68, 141
    legislation of early Congresses, analysis
        of, 122–23
    potential foreign aggression in
        borderlands, 28
    sovereign status, 30–31, 32
    trade with, 27, 31, 32, 93–97, 98–99, 138–39
    treaties, 32, 138–39, 141
    voting rights of Indians, 143–44
industry
    defined, 83
    promotion of manufactures and industry,
        83, 84, 86, 87, 97–98, 99–100, 102–3,
        113, 121–22
infrastructure, regulation of, 9–10, 11–12,
        13–14, 135–36
inheritance laws, 102–3, 111–13, 116, 129–30

Innes, Joanna, 108
*An Inquiry into the Nature and Causes of the Wealth
        of Nations* (Smith), 86–87
Institutions politiques (von Bielfeld), 84
insurance companies, incorporation of,
        125–26, 136
interference with contracts, 27
Interior Department, 98
internal-external axis of early modern
        confederations, 76
"internal improvements", 135–36
internal peace, 87
internal police, 39–40, 74–103
    British model, 78–81, 86, 87–88, 113
    class of powers labeled internal police, 98–99
    Congress and Supreme Court, regulation of
        internal police of states, 149
    delegation of supervisory authority, 103
    early legislation, 113, 122–23, 125–26,
        128–29, 130–31
    explained, 12–13, 39, 77–78, 79, 80–81, 83–88
    "internal polity", 78–79
    See also residual power of states
"internal polity", 78–79
internal *vs.* external powers, 39, 131–32
international commerce, 25, 28, 29, 43–49, 57–58,
        62–63, 67–68, 73, 135, 136, 137–38
    Britain, commercial discrimination against
        U.S., 106
    Caribbean/Gulf Coast trade, 44–45, 47, 49, 50,
        65, 138–39
    commercial diplomacy, 33–34
    customs and customs duties, 5, 30, 57–58, 62,
        122–23, 135, 137, 140
    early legislation, 106, 117–21, 122–23,
        130–31
    enumeration of powers, 93–97
    and internal policing, 83, 87, 98–99, 102–3
    law merchant, 30
    Mediterranean trade, 5, 45, 53, 140
    navigation acts, 26, 64–65, 79, 96t, 98–99
    prizes captured by American privateers, 52–53
    slavery, 63, 64–66
    and standard of living, 43–44
    taxation and customs, 5, 27, 30, 52–53, 55–56,
        57–58, 62–63, 64, 65–66, 122–23, 135,
        137, 140
    transition to liberal democracy and market
        economy, 142
    treaties, 26
    world power status of U.S., 142
    See also Atlantic marketplace; maritime issues
international relations. *See* diplomatic relations
internationalist interpretations, 7. *See also* Unionist
        interpretation
interstate commerce. *See* commerce and trade
Iredell, James, 105

Ireland, 81–82
Iroquois (Six Nations), 46

Jamestown and Plymouth Plantation, 18–19
Jay, John, 49, 71–72, 138–39
Jefferson, Thomas, 38, 55–56, 89, 106–7, 123, 138, 140
Jeffersonian ideology, 9–10, 16–17, 141
Jeffersonian Republicans, 9–10
Jensen, Merrill, 7–8
Johnson, Samuel, 21, 84–85
Journal of American History, 16
judiciary/judicial branch of government, 59–60
    expansion, 74, 77
    federal courts, 27, 33–34, 55, 61, 71, 73, 74, 77, 105, 107, 122–23, 149
    list of police powers to be exercised by state governments, 102–3
    local courts, 114, 124–25
    state laws, constitutionality, 60–61
    Supreme Court of U.S., 27, 33–34, 61, 73, 105, 149
jury duty, 148
justice
    defined, 87
    "private justice", 101 (*see also* internal police)
justices of peace, 114, 124–25
von Justi, Johann Heinrich Gottlob, 84–85, 86

Kameralistik or *Kameralwissenschaft,* 84–85, 86, 87
Katznelson, Ira, 117
King, Rufus, 58–59
kyrios (head of household), 145, 148, 149

de Laforêt, Antoine, 100–1
laissez-faire, 103, 114
Lapinski, John, 117
law merchant, 30
law of nations, 4–5, 19–20, 27, 29, 30–31, 43
Of the Law of Nature and Nations (von Pufendorf), 41
The Law of Nations (de Vattel), 36, 85
Lectures on Jurisprudence (Smith), 87
Lectures on Law (Wilson), 131–32, 146–47
Lee, Richard Henry, 40, 56, 68, 71, 102
legal tender. *See* currency and legal tender
legislation
    analysis of legislation of early Congresses, 104–32, 112*t*
    classification schema, 108–9, 111, 112*t*, 117–21
    "demand-led" legislation, 114
    gaps in legislative activity, 117–21
legislative history, proceedings of Constitutional Convention, 56, 70, 88, 90, 91, 92, 100, 105–6
leisure, 148
L'Enfant, Pierre, 104

Letters from the Federal Farmer to the Republican, 76, 102
letters of marque and reprisal, 42
liberal democracy, 142, 144–45
liberalism *vs.* republicanism, 16–17, 147
licensing, within police powers to be exercised by state governments, 102–3
limitation of federal power. *See* enumeration of powers
liquor, taxation, 140
Livingston, Robert, 104–5
Locke, John, 37
Louis XIII, 81–82
Louisiana Purchase, 141
luxuries, sumptuary laws, 93–97

Maclay, William, 104–5
Madison, James, 9, 10–11, 20–21, 23, 34, 51, 52–53, 54–56, 58–62, 63, 64, 66–67, 71–73, 88–90, 91–92, 93–97, 98–100, 106–7, 138
Maine, 79
manufactures/industry
    definition, 83
    promotion of, 84, 86, 87, 97–98, 99–100, 102–3, 113, 121–22
maritime issues, 42, 44, 64
    Barbary States, 5, 45, 53, 140
    crimes, 42
    import duty on prizes captured by American privateers, 52–53
    prize courts, 42
    ship construction, 44
    shipping interests, 25, 26–27, 44, 63
    See also navigation of waterways
market economy
    marketplace regulation, 12, 42–43, 82–83, 86, 87, 93–97, 129
    transition to, 142
    See also commerce and trade
marriage
    police powers to be exercised by state governments, 102–3
    rights and duties of husbands and wives, 143–44, 146, 147, 148–49
Martin, Luther, 91–92
Maryland, 48–49, 53, 58, 65, 69, 79
Mason, George, 61–62, 68, 71, 74, 91–92, 93–97
Massachusetts, 63, 65, 69, 90, 91, 142–43
master and servant, rights and duties, 146–47, 148–49
master of household, 145–46, 147, 148
Matson, Cathy, 17–18, 25
McIlwain, Charles, 18
McLaughlin, Andrew, 18
McNut, Alexander, 79
meat regulation, 82–83
Mediterranean trade, 5, 45, 53, 140

mercantile contracts, within police powers to be exercised by state governments, 102
mercantilism, defined, 44
Mercer, John Francis, 64–65
Mexican American War, 141
Mexican Cession, 98
Mexico, 47
military defense, 2–3, 27, 28, 72, 141
  British military, postwar presence in U.S., 5, 20, 46–47, 53
  early legislation, 117–21, 122
  fiscal-military states, ix, 109, 131
  states, military force by national government, 61–62
  world power status of U.S., 142
militia service, 61–62, 70, 71, 100–1, 102, 148
Millar, John, 86–87
mint of U.S., 122–23
Mississippi River, Gulf Coast trade, 44–45, 47, 49, 50, 65, 138–39
Mississippi River Valley, fertility, 31, 46, 47
modern liberal democracies, 145–46
modernization narratives, 142
monarchies vs. republics, 36
monopolies, 87
Montesquieu, 19–21, 36–37, 75–76
morals, within internal police definition, 39
Morocco, 139–40
Morris, Gouverneur, 60–61, 64–66, 90–92, 97–99
Morse, Jedidiah, 46
municipalities
  creation, 102–3, 129, 136
  police powers, 81–83, 84, 102–3

native Americans. See Indian nations
natural law, 19–20, 84, 85, 87
naturalization of citizens, 55–56, 130–31
navies/naval powers, 28, 44, 64–65
  naval courts, 42
  See also maritime issues
navigation acts, 26, 64–65, 79, 96t, 98–99
navigation of waterways, 26, 53, 64–65, 79, 97–99
  early congressional legislation, 116–17, 122–23, 126–28, 130–31
  Mississippi River, 49
"necessary and proper" clause, 70, 92, 93, 114–15
negating state laws. See veto power
Netherlands, 22, 23, 47–48, 81–82
New Hampshire, 65, 69
"New Ireland", 79
New Jersey, 53–54, 58, 65, 79
New Jersey Plan, 57–58, 62
New York, 58, 63, 68, 69, 84–85
New York City Hall, 104
non-whites, voting rights, 143–44
North Carolina, 53–54, 64–65, 69, 79, 91

Northwest Territory and Northwest Ordinance, 17–18, 26–27, 31–32, 33–34, 116, 117, 138–39, 148–49
"Notes on Ancient and Modern Confederacies" (Madison), 54–55
Novak, William, 80–81, 103, 108, 114, 123, 128, 129, 142–43
Novanglus, 38. See also Adams, John
Novus Ordo Seclorum, 19–20

Observations on the Commerce of the American States (Sheffield), 44–45
oeconomical, use of term, 146
Of the Law of Nature and Nations (von Pufendorf), 41
Ohio River, 4–5, 26, 31
Ohio River Valley/Ohio country, 46, 47, 138
oikos (household), 145
Onuf, Peter, 7–8, 17–18, 20, 21, 25
opulence (property and plenty of the state), 86–88, 103, 114
Osgood, Samuel, 105
Ottawa people, treaties with, 46
Otto, Louis Guillaume, 100–1

Paine, Thomas, 21–22, 147
paper money, 6, 16–17, 27, 30, 35–36, 48–49, 61, 70, 83, 90, 91, 99, 144–45
parent and child relationship, 146, 147, 148–49
Paris Peace Treaty. See Peace of Paris
Parliament, British, 9
  comparison of legislation, 108–17, 123, 124, 131
"partial consolidation plan", 76
party politics, 106–7, 117, 142–43
patents, early legislation regarding, 117–21, 122–23, 131–32
Paterson, William, 58, 62, 63
patriarchal authority, 31–32, 145–46, 147, 148, 149
Peace of Paris, 3–4, 44–45, 46–47, 50
Peace Pact: The Lost World of the American Founding (Hendrickson), 21
peace treaties, 3–4, 5, 22–23, 26–27, 44–45, 46–47, 50
Pearl, Christopher, 129–30
Pennsylvania, 53–54, 63, 69, 74, 75, 77, 79, 90, 100, 136, 140, 142–43
  comparison of legislative activities, 107–32
  state constitution, 123–24
people
  elections by "the people" or by the states, 89, 143–44
  popular consent and popular participation, 74–75
  popular sovereignty vs. agreement between states, 35–36

popular understanding of U.S.
  Constitution, 133–34
"private oeconomical relations" of
  individuals, 146
single American people, 134
'We the People of the United States', 134
The People's Welfare (Novak), 114
*Peripheries and Center: Constitutional Development
  in the Extended Polities of the British
  Empire and the United States, 1607-1788*
  (Greene), 18
perpetual unions, 41–43
personal legislation (estate and inheritance
  legislation), 111–13, 116
Pew Research Center, 133
Philadelphia Convention, 1, 13, 20–21, 25, 34, 35,
  53–73, 105–6
  adjournment, 68, 74
  Committee of Detail, 62–63, 64, 65–66,
    92, 97–98
  Committee of Style, 35, 92, 99–100
  delegates, 56
  proceedings, 56, 70, 88, 90, 91, 92, 100, 105–6
  ratification process, 68
  reconfirmation of states as principal political
    organization within federal union, 67–68
Philadelphia police, 81–83
"Philadelphia System" (Deudney), 21
Pinckney, Charles, 58, 64–66, 90, 91–92, 93–100
Pinckney, Thomas, 138–39
Pinckney Plan, 58
Plymouth Plantation, 18–19
Pocock, John, 16–17, 18, 33, 143
polarization in Congress, 117
police, 81–86
  defined, 81–82
  See also internal police
police power, 12–13, 80–81, 93–97, 96*t*, 98–99,
  102–3. *See also* internal police; residual
  power of states
policy, explanation of term, 83, 84, 85
politeia (internal police), 39. *See also* internal police
political modernization, 143
political parties, 106–7, 117, 142–43
"political" rights, 146
poor laws, 82–83, 102–3, 117–21, 128, 148–49
post offices and post roads, 42–43, 93–97, 98–100,
  105, 116–17, 122–23, 130–32, 136, 141
Postlethwayt, Malachy, 86, 87–88
preamble, 35, 114–15, 134, 135
president of U.S., 29, 70
  first inauguration, 104–5
  popular election, 89
Principles of Political Oeconomy (Steuart),
  87–88, 116–17
private debts, within police powers to be exercised
  by state governments, 102

"private justice", 101. *See also* internal police
Progressive school of interpretation, 6–8, 14–15,
  16, 30, 33–34
property rights, 9–10, 11–12, 13–14, 87,
  136, 148
  in Britain, 111–13, 131
  early legislation, 112*t*, 115–17, 122–23, 129–30
  freeholders, 31–32, 143–44
  within police powers to be exercised by state
    governments, 102
  slave owners, 144–45
  title to property, 102, 129–30
  and voting, 146–47, 148
proportional representation, 55, 58–59, 66–67
Prussia, 139–40
public debt. *See* indebtedness
public finance. *See* fiscal matters
public health regulations, 39, 128
public lands, 12, 46, 138
  surveyors and land offices, 138
  See also trans-Appalachian west
"public police", 80–81
public relative rights, 146
public ways. *See* highways and streets
von Pufendorf, Samuel, 36, 41

quorum, 53, 57, 104

"radicals" *vs.* "conservatives", 7
Rakove, Jack, 18
Ramsay, David, 78
Randolph, Edmund, 57–58, 61–62,
  68, 74, 89, 91
ratification of Constitution, 68–73, 102
Rawson, Susanna, 45
reactive state
  Britain as, 109
  defined, 109
  U.S. as, 131
Reading act, 129
redistribution of wealth from "ordinary people" to
  elite, 99
regional confederations, 9
relative rights *vs.* absolute or universal rights,
  145–46, 147
religion, 9–10, 11–12, 13–14, 102–3
republican system of government, 2, 21–22, 23–
  24, 26, 31–32, 70, 74–75
  Congress as representation of American people
    or of sovereign states, 40, 59–60
  consent and participation, 74–75
  elections by "the people" or by the states,
    89, 143–44
  liberal citizenship *vs.* republican
    citizenship, 147
  popular understanding of U.S.
    Constitution, 133–34

republican system of government (Cont.)
"private oeconomical relations" of
individuals, 146
ratio of legislators to electors, 74–75
republic, explanation of term, 144–45
single American people, 134
'We the People of the United States', 134
requisitions system, 2, 48, 49–53, 55, 57, 62
residual power of states, 74–103
British model, 110–11
Congress and Supreme Court, regulation of
internal police of states, 149
economic development, state driven, 142–43
expediency, 86–87
Federalist and Antifederalist agreement, 103
fiscal power, 76
list of powers to be exercised by state
governments, 102–3
means *vs.* ends, 101
popular consent and popular
participation, 74–75
property and plenty of the state, 86–88
taxation, 75, 87
See also Antifederalists and anti-federalism;
enumeration of powers; internal police
Revolutionary War. *See* American War of
Independence
Rhode Island, 52–53, 56, 68, 69, 99
rivers, 47
in Britain, 113–14
list of police powers to be exercised by state
governments, 102–3
Mississippi River, 49
Ohio River, 4–5, 26, 31
types of statutes enacted by early Congresses,
112*t*, 115–17
See also navigation of waterways
roads. *See* highways and streets
Robertson, William, 83
Rowson, Susanna, 45
Rush, Benjamin, 21–22
Rutledge, John, 91–92

Sadosky, Leonard, 7–8, 21, 30–31
Saler, Bethel, 32
"The Savage Constitution" (Ablavsky), 31
Schuylkill companies, 127–28
secessionist movements, 5, 17–18, 53
sectionalism, 25–26, 62–63, 89, 100, 142
security of nation. *See* defense of nation
Senate of U.S., 59, 62–63, 70, 89
analysis of legislation of early
Congresses, 104–32
"aristocratic", 143–44
average number of statutes enacted by early
Congresses, 115
See also first sessions of Congress

settlement expansion, 28
Louisiana Purchase, 141
See also Northwest Territory and Northwest
Ordinance; trans-Appalachian west
Seven Years' War, 78
sewers, 82–83
Shammas, Carole, 145–46, 149
Shawnee people, 46
Shays, Daniel, 53–54, 57
Shays's Rebellion, 53–54, 57
Sherman, Roger, 57–58, 60–61, 67, 90–91, 92, 99,
100, 101
shipping. *See* maritime issues
signatories to U.S. Constitution, 68
slavery, 25–27, 45, 63–66, 91, 142, 148–49
federal protection, 25–26, 66, 67–68
list of police powers to be exercised by state
governments, 102–3
property rights of slave owners, 144–45
social rights of slaves, 146–47
three-fifths rule, 66–67
Slaves in Algiers (Rowson), 45
small states, 57–58, 59–60, 63, 64, 65, 89, 91–92
New Jersey Plan, 57–58, 62
redrawing borders to create states of equal
size, 89
Smith, Adam, 84, 86–88, 93, 100, 103
social policy, 117–21, 136
"social" rights, 145–47
"society of societies", 19–20, 36
socioeconomics. *See* class issues
South Carolina, 64, 65, 68, 69, 91
Southern Quarterly Review, 145
sovereignty
under Articles of Confederation, 43
of colonies, 40
of Indian nations, 30–31, 32
of states, 19, 24–25, 58–59
Spain and Spanish Empire, 25, 30, 44–45, 47–48,
49, 53, 83, 138–39, 141
Spirit of the Laws (Montesquieu), 19–20, 36
stamp tax, 57–58, 62
state constitutions, 21–22, 29, 34, 61, 114,
123–24, 143–45
states
under Articles of Confederation, 1–3, 36–43,
48, 49–53, 55, 57, 60–61, 62, 67–68
Congress as representation of American people
or of sovereign states, 40, 59–60
constitutionality of state laws, 60–61
as corporations, 34, 58–59, 74, 100–1
division of legislative power, 7–8, 9–10, 12,
13–14, 136, 149
and foreign affairs, 4–5, 30, 139–40
growth of number of states in union, 107–8
independence and union as inseparable
concepts, 26

interstate commerce (*see* commerce and trade)
interstate relations and conflicts, 2, 5, 11, 17–18,
    20, 23–24, 25–27, 35–36, 38–39, 43–44, 49,
    62–63, 67, 89, 100, 122–23, 134, 142
legislation, analysis of, 104–32, 112*t*, 125*t*
legislature privileged over executive, 114
means *vs.* ends, expansion of national
    government, 101
military force by national government against
    states war, 61–62
militia service, 61–62, 70, 71, 100–1, 102, 148
and national debt obligations, 47–51
"principal care of persons, property, and
    reputation", 123
Progressive *vs.* Unionist interpretations of
    Constitution, 6, 8, 13–15
secessionist movements, 5, 17–18, 53
sectionalism, 25–26, 62–66, 89, 100, 142
sovereignty, 19, 24–25, 58–59
supremacy clause, 61, 71, 75, 76, 91–92
tables listing federal and state powers, 94*t*, 96*t*
taxation, 71
transformative role of national political
    institutions and policies, 142
union and independence as inseparable
    concepts, 26
voting, suffrage requirements, 143–44
war, prohibited from waging war, 27, 30
Washington's letter to, 1–3
well-ordered societies, 81–82, 84–85, 86–88,
    103, 114, 129
See also Antifederalists and anti-federalism;
    enumeration of powers; residual power of
    states; small states
Steuart, James, 84, 86, 87–88, 116–17
streets. *See* highways and streets
sumptuary laws, 93–97
supremacy clause, 61, 71, 75, 76, 91–92
Supreme Court of U.S., 27, 33–34, 61, 73, 105, 149
supreme law of the land, 12, 21, 30, 31, 61,
    77, 139–40
"surrogacy," strategy to stretch enumerated
    powers, 73
surveyors and land offices, 138
Susquehanna, 126–28
Sweden, 44–45, 139–40
Swiss Republics, 22, 23

tariffs. *See* customs and customs duties
taxation
    under Articles of Confederation, 48, 49–53,
        57–58, 62, 64, 65–67, 71–72
    customs duties and tariffs, 5, 27, 30, 52–53,
        55–56, 57–58, 62–63, 64, 65–66, 122–23,
        135, 137, 140
    early legislation, 117–21, 122, 140
    federal fiscal powers, 35–36, 62–63, 75

and internal policing, 83, 87
requisitions system, 49–53
residual power of states, 75, 87
Shays's Rebellion, 53–54, 57
slave trade, 64
stamp tax, 57–58, 62
whiskey rebels, 140, 141
term limits, 71
territorial expansion. *See* trans-Appalachian west
territorial possessions of U.S., 12, 98
Texas, 141
Thelen, David, 16
Theory of Moral Sentiment (Smith), 86–87
three-fifths rule, 66–67
title to property, 102, 129–30
Totten, Robbie, 7–8
trade regulation. *See* commerce and trade
Traité de la police (Delamare), 84
trans-Appalachian west, 4–5, 14, 17–18, 20,
    135, 137–39
    under Articles of Confederation, 49–50, 53
    communications with, 100
    early legislation regarding, 121*t*,
        122–23, 130–31
    economic success dependent on, 31
    foreign interest in, 8, 11, 25, 28, 46–47
    post-war presence of British traders and army
        posts, 46–47
    rapid population growth of early 19th
        century, 46
    transfer of territory from states to
        Congress, 31
    Treaty of Paris, 46
    See also Indian nations; Northwest Territory
        and Northwest Ordinance
transportation
    early legislation, 116–17, 126–28
    police powers, 87
treaties
    Articles of Confederation as treaty
        organization, 19–20
    constitution as treaty, 11, 22–24
    enforcement powers, 4–5, 19–20, 28, 29,
        30, 139–40
    Indian treaties, 32, 46, 138–39, 141
    law of nations, 4–5, 19–20, 27, 29, 30–31, 43
    Peace of Paris, 3–4, 44–45, 46–47, 50
    supreme law of land, 12
    table of early treaties, 121*t*
    "treaty-worthy", 28, 29, 30
Treatise on the Police of the Metropolis
    (Colquhoun), 81
Trudeau, Garry, 133–34
trusts, 113–14
Tucker, George, 37, 131–32, 146–47
turnpikes, 113–14, 122–23, 136
Tyler, Royall, 45

union, 35–73
    common good of union, 2–3
    independence and union as inseparable
        concepts, 26
    "more perfect", 35
    perpetual unions, 41–43
    of sovereign republics, 1, 2, 3, 4–5, 7–8, 9
    structure *vs.* purpose, 10–11
Unionist interpretation, 7, 8, 13–15, 17–18, 33–
    34, 134, 136, 142–49
universal rights *vs.* relative rights, 145–46, 147
universities and colleges, 99–100, 102–3, 128
U.S. Constitution
    amending *vs.* replacing Articles of
        Confederation, 9, 23, 35–36, 53–54,
        57, 105–6
    Bill of Rights, 72–73, 76, 107
    Committee of Detail, 62–63, 64, 65–66,
        92, 97–98
    Committee of Style, 35, 92, 99–100
    compromises within, 9, 58–60, 89
    drafting (*see* Philadelphia Convention)
    meaning of term "constitution", 10–11, 23
    as organizational solution, 134
    preamble, 35, 114–15, 134, 135
    procedural amendments, 72–73
    as pro-slavery document, 25–26
    publication, 70
    ratification, 68–73, 102
    signatories, 68
    supreme law of the land, 12, 21, 30, 31, 61,
        77, 139–40
    as symbol of nation's ideals and values, 33
    tables listing federal and state powers, 94*t*, 96*t*
    See also Philadelphia Convention
Utrecht peace treaty of 1713, 23

Van Cleve, George, 25–26
de Vattel, Emer, 21, 24, 27, 28, 36, 85, 87–88
Vermont, 79
veterans, 2–3, 47–48, 122, 124
veto power, 41, 88–92
"Vices of the Political System of the United States"
    (Madison), 54–55, 99
Vienna peace treaty of 1815, 23
Vining, John, 98–99
Virginia, 48–49, 52–54, 63, 69, 90, 91, 100,
    143–44, 146–47
Virginia Declaration of Rights of 1776, 21–22
Virginia Plan, 57–58, 59–60, 61–63, 66–67, 68,
    89, 90–91
"A Virginian" (pseudonym), 101–2
von Bielfeld, Jakob Friedrich, 84, 87
von Justi, Johann Heinrich Gottlob, 84–85, 86
von Pufendorf, Samuel, 36, 41
voting. *See* elections and voting

Wabash people, 48–49
Waldstreicher, David, 25–26

war, 36–37, 39–40, 43, 71–72, 73
    as constant danger, 23–24
    European wars, 136–37, 140, 141
    fiscal-military states, ix, 109, 131
    foreign aggression, 28
    law of nations, 4–5, 19–20, 27, 29, 30–31, 43
    peace treaties, 5, 22–23, 26–27
    states, military force by national government
        against states, 61–62
    states prohibited from waging war, 27, 30
    See also military defense
War of 1812, 137, 141
War of Independence. *See* American War of
    Independence
Washington, D.C., 107
Washington, George, 5, 13, 55–56, 136, 137–39,
    140, 141
    letter to states at end of war, 1–3
Washington administration legislation,
    104–32, 141
    average number of statutes enacted, 115
    "demand-led" legislation, 114
    gaps in legislative activity, 117–21
    types of statutes enacted, 112*t*, 115–17
water pumps and sewers, 82–83
The Weakness of Brutus Exposed (Webster), 77
Wealth of Nations (Smith), 87–88
Webster, Noah, 50–51, 55, 77, 78–79, 84–85, 147
Webster, Pelatiah, 51, 55, 61–62, 77
weights and measures, 42–43, 82–83, 86, 87, 93–
    97, 98–99, 113
welfare state/poor laws, 82–83, 102–3, 117–21,
    128, 148–49
well-ordered societies, 81–82, 84–85, 86–88, 103,
    114, 129
West Indies/Gulf Coast trade, 44–45, 47, 49, 50,
    65, 138–39
western expansion, 28
    Louisiana Purchase, 141
    See also Northwest Territory and Northwest
        Ordinance; trans-Appalachian west
Westphalia peace treaty of 1648, 23
whiskey rebels, 140, 141
white people, 23–24
    extension of rights in 19th and 20th
        century, 149
    settlers in trans-Appalachian west, 26, 28,
        31–32
    voting rights, 143–44
Williamson, Hugh, 64–65, 90
Wilson, James, 37, 38, 77, 90–91, 131–32,
    146–47
women, rights and duties, 143–44,
    146–47, 148–49
Wood, Gordon, 7–8, 16–17, 33
world power status of U.S., 142
Wyandot people, 46

Zuckert, Michael, 20–21